SIT DOWN AND PLAY

Elsa J. Baker

Sycamore Press
P.O. Box 597
Ocean Park, Wash. 98640

*This book
is dedicated to
music and everyone
who enjoys it.*

Library of Congress Catalog Card Number: 87-90545

Cover design by
Bernice Kehoe

Published by
Sycamore Press
P.O. Box 597
Ocean Park, Wash. 98640

Printed and bound in the
United States of America

CONTENTS

ACKNOWLEDGEMENTS

A great chord in "G" for my husband and co-musician, Kenny, for his patient listening and realistic editing.

Strike another chord for early encouragers such as Lois Gross, Creative Writing instructor for the Fort Steilacoom Community College in Steilacoom, Washington; for Arlene and Bruce who never doubted Mom was piano-struck; and for friends like Florence Krummel (wife of my compatriot, Bernhard, in early piano times), who thought my writing of this book might take forever.

Strike a third chord for son, Kenny Jr. (Fr. Kenneth Baker, S.J.), who took it upon himself to make forever happen a little sooner.

Ocean Park, Wash.
March 17, 1987

INTRODUCTION

Sit Down and Play

Sit down and play what? The Piano of course. Was there ever anything else? It was my good fortune to arrive within the 1912 set of girl babies labeled: "Born with musical tendencies." I would suppose some greeted the world with violin bows in hand, while others soon began to warble like larks. However my lot was cast with the group whose infant brains came pre-programmed with the key progression of a piano.

Throughout her long life, my mother attested to my teetering atop our highly-wound piano stool carefully testing and sounding out each key of our Kimball upright—at age two and a half. Before my third birthday, separate notes were being strung together in simple but definite tunes. A slower left hand then began to counter with a supportive key or two. Dared she let herself interpret what was to her, a handwriting upon the wall? The letters, so apparent through a mother's pink tinted glasses, seemed to spell out "C-H-I-L-D P-R-O-D-I-G-Y!" I imagine there was some alarm on her part. There shouldn't have been.

Instead of fostering a Concert pianist, a brilliant Composer or compelling Virtuoso, my guiding stars opted to manage and design each chapter of my life in a unique fashion. In knowing retrospect I now choose to think the early wall writing bespoke: "This child will be asked to sit down and play throughout her life." And I would not, were it possible, rearrange one note.

But where to begin? With the opening bars I suppose, as any piece of music does. Or as I was to learn later, "From the Top."

Elsa J. Baker

6

PART I

VERSE

I

A Most Elementary Audition

The very first request to sit down and play took place in that era of two and a half. It was, as my mother related it for years, a colossal embarrassment to both her and her traditional afternoon coffee hour. Naturally I do not remember the incident, but I can well visualize the setting as many of the accessories in the scene are still loved possessions of the family. I would say the best Austrian embroidered cloth (Mother then only four years distant from Germany) was upon the table, as were the silver coffee service, the handpainted eggshell china cups and plates, and the initialed linen napkins. And why not?

While recently attending an important Tacoma Theater concert, mother had met the pianist of an ensemble. Would Madame consent to an afternoon coffee and perhaps give audience to a young daughter's exploits of the piano? Evidently Madame consented. All had been in perfect readiness, coffee hand-ground and brewed, Ladyfingers daintily fanned across a plate. This delicacy, and how I prized them, had most likely been home delivered by Tacoma's gourmet grocery, "Roberts Bros."

Came the moment of my presentation at this cosy affair, where all I had to do was climb up on the piano stool and do what I usually did there. Mother was only slightly annoyed at my fleeing the parlor after one look. Had she followed me in hot pursuit instead of holding her post as polite hostess, no story would have ensued and annoyance wouldn't have turned into social agony. What she saw at my reappearance after being called, was her little child prodigy casually toddling into the room, dangling her small white enamel potty from one hand. Mercy! Before I could position it upon the Axminster rug, I was whisked away in a flash. The rest of the story became lost in time, at least I can't remember hearing much else beyond mother's utter discomfiture.

Sometime after the impressive touring artist left Tacoma, Mother cast out another exploratory line. She needed help. Was it too early for beginner's lessons or was she being foolish? Evidently she reached a conclusion to proceed and follow her original impulses. For the new doctor's wife, to seek advice from within the ring of Tacoma's cloistered German community was entirely natural. Two birds with one stone! For added substance, this instructress was also an accomplished concert pianist and specialized in music theory and other approaches rarely offered by run-of-the-mill elementary teachers. Fräulein Fritsch would be consulted.

2

Regulated Roots

"Now you just come and sit at this little table," Fräulein Fritsch was taking me by the hand. Mother was out in the offing. Once at the low table (my own memory now takes charge), a long sheet of heavy paper was unfolded before me. Neat spaced lines of inky blank stretched across the sheet like railroad tracks. I remember best the pleasure of reaching into a box filled with black wooden notes, about the size of a clothespin. Next came the fun of being shown how to place them right upon or right between the black lines. The exercise lasted several months and held all the charm of Stevenson's "Child's Garden of Verse" for me. My acquaintanceship with sighting and writing music symbols along with this teacher's form of specialized training became quite well established before I even heard of the A B C's. The end came when my age of pre-five was judged a bit young for further theory. As a parting memento Fräulein Fritsch hand-copied one of my mini-compositions into a manuscript book, which still occupies space at the bottom of my piano bench. Its faded cover bears a treasured and dim photo of the then quite new "Stadium High School," with bay back-grounded Bowl.

The conclusion could also have been prompted by the weekly testing of mother's lifelong fear of dogs, namely a medium sized white dog. His greeting for us, about a block prior to the home of his mistress (the Fräulein), was an overdone succession of exuberant barking, leaping and prancing. "Be careful, don't pet him," mother would warn. "Yes I see his pretty fluffy white hair, but he's a "Spitz" and cannot be trusted." Mother's explicit accent of the word "Spitz" was enough to convince me. In child fashion I took the name literally, waiting for him to turn on us and spit. So it was farewell to Fräulein Fritsch and her Spitz, a statement more easily articulated by those of German tongue! Beginner's regular lessons became the self-evident choice. We were moving to another section of Tacoma. Mother would then locate a reputable teacher. Hopefully a dogless one.

3

Under Pinnings

Though thoroughly intimidated by each of them, my piano teachers were the prime promoters of learning it right, or not at all. Mine had a universal method of keeping a student's nose pointed down the middle of the road, a narrow one at that. They were of course, of another era. Other youngsters may have enjoyed more casual relationships with their mentors, such as discussing personal preferences and other such fripperies. But not mine. In all fairness I must say, this was not a popular trend during these years.

Compliments from my teachers? They were as precious as jewels. Again, a prevailing custom. The praising system evidently had not caught on as yet. The lack went right by me, unnoticed. With mother holding to a similar theory in the upbringing of her children, you can bet I was well accustomed to the atmosphere. Thus the possibilities of remaining humble and unaffected were excellent as well as of long duration. Mother supported each teacher totally, paid them promptly and effected a reasonable facsimile of their tactics during my home practice hours. I discredited neither.

Recallings of harshness or over-severeness are non-existent. Nor do I remember unfairness of favoring of superior students. Their small circle did not always include me, though I steadily hovered at the outer edges. My warming of teachers' hearts was an ability to memorize rapidly and "play by heart" as it was termed then. Later the inborn trait of transposing came to light and to my reward, as both were so often the downfall of many students.

Thinking back on these hallowed teachers, I wonder why each one was so entrenched in unflagging discipline with no fancy trimmings. One would think somewhere in their midst, a maverick would have surfaced. And so it was 100% respect and effort. It's easy to picture them now, floating about in the upper realms, guiding cherubic angels through no-nonsense harp lessons and making sure angelic head-sizes never exceed their golden halos! "Taking," as lessons were then termed, was nothing to set one apart. Every one "took" and usually it was the piano. An early question in the childhood structure when sounding out a playmate was: "Who are you taking from?" Geographic proximity often chose the teacher, as well as access to a streetcar line. Entering the first grade at Washington School must have taken priority as the year's important event, as I barely remember my first piano teacher. What remains of her in my memory is only her generous frame and the tall many-windowed house from which she taught. Never to be forgotten however were the shiny gold stars awarded for effort and success. Each was glued to the spot where victory was won, to remain there forever. For me they shone as brightly as any in the heavens above.

Before she could introduce her methods of beginning to me, I proudly informed the new teacher I could already play "Yankee Doodle." Evidently she was not awestruck as it seemed she placed a great amount of importance on playing correctly from the written notes, as opposed to wandering off at will. "Yankee Doodle" was not hard to come by as everyone was either humming or whistling this pepper-upper of World War I. The nonsensical lyrics seemed to please young and old alike, and I loved picking out the tune for the pure fun of it.

During first teachers and Yankee Doodle time, two serious and contrasting conclusions took place. The first, noticeable to even a six year old, was the air of rejoicing with the end of a war. The second was not so joyful. Mother was divorcing my doctor father. Too young to comprehend these problems, I only knew it as the physical disappearance of a father whom I was never to see again. We moved to another Tacoma house on Union Avenue, close to what mother called "The Black Forest," or today's many-treed Puget Sound University campus. Lessons, I suppose, continued but what I remember most is my vigil of curb sitting in front of our Bavarian type home. My object was simple—to hail down my father whom I felt sure was looking for our new house.

After a period of some two years my brother and I were sensibly adapting to a very fine and willing step-father. If adjustment or resentment phobias threw us out of line, the incidences are forgotten. From him came vigorous interest and support in furthering his newly acquired young pianist. He was spared the early one hour practice sessions before school, a time of day when he was on foot, bound for the streetcar and his office. What he heard were the more finished products of my labors. Now and then he would ask me to play for him after dinner, and the dishes of course. His most favorite request, and I liked it too, was a piece called "Hungary." True to its name the four pages were full of galloping horses and charging Hungarians, whose exploits were accented in heavy minor chord strikings. While pouring on this fiery Hungarian paprika, I would spy him placing a large coin onto the lower end of the piano. Mother frowned on this little act and for me the fifty-cent piece was an unrecognizable coin. It even refused to slide through the designated slot of my litle metal-grilled savings bank! His meaning however was very clear to me, he was pleased. And so I tried all the harder to please him. The magic formula remains as effective today as in those long ago years.

Life at age seven and eight brought about more than the realization and acceptance of a kind step-father. If Christopher Columbus counted his year of 1492 to be a great significance with the discovery of a new world, so did I rate my year of 1920. My discovery was a new world of music, and made within the confines of neighborhood blocks and required no royal financing. All I needed was what I already had—plenty of free time outdoors, a pair of curiosity-bent ears and a transcribing mind. Fate had decreed all to be freely given unto me. The new discovery proved to be none other than POPULAR MUSIC! Strong as it may sound, the very existence of it was a complete surprise.

Like most active children, most waking hours were spent outside, which in Tacoma's yards then meant lots of empty lots and homey sidewalks. Though no radios were in evidence yet, music still pervaded the air. Without benefit of amplifiers, indoor sounds broadcast themselves out into the open air, more easily heard in the summer months of course. Every screen door in the block qualified as a broadcaster of the good news for me. And music from within there was, as the item for producing it (a piano) was almost a frontroom fixture. Secure and loved and fancily scarved and photo bedecked, these keyboards felt the touch of many an inquiring finger. Picking out a tune either by imagination or written notes was the available method for keeping up with the latest hits. Evidently no one wished to be caught napping back in the '20's either.

Since I had never heard the term "Pop Music," I had no name for the pleasant tunes floating their way into my heart via the screendoor route. I only knew they appealed to me instantly. How I longed to bring them home to our Kimball, as I felt transferring each one from mind to key would bring great delight. The delight was not immediately forthcoming for I was rarely alone in the house to set up what I knew would be a rather secretive experience. Formal music training was well begun now, and I felt in my bones that the two kinds of music were worlds apart, at least for me. No such shilly-shally was about to cloud the home atmosphere, period. I had vaguely heard mother and teachers alike refer to modern music as "trash" and other derogatory terms. However, there was a way. Just memorize the pretty tunes by keeping ears open around all the screen doors, and then file them away in my head for another day. It would have to be when I was alone in the house, which was seldom. The process was like bringing home the dress you had admired in the storewindow, and then having to hang it away in the

13

closet, without even trying it on. The opportunity for slipping one on for size was not as far away as I thought.

My forbidden fruit of Pop Music carried more than the power of temptation, it also deafened my ear. Not even the musicianship of these parlor pianists failed to dull my appetite. Perhaps enthusiasm pardoned any lack of expertise and I wonder what might have happened had a creditable jazz pianist lived in our neighborhood! Actually the laborious note picking was to my advantage. All the needed repetitions as fingers doggedly plodded their way, backtracking and repairing mistakes enroute, aided my committance. And so I bless all those unseen but heard pianists seated at their palm flanked uprights, earnestly attacking "Stumbling," "The Sheik of Araby" and the reigning favorite, "Go Feather Your Nest." With sheetmusic going for twenty-five cents a copy, most piano racks held a fair-sized collection.

The buying of a piece of music was no pig-in-a-poke transaction. Downtown five and dime stores boasted "live-in" pianists who methodically ground out a number of bars from your selection, at no extra charge. The buyer listened with the privilege of making the purchase, or just standing there with an appropriate remark denoting it was no sale. Oh to be one of these popular-with-the-public piano players, playing out samples of everything that was coming out and filling most of the air among the pot and pan department, cups and saucers, laces and trims and the counters of Tangee cosmetics, Brilliantine and Pomades. My mind reached a firm conclusion: Popular Music was the only road to go, and at the road's end was Piano Paradise. A small glimpse up the road was about to take place.

Mother was paying a rare social call on one of our close neighbors and I happened to be along. Sitting and chatting (Mother and the other lady), my eyes wandered beyond the maroon velvet portiers between parlor and dining room. Right there on the piano rack stood several colorful copies of popular sheetmusic! A bit later when Mrs. Morris said to Mother, "I understand your daughter is studying the piano. Do you suppose she would be able to play those two songs up on the piano? I'd just love to hear them, as they're my favorites." Mother had to acknowledge my ability to sight-read, and I was promptly dispatched to the piano bench. Once there I was momentarily distracted by the many little gold tassels dangling from a crushed velvet scarf atop their piano. We had nothing like that decorating our Kimball, nor did my teachers. I wasn't distracted very long for right in front of my wide open eyes was a most exciting picture. The entire front of the first sheet of music held a vision which up to now had only been a fantasy in my mind. A beautiful galleon, full sails billowing upon a wavy blue sea! The minute I saw it I felt sure it had to be "Loveship," and sure enough the title printed above the white sails read "Loveship." Reading and playing it was a breeze for I had listened in on it many times and knew it well within my mind. Mrs. Morris was all smiles beaming at Mother with, "Isn't that lovely . . . it's so pretty." Mother must have twitched at the selection and probably wrote the whole thing off in the name of social decency. As for me, my cup ranneth over.

4
The Great Green Book

Heaven, mother and fate are to be thanked for what suddenly stood on the music rack of our Kimball one fine day. Two new books, each covered in brilliant emerald green were flaunting ther newness amid the usual monochromed study material. A stop at Sherman & Clay's marvelous music store on one of mother's downtown shopping trips had brought forth this all important purchase. While our home library was excellent, it suffered no invasion of contemporary, or popular music. This would have been akin to deliberately adding slang words to a good English vocabulary! Though neither book was intended for me (mother still played then), I soon found time to give them the once-over. Outside of practice time of course.

"Grand Opera At Home," the first to be opened fell into disfavor after only a few scannings. An added feature of this book was a condensed story content prefacing each opera therein. Reading this intense drama, made even more lurid by the abbreviated form, gave me my first shocking news of what all those operas were about. Familiar and appreciated as many of the melodies were, by way of our phonograph or mother's excellent whistling, I found it hard to ignore the violence factor after that. All those stabbings and pools of blood. How could people sing about that? And if that wasn't enough, most all the endings were SAD.

One peek at the second Green Book, "Songs the Whole World Sings" had me off like little "Alice" to a Wonderland of Music. With each page I stepped through the looking glass into a new world. Printed upon the flysheet was, "A Collection of More than 200 Sentimental, Home,

College, Patriotic, Operatic, Sacred, Southern, National and Children's Songs"! Had I been the publishers I would have dared to add the cliché, "A Gamut of Emotions Lies Inside." But then it might have spoiled the fun of discovery. The cover suggested little—a verdant green front, bordered in pure white Grecian columns, entwined with formal garlands of white roses. Hardly a hint to the fascinating fare inside. Once there the pages still suggested nothing beyond black and white notes and words. Not a single interesting sketch, squiggle or decorative touch. Compared to methods used now for turning learning into painless adventure, Green Book was a low-cost utility edition. Nevertheless I was captivated, and not just for the moment but throughout my life. Green Book did it without bending over backwards even a little bit!

Totally unaware of the fact, geography, history and social studies subtly wove themselves in and out of the many pages. Far flung places such as Scotland, Ireland and Italy (the world was larger then), came to musical life right before my eyes and ears. How proud I was to claim an acquaintanceship with the national Anthem of such a country as Serbia. Never mind the unmelodic tune, that just made it more exciting. The bluebells and heather of Scotland became very real as I played and sang along about "bonnie lassies" yearning for their "laddies," who were off fighting the endless wars of the clans. No wonder my smugness when two years later our fourth grade class was introduced to "The Bluebells of Scotland" during the morning singing period. At this young age I had not seen an ocean as yet, but I feel sure that "Sailing, Sailing, Over the Bounding Main" brought me closer than pictures in books. I literally rolled myself across enormous waves each time I played this rollicking song.

As far as the Civil War was concerned (whose study came along later), Green Book rendered me unable to take sides. Not after meeting Stephen Foster and his loving Southern Songs. For me, Stephen Foster and Abraham Lincoln stood side by side as national heroes. A large lump managed to form in my throat each time when Old Black Joe intoned: "I'm coming. . . . I'm coming, for my head is hanging low . . ." If it was racism, it was without malice. I was too young to know that what I held so dear were songs destined to go on and on. Maybe forever.

It never occurred to me to doubt the validity of all the lyrics. If they stated a fact, it was a fact, all of which helped plant early seeds as to the world and the customs of its people. I was even moved to the point of regretting the teasing I gave my brother over his uncontrolled homesickness. Not after the lines in "Home Sweet Home" sunk in, and I realized with some shock that persons actually "died away" in the process. Now I knew his case was a legal one.

While Green Book Two did contain an Opera section, it remained true to its format by staying just with Light Opera and much less mortification. What could be lighter and frillier to play than "Woman Is Fickle," as you whirled away in its fast three-quarter time? And who cared if woman was depicted here as "false altogether, light as a feather borne on the breeze"? If I had recognized the poking of fun at a woman's frivolous mind as discriminating, I wouldn't have cared. No one else did either, at the time.

Public school formats then included patriotism on a daily basis, complete with flag salute, followed by "My Country 'Tis of Thee," but nowhere did I feel it more keenly than right at our piano with Green Book. When it was my own fingers triumphing across "Columbia the Gem of the Ocean," the red, white and blue unfurled in full color. When I struck up "The Star Spangled Banner," I all but bent the flagpole. In the middle of it I would look down sideways at my arm and watch the goosebumps popping.

I wish to add a few words about the "Sacred Songs" segment, where my first hymns were tried and felt. Though Sunday School was a weekly affair, accompanying my chum Ruthie to their Norwegian Lutheran church, the two of us never stayed on for the church hour. Just as well as I recall the sermon was preached in Norwegian. Consequently, church music for me did not reach beyond "Jesus Loves Me" or "I'll Be a Sunbeam for Him." Besides that, regular eleven o'clock service was for grown-ups and represented a mysterious kind of never-never land. Therefore the playing of real hymns gave vague feelings of treading in unknown territory, instead of bestowing comfort. However I felt the hymns inspiring, if fearsome and duly learned each one . . . and never forgot them.

Although Green Book's index did not list such items as "Spooky Music," I came across one sufficient to cast an eerie spell over my entire being each time it was read and played. Who would suspect this book to furnish my first insight into the world of occult powers? Though "Grandfather's Clock" was not my favorite, I played it now and then to convince myself such a thing could happen. As I said earlier, if the lyrics stated a fact, that was good enough for me. The way I arranged this do-it-yourself drama was to begin the piece at a slow pace, in order to prolong the finale. It seemed Grandpa had owned a huge timepiece "too large for the shelf, so it stood ninety years on the floor." What Grandpa didn't know (but I did) was that both he and his faithful clock would bow out of this world at precisely the same moment. Midway into the fateful demise, I would be torn between holding a perfect tick-tock beat or slowing down the action. My heart would actually palpitate as it went on, "Ninety years without slumbering, tick-tock . . . his life seconds numbering, tick-tock, tick-tock." The end of the next line is where tension set in as I made the appropriate quarter rest which followed the phrase, "But it stopped" (played staccato). Then came the word "short" (struck dramatically) "never to go again"; now came the slow ritard and the spooky finale, "when . . . the . . . old . . . man . . . d—i—e—d!" The whole thing was so inevitable. Maybe this is why in later years when I saw an old and lonely person sharing the living room with an old and slowly ticking clock, the same cryptic feeling was recalled.

Such were but a few of the effects from Green Book's contents. I am certain it talked, taught and entertained in a most remarkable manner. It became my personal invitation to put on a pair of musical glasses and see what went on in this world. I like to think we were fated to meet.

5

The Runaway Rivulet

The natural curiosity of childhood carried right into the written world of music too. For the time being, any detours from the well marked musical road were found by picking my way among Green Book's exciting pages. Being less than a perfect child I yielded to the temptation of straying from the path one day, and took myself down an unmarked sideroad. The unapproved byway, so beckoning and attractive, proved to be a short road that dwindled into a sorrowful swamp.

Intermediate lessons were underway with a Miss Pauline Endres in a downtown studio no less. Getting there involved a transfer from the Kay Street car line to the cable car that jolted at a terrible slant over a staircase set of hills, to the bay levels of downtown Tacoma. Mother considered a third grader too young for such a commute and appointed my elder brother Hans as escort and protector from the perils of city traffic. Each Saturday morning found him safely depositing me inside the foyer of the red-bricked Chamber of Commerce Building (now site of Winthrop Hotel). Facing the fancy grillwork of the birdcage elevator, I would pause with leather music case in hand, with my straw sailor hat listing heavily to one side. Were it not for Mother's sewn in elastic chinstrap on my skimmer hat, I might have arrived with no hat at all.

Several crossings of busy intersections amid autos, delivery vans and rattling streetcars had a direct bearing on my chapeau's condition. Without benefit of modern traffic lights and with no whistle-blowing policemen on duty in the early morning hours, Hans had to devise his own system for my safe crossings. And it had to be one not requiring us to walk side by side in a conspicuous sister and brother fashion. So we proceeded down the sidewalks in single file position, with me in the lead. When the curb was reached he gave me his version of a stop or go signal before stepping into the open street. A distinct prod in the middle of my back meant it was safe to go ahead. But when a halt was necessary, Hans would give a typical big brother yank on the back ribbons of my hat. What a chance to get even! More than once I had to be jerked back to curbside. It must have been the dependable quality of sewing found in purchased items then, for the ribbons held fast. Mother's firmly attached elastic chin band served to ward off strangulation.

As the birdcage elevator clattered and shook to a stuttering foothold at the third floor, only a short distance of hallway remained to be covered. Up and down its side stood a row of closed and heavy oak doors. Never in a great hurry for the great weekly appraisal of my worth, my footsteps dragged by a door marked, "Frederick Wallis, Voice," in hopes of catching stray soprano arpeggios from within and buying some time. When the voice rose up the scale in perfect half-tones, I sensed the drama of chromatic steps in music. One more door to pass and I'd be there. My teacher's name, printed in straight black letters upon a swirled and frosted pane read: Miss Pauline Endres, Piano.

Though Miss Endres was younger, prettier and less formidable than previous ones, I soon would learn her heart had a high melting point when pressed. One fine Saturday morn while waiting the finish of an earlier student's lesson, my ears turned pink with envy. Seated upon a straight-backed oak chair, I hear lilting runs all bubbly and frothy tumbling from her fingers. Why did she have such a much nicer and faster fingered pieced than any of mine? As she folded back the last page and turned the music around, I leaned from my perch to read the bright blue letters. The title said, "The Rivulet." Instant desire overcame me to the extent of speaking up bravely and asking to have it for my assignment. Evidently Miss Endres did not find it in her heart to refuse such a deadly earnest plea. A copy was issued to me that very day, provided I worked on it after other work was completed. Smitten with joy I agreed with all my heart.

By chance, or predestination, the Third Grade teacher at Franklin school was setting up something rather unusual. A little afternoon class program no less, just for our room. Since volunteering piano solos was not by habit, I must have been drafted for the event. Why I don't know, but at my next lesson, Miss Endres was dutifully notified of the program. An out and out mistake. To my dismay I heard her say quickly, "I think this is a very nice idea of your teachers, and I think you should play "The Little Shepherdess" for your number. It is very fitting and has such a sweet melody." The next statement came to me as a surprise: "And you play it well." As no rebuttals or questions were indicated, I swallowed a rising lump of disappointment. First of all, my ego was insulted. Who wanted to play such a simple and dull piece in front of everyone in the class? My dislike for "The Little Shepherdess" and her simple ways had begun to mount from the day I carried her home in my music case. Naturally it grew throughout all the countless repetitions.

Came the program day, making itself very forceful now, the formerly soft voice of the little red devil who had been making suggestions to me for a week, began to insist in a more pressing tone: "You know," it said, "You don't *have* to play that piece. The Rivulet would be much more fun. Why not switch? You have it memorized. Just think how your classmates will ooh and aah when you play the fancy and long runs. And you can speed it up real fast. They'll be sure to take notice. After all Miss Endres will be far away downtown in her studio. She'll never even know you did it, so go ahead, play 'The Rivulet' instead." And I did. With barely a qualm the simple little shepherdess was cast aside and replaced by something much showier. I must have felt it was my chance to get even with her for being such a plain and simple character.

"And tell me please . . . how did your piano solo go . . . the one you played for the class program?" Miss Endres was peering down at me. It was several days after my defection and we were about to embark upon another lesson period. Her brunette ear-puffs, so perfectly ratted and circled, almost touched the pink discs of rouge on either cheek. I was noting how the glassy blue beads around her neck matched the flowers of her pretty blue dress. The questions was unexpected and seemed to hang in the stilled air of a suddenly chill studio. Why did I have to be here? She had me dead to rights. Instead of just saying "fine" my bravado deserted and left me giving out the whole story. We had just recently studied about George Washington at school and his telling of the truth had turned out well. But not for me. My penance was intoned thusly: At the upcoming Spring Recital Miss Reitz will perform one number, "The Little Shepherdess"! How could Miss Endres be so pretty, and yet so cruel? Strong feelings of revolt rose within my breast, but in my heart I already knew they'd never be carried out. Besides, mother would support Miss Endres one hundred percent.

All the while life and lessons with Miss Encres were falling into their own cycle of time. Rebellion's price had been paid and the sting was fading. Best of all the lowly shepherdess had been put out to pasture, where I thought she belonged. No doubt Miss Endres felt she had done her duty in showing me simple can also be beautiful. Progress continued and now I began to shake hands with Frederich Kuhlau's Sonatinas, Carl Czerny's School of Velocity (which term I associated with a bicycle) and other stern appearing books. Most of them in my opinion then and now, were willfully perpetrated to shamefully embarrass your lazy fourth finger. To my joy a Suite of Edvard Grieg's compositions was soon being carried back and forth in the leather case. In spite of his three, four and often five sharp signatures, which resembled the flock of blackbirds on a fence, his melodic music had instant appeal for me. In today's parlance I was now "relating better to my assignments." Whether mother sometimes caught glimpses of the long ago wall inscription when I was three, I do not know. Nor do I know if she considered my interest for Grieg anything outstanding, but I would assume she did for she followed each step quite closely. As I have mentioned before, loud praises were not sung in my presence. Mother, who was anything but uncaring, was simply steeped in German culture in the whys and wherefores of bringing up children. I'm sure it was deemed to be in my best interest.

6

The Fifth Terror

Centuries ago a wise Chinese philosopher sat down and made a listing he entitled: "The Four Terrors of Life." He saw them as EARTHQUAKE, FIRE, FLOOD AND FATHER. One must assume music recitals did not exist at his time of writing. I am absolutely certain any student of any musical instrument would fully support and recognize RECITALS as Terror Number Five! Nearly every one of mine was a fear-ridden date with destiny. You simply became very unwell when the time came to perform. Clammy fingers, burning cheeks and a dreadful sensation in your middle reduced what talents you possessed into quivering submission. Placing yourself on a piano stool in front of all those people, in front of an unfamiliar instrument whose keys were alreay slick and damp (unless you played first) used up your adrenalin supply for a week. How could you possibly sit down and play *anything?* Like a carved statue, the keyboard only stared back at you, willing to go ahead if you were. But you weren't ready—ever.

The only pleasant memory I have of any recital is my first one. Innocence was responsible for my bliss. By virtue of being the youngest, my number was the recital's opener. Confident and happy I ran through the little familiar number so well known to program audiences, "The Merry Farmer." The definite pattern and harmonic tonic chords were to my liking as was the artist's concept of country life sketched upon the cover. Here a smiling farmer cheerfully dug away among neat and weedless rows of abundance, all rayed in yellow sunshine. I simply liked the whole package and the first recital came off without scars, but the condition was not to last.

About a year or so later, maybe I was seven by then, my program contribution provided the sole comic relief in the tension filled atmosphere. All nerves were on edge, the students, parents and recruited friends alike. Due to lean pocketbooks, most teachers rented halls which were of similar decor. Austerity trimmed in dust. Their musty indifference lent no warning to trembling hearts. Slippery wood floors echoed every human step and stiff rows of cold fold-up chairs stood like a death watch. The stage of concert size rivaled a desert for barrenness, except for a lone piano and the erect rod of the American flag at the right wing. A far cry from homey.

A new dimension, possibly designed to lend some color and warmth, was to enhance this recital. The youngest daughter of a locally prominent florist (the Ghilarducci family) was one of the pupils, so her proud parents had judiciously decided to honor *each* performer with a floral bouquet. After all, how would it look to just present their very own with flowers? Somehow I wasn't clued in on the gesture, or maybe the parents' intention was to surprise each soloist. In this particular rented hall the pupils had all been secreted backstage, with no view of the audience out front. What a twittering cluster of flowered voile, starchy laces and showy sashes, each little heart a victim of suspense. Any moment now our teacher would be stepping onstage, where each number would be announced to a shuffling and rustling background of programmes and resettling bodies.

I was youngest, and first. Nothing to do now but step out onto that open area of stage and force myself forward to the piano. My selection was something from a suite of meadow meanderings (not a new locale for me), with which I feared no breakdown as it had been thoroughly memorized. In my habitual gymnastic fashion, I did a flying twirl from the piano stool almost before the last note died away, sailing myself across stage to the exit.

To the entire assemblage's delight, the poor floral bearer emerging from the other side, outstretched bouquet in hand, never had a chance. Pfft . . . I was long gone into the wings, as if the devil himself were behind me.

Though I sensed something was following me, fright precluded even peeking over my shoulder. The chase was on and any applause was replaced by contagious laughter at the unrehearsed comic skit. Into the opposite wings he pursued his recipient, finally cornering me backstage. Not to be outdone he propelled me back onstage again amid a regathering wave of laughter. Here, as my parents described it, he anchored me firmly with his one hand and practically thrust the bouquet into my bosom.

My then quite new stepfather agreed it was the high point of the whole recital. His only regret was that we hadn't gone around the track one more time! It remains the lone ice breaker and only comic relief (enjoyed by the audience) of my recital career.

7

Summertime's Pianos

No more teachers, no more books began echoing through the play yard of Franklin Elementary School about the last few weeks of May. The lid would soon be off. At our house on Melrose Street the rosebeds were budding up and like most pupils, Hans and I as brother and sister checked off the remaining days upon the kitchen calendar. While his anticipation matched mine, he found himself unable to enact his part in mother's plans for our vacation time. Still clinging to the German tradition of sending youngsters off to the country during summer, she put together the best of everything to make an enviable vacation package. Without so much as a single relative within the whole United States, it was a Godsend to have selfmade "Tantes" (German term for Auntie) as the plans certainly revolved around them. First and closest was our Tante Krummel (Adele Krummel). Significantly and in the name of German fellowship she had been the very first to call on mother after the arrival of the new German doctor's family. From that gesture sprang an abiding friendship and close family ties that endured unto a second generation. Tante number two of the summer coalition was Tante Lottie (Lottie Krull) a more casual friend within the German clique. That these two offered perfect summer settings had to be part of God's generosity and my good luck. How the logistics were worked out is unknown to me, but I would suppose some sort of a reciprocal pact was made as mother was a poor receiver of anyone's largesse, be they Tantes' or anyone else's.

On the very first run Hans had become so violently homesick, he had to be returned with haste to the city. With distances a larger factor then and not wishing to rerun the risk, he was the first to agree that his misery ruled him out of the game. The plan went ahead with me as the sole party to carry on tradition, but I was moved to add an additional clause to the contract, in spite of delight and gratitude—one which would cover *any* stay *any place* that exceeded an overnight stop. No pianos in said homes—no go. Quite an ultimatum from a child not given to vindictiveness! A few such outings at piano-less homes had brought the fact to light. It could be I felt this in some way would provide me with a quirk that was all my own.

Brother Hans was not left out in the cold. I recall at one of the first returns from one of the Tante's, he was busily attaching wheels to some kind of a sidewalk racer, which kit he had received while I was away.

Strange to say, I felt no urge to taunt him about his homesick problem, and for good reason. Never one to doubt the authenticity of Green Book's songs and lyrics, I was well aware that homesickness was not only drastic, but legal as well. Playing and singing through the explicit verses of "Home Sweet Home" painted a picture not easy to forget along with implied possibilities of just pining oneself right out of this world. Like most children I never stopped to think how mother must have adjudged her up to now, two offspring's reaction to the summer plan. One had a proven case of acute homesickness and the other threatened her own disease, a piano-sickness.

Neither our beds of blooming roses or mother's vacation traditions swayed my piano teachers into declaring a summer moratorium. "Just to keep our fingers nimble," prefaced an outline for daily, but unsupervised practices. Weekly lessons were cancelled till Fall. The loopholes of this little honor system posed no temptations to me. Not that I was so honorable, I just required a daily contact with the piano.

Far from being an aesthetic child, I welcomed summer's extra hours for real physical exertion at one of my favorite accomplishments. It had to do with fancying myself to be a daring gymnast, homemade of course with no help or coaching. The wherewithal was right at hand in our own backyard. Visible from blocks away, two towering support posts held a rigid lateral beam, upon which firmly bolted swing and rings were hung. The whole concept was a product of my stepfather's true German thoroughness, measured out in Atlas proportions. Any safety insurance writer would have been happy to endorse it. No wonder my hands could just circle over the sturdy ropes of the swing. They were originally designed for fastening an ocean liner to a dock and tightly twisted in marine quality Manilla hemp. Much of my outdoor world began to be viewed from an upside-down position, swinging boldly through the air, head straight down with both knees clamped onto a pair of industrial weight metal rings. Mother, who saw my monkey-like acrobatics as a continuous exposé, and in the name of decency, took to her seldom used sewing machine. What came forth were several pairs of black sateen bloomers, whose ballooned legs were indubitably controlled with a length of elastic that snapped shut with the vengeance of a bear trap. The upside-down bloomer picture evidently soon paled also, for the next item of my gym attire was what I'd always wanted. A pair of khaki knickers! A provision was attached: "To be used solely for gymnastics." Their style, painfully revealed later in our family albums, was square necked, saggy and baggy, with one drooping sidepocket on either hip. Before long the better part of summer found me inside of them, which only goes to prove, every mother has her breakdown point.

25

Though only nine summers old now, I could still dimly remember some scenes from other family summers, the ones that preceded any worries about being without pianos. I could reach back as far as when Tahlequah was called "Clam Cove." Our father, after his day as a doctor, usually jumped aboard the little "Elsie" launch in Point Defiance, and crossed the bay to our beach house on the other side. German togetherness thrived in Clam Cove too, with other nearby cabins and homes belonging to the Krummel's, the Kloepper's and the Arnold's. After the separation of my parents, we were only a unit of three and Clam Cove summers were over. Next came a sort of tent-house on the shores of American Lake where the proximity of the Krummel's like abode must have put a crimp in mother and Tante Krummel's summer. Bernhard (their son) and I managed to run two successive cases of measles over the better part of the season. Fortunately neither of us had what was called "the hard measles," making it possible for both mothers to at least be at the lake. Some years later, when mother re-married, saw the beginning of what I like to call the Tante summers. Though mother accompanied us to our destinations, she returned soon to her new home and husband. I didn't know it then, but it was the prelude to a new family. Then when after a few traumatic episodes where my brother's longing for home became unbearable, the whole package just sifted down to me. A whole new world of summertimes and summer pianos was ready to roll. It was time for me to pick up my little suitcase and proceed.

"Yes, little lady, we'll see you get off in Adna—in fact we make a mail stop there." Procedure Number One was underway and believe me I needed the assurance of the conductor on this first train trip on my own, at age nine. Naturally Mother had seen me off at the domed Union Station in Tacoma with full instructions for every eventuality concerning the role of traveler and house guest. The first out-of-town fun was stretching ahead over shiny rails that clickety-clacked under the rolling iron wheels of a magnificent train. Far away after about three and a half hours, I would be alighting in Adna and be taken into the family scene at the Krummel home, with Tante Krummel in charge. Though both summer junkets were well within a one hundred mile radius of Tacoma, they spelled distance for most folks, and for a young child the word distance was spelled with a capital "D."

The train had made only a reluctant pause in Littell and I knew it was my signal to reclaim my suitcase way up on the overhead rack and adjust the rubber band designed to keep my sailor hat from flying and then stand in the aisle while bracing myself for any manner of a jolting halt. Heaven forbid any tottering into another passenger's lap when you were nine and had ridden trains before! As the full swoop of Adna country began to slow down and I knew that real soon I'd be jumping off onto the wooden platform and step right into it, I could barely contain myself. After all I wasn't just going to *anybody's* house, but to the Krummels who were all dear to me and whose domain included a huge general merchandise store smelling of oily wood, coffee beans and hardware. Housed in the back corner of the store was the sanctum of a United States Post Office where "Pop" Krummel, as he was called, reigned as Postmaster. Not only that, the whole rectangular wooden building's upstairs hosted the Lewis County Grange. Directly across the street was the Krummel home, a comfortable bungalow with porches fore and aft, set off by grassy spaces, rose trellises and a kitchen garden. On cloudless days, which were many, Mt. St. Helen's and Mt. Adams swam on a faraway blue horizon from a foreground of yellow fields, dairy barns and fertililty. I lost no time in becoming thoroughly country struck at each visit.

If the grass was greener away from home, so was the piano playing. For one thing, informal or even mundane music was not verboten in Adna. The whole Krummel household drew breath in less rigid climate than ours at home. This might have been due in part to Tante Krummel's intermittent clerking at the store. Be that as it may, the musical air was thinner, despite Bernhard's many hours of practice with the advanced classics. Even their Victrola was not in error when it spinned the eldest son Carl's new record of "Underneath The Mellow Moon." I lost little time in learning every note and word of this pleasant waltz. It would have had my vote for the Gold Record of the Year, had such honors existed then. Another differing factor was the audience. At home it was mother or teacher, who both saw eye to eye in dogmatic approach. Here in Adna the listeners could run from an aproned housewife still clutching a pungent bag of hand-ground coffee, to a shy, stubble-faced logger from up Bunker Hill way. Both had been spontaneously recruited only moments earlier thusly:

"You must come over to the house with me. It won't take but a moment," Tante Krummel would carry on from across bolts of yardage spilling across the counter. "My best friend's young daughter is here with us for a visit. She can just sit down and play most anything you ask for. Isn't it remarkable at her age? Now you be thinking of one of your favorite songs whilst (one of Tante's well-used words) we march on over."

The remarkableness was largely the result of my love for Green Book's many pages and my easy memorizing. To that I had now the opportunity to play the pop tunes tucked away in the back of my head.

The impromptu listeners usually trailed Tante into the front room rather shyly. On their faces was a look of quizzical concern. One could not blame them for that. How did they know what was in store for them? Just could be Mrs. Krummel was proudly overstating the facts. How embarrassing a situation could take place if this were true, and what in the world *was* their favorite song?

Since most had not the foggiest notion of what to ask for on such a short notice, it was often up to me to make a suggestion. To my delight, when I offered a particular song with the feeling it could be something they'd like, it sometimes turned out to be just that. Seeing their faces light up in surprise was half the fun and helped take some of the fright out of the skinny girl at the piano. When at times a request did come forth, by some lucky quirk and the backup support of Green Book, my batting average was quite high. Conversely, had I been asked to sit down and make polite conversation with these strangers, I would have struck out in a hurry! Had I been able to express it with an adult's reasoning power, I would have thought: "It sure is a lot easier to let the piano take over for me."

As soon as these little mini-performances were finished, no time was lost in picking up the thread of whatever had been going on before. All activities inevitably led to the high spot of the day. . . . SWIMMING. Afternoons were for splashing and swimming in the meandering Chehalis River, with its smooth sandy bottom and harmless current. Clusters of riverbank bushes rescued our modesty and became snug undressing rooms. In between dips and daring "Preacher Seat" jumping, the toasty warm sand, so fine and sugary, was great for getting warm all over as you flopped yourself into a scooped out space and covered up.

Such were the delights of nature in the nostalgic Adna summers. All of them only a few pastures and a fence-squeeze away.

The little functional straw suitcase barely had time to cool its heels after the trainride south and back, before being re-packed with almost the same summer collection. Within again, among the necessities, lay a pair of limp canvas waterwings, my semi-kneelength black wool bathing suit with the white stripes, prudently purchased to allow for certain shrinkage and "growing into," and of course a Sunday dress and my trusty knickers. Our kitchen calendar soon read, "Ilse to leave for Aunt Lottie's," leaving only a scant two weeks for leveling off at home, getting reacquainted with our yard, now with all rosebeds fully abloom, and playing with Ruthie Hansen, my closest friend. I don't remember any statement put to me directly, but I'm sure mother must have felt gratified over how good I was at living out her instilled customs of a proper summer, for I was all set and ready to sail again.

Part Two, or the Tante Lottie portion of summer, officially got underway when the propellers of a big white Ferry ruffled the saltwater around the Steilacoom dock pilings. The underfooting of solid ground would soon be replaced by the throbbing decks of a boat. There it sat, looking for all the world like a protective mother hen, ready to enfold an oncoming batch of cars under her wings. Upper decks shone invitingly with outside benches or enclosed seating. Much earlier in the morning a small bus had jittered mother and me from Tacoma to the historic bayside town of Steilacoom. Having just done my first solo trip by rail, I now would undertake another one, only by water this time. I was still the sole family representative as Hans's homesickness was still in effect. This summer he and his close companion Pete Hansen were well into the throes of baseball fever. Our Melrose Street home was but three or four blocks from Peck's Field, and he and Pete had laid claim to their favorite knotholes in the board fence for glimpsing the Tacoma Tigers.

A few bugaboos still remained to be met before becoming the independent sailor, the first of which managed to catch one unaware no matter how you braced yourself for it. All of a sudden from within the mild bustle of the little harbor, a tremendous blast would literally split the air. All else ceased for the moment. It seemed to rise from the deepest innards of the ferry and shoot upward into the heavens with an authoritative roar, bouncing back and forth from warehouses and shores in a series of echoes, as your deafened ears regained normal hearing again. The ferry's imminent sailing was never in doubt. My other worry was missing the whole performance, and the ferry too. However the bus always reached the dock in time. After mastering the foregoing came the moments of wistfulness, standing on the back apron of the boat, waving to a mother who faded slowly into the distance. This period was short as the fascination of Puget Sound's watery byways, secluded coves and inlets, especially in these earlier times, was like a picture book. Just maybe today, deckrail leaning and peering into the clear waters would reveal the awesome red jellyfish!

In between were hootings and arrivals at several docks where onlookers waited or sat here and there on each wharf awaiting the incoming boat. Lazy fishlines dangled into the waters as young freckled and barefoot boys paused amid the clanking of chains and suddenly churning waters. Even a child could sense how the charm of summer seemed to cast a special spell upon an island. Soon I'd be a part of it, just a few bays away in Longbranch. Once there, only a crossing of little

Filucy Bay remained before reaching Aunt Lottie's beach cottage. As the gangplank bridged each passenger from ferry to anchored dock, the bustling and greetings filled the air. Life here, it was soon apparent, became a watery affair. High and low tides helped set the day's pattern and rowboats were a way of life.

But not yet. For now it was a scattering of seagulls and goodbye to another sleepy island village. The friendly looking small store and dirt road, winding up and away from the harbor, grew smaller and faded away as the ferry chugged out into another aisle of water. Unlike the train trip to Adna, no uncertainty existed as to getting off at the right place. The one-and-a-half hour's run terminated in Filucy Bay. Here the captain merely switched ends of the boat, stationing himself in the wheelhouse there. To me this seemed a most ingenious arrangement. What happened to incoming passengers, announced or unannounced and in need of getting to the other side, had been neatly figured out. Each family home on these shores had a unique code system worked out with the ship's captains. Two long hoots of the ferry's horn alerted the Mahncke's they had someone to pick up at the dock. A long and a short blast was for the Krull's, and so on. Not too many complicated combinations were necessary in these times of only scattered homes. Bridges then were only dreams of the future. Much like the old rural partyline, these horn signals gave out a lot of information as to Filucy Bay's social scene. I don't believe surprise visits were overly common, and when they did happen, the hosts could be reasonably sure the guest would arrive ham in hand. Farm chicken was available at times and butter clams were everywhere, but ham was a city treat that could overlook the absence of refrigerators.

Sure enough now, the ferry's motors slowed to a drone as we sidled into the bay and two code signal hoots echoed themselves around the circle. One, to my reassurance, was Aunt Lottie's call and though all had been arranged previously, it felt quite impressive to be so hailed among the saltwater coves and sandy points.

Being greeted by Tante Lottie almost overwhelmed me at first . . . each time. Her approach to life leaned heavily toward a Pollyanna form. While my eyes took in favorite landmarks and legs adjusted to firm ground, her glowing voice was already proclaiming the bounteous gifts in store for us. I could not say I found fault with her concept (some did), but it took a bit to get into the swing of so many gloriouses, wonderfuls and thankfuls. No time was lost in getting down to the lower floats where the rowboats were tied. The almost vertical tilt of the adaptable footbridge to the water's level meant the tide was now at low point. With one hand clutching the handrail and the other my straw suitcase, my

Mary Janes had to grasp hard at each cleat of the descent. A few days later would find me almost flitting up and down, just like an old salt.

"It's just an old has-been." Tante Lottie was apologizing cheerily. "But we are so grateful just to have had it brought out here." I was being introduced to the cottage piano, which I had already ascertained before going there would be in the small house. "I just can't imagine," sang her voice, "why the middle pedal was ever added. Perhaps just for the novelty of it." I looked down at what appeared like three ordinary foot pedals, instead of the customary two. She continued, "The tone is not pleasing at all and we try not to use the extra pedal . . . just make believe it isn't there." "I'm sure Ilse (my German name used at home and by Tantes), you will not be pleased by it either." What surprised me more than the third pedal was Tante Lottie's voice delivering an uncomplimentary remark. "It's called," she sang from the little closet where I was to hang up my things, "a Mandolin pedal." About here is where the desire to try out such a unique item began to take root.

Truthfully, once the twangy tones were heard I could hardly stand them myself! Not only that, the whine insisted to hang on and overide all else in its path. Consequently, the pedal was only resorted to for an added effect when other kids dropped in and we wanted to play and sing. An almost daily occurrence. Though Tante Lottie was apt to be outside during these sing-a-longs, I'm sure she heard the tinny tones of "No No Nora" and such jangling off the barnacles and butter clams of peaceful Filucy Bay. In Longbranch the lid was also off as to music choices, as long as the daily exercise period had been done. The carefree weeks drifted by with days of water, clams, sunshine and always the necessary piano to round out the picture of complete summer.

Though it was several summers distant, the old piano's mandolin pedal was to have the last word with me. One particular afternoon, of what was to be the last of the idyllic Longbranch visits, I unknowingly set off the spark. A high tide had decreed mid-afternoon to be swim time, and with young guests over at Mahncke Point, five or six of us had swum in the sandy cove there. After the water fun, now accomplished without the childish waterwings we had all begun with, all had trooped back over the winding huckleberry fringed path to where the only piano was . . . Aunt Lottie's. Heretofore no one else had been able to play in the fun fashion needed for a group of giggling girls, so I lost no time in taking over and sitting down at the piano. "Row Row Your Boat" went round till breakdown point and then I played a fast clip on a march I loved, "Under the Double Eagle." This of course set the whole lot to prancing about the room. Over impressed at inciting such action, we hardly drew breath before bawling out, "Ma, He's Making Eyes At Me," followed by another rouser. Through the cottage window I could see Aunt Lottie sitting out on the bulkhead steps, a wall that kept Filucy Bay's high tides from swishing up the porch steps. As far back as "Ma, He's Making Eyes At Me," nothing would do but to depress that middle pedal for all it was worth. Without a doubt this is where it fitted and soon hilarity took over our little soirée. We managed one more chorus, twanging all the way, before giving out. Standard count is thirty-two bars in popular music, so multiplied by even just three, an awful lot of rasping had filled the air. My heart was telling me once more how much I loved playing here, right on the rocky beaches of this friendly bay, with the swooping branches of red-skinned Madrona trees often overhanging secret coves at high tide. I loved my view from the keyboard as I could beam straight across the water to Longbranch proper. From the cottage window the little village appeared as a little scene created by toy building blocks, with the simple white spire as its tallest point. I knew it then and I know it now. Being at Longbranch was summer's second helping of Manna from Heaven. But back to the significant pedal.

From the corner of my eye I saw Tante Lottie's tall figure ascend the steps to the long front veranda. There was no stopping at her wicker rocker, the one with the flowered cretonne pillow. Instead I soon felt her standing right behind me, as the last measures droned away. The gaudy whangs were still floating and hanging in the warm air. I wondered if they'd ever die away and then finally it was quiet. Very quiet.

"And now Ilse," came her cultured and very calm voice, "Don't you think it might be nice to ask one of our visitors if *they've* anything *they'd* like to play or perform? Perhaps someone can recite or might possibly play the piano too." Silence. Then without acidity or sarcasm she leveled me with, "You cannot be the *whole* cheese all the time." I can still see the dark blackish brown on the old piano's arm as I stared downward. Would there be more? But that was all and the moment, long as it was, passed with Tante cooly proceeding into the small kitchen. We carried on briefly, but the heart had gone out of it. To my secret joy, no one could or wished to add any further talents to the affair.

That night as I lay in my cot beside the front window, the words kept going round and round in my head. Over and over I heard, "You can't be the WHOLE CHEESE." The size of the cheese seemed to grow into an enormous block with each repetition. Had Aunt Lottie been at a loss of adages at the moment and forced to consult Ben Franklin's Almanac, she couldn't have improved upon her choice. Unbeknownst to her she had not only cut my water off, she had likened me to an article of food I then found most unsavory and impossible to eat! The analogy possibly lengthened my acceptance of cheese as palatable food.

Somehow the advice lived to haunt me for a long, long time. The opportunities for causing it to flash upon my mind seemed to crop up every now and then throughout later playing years. I wish in all honesty I could say they were heeded without fail, but at least I had a necessary sense of awareness. Though I did learn later to appreciate the world of cheeses, my conscience is forever marked with its connecting link to my musical ego. Aunt Lottie never referred to the incident again, and she lived on to a cheery ripe age. I've always chosen to put part of the blame on the rasping mandolin pedal going at full volume. There is a straw for every camel's back.

8

A "Noted" Excursion

Without benefit of airmail, two cent postcards suddenly flew back and forth between Tacoma and a little town named Adna. On their surfaces were written specific dates, hours and suppressed excitement. Something was afoot. Evidently revelation beforehand of a Seattle journey, half of whose focal point was to center on me, was not the way to go. The other half of the focus was Bernhard, one-and-a-half years my senior and son of mother's best friend Adele Krummel. Contained within the postcards was the complete strategy for quite an ambitious undertaking, prompted by parental curiosity as to a steering direction for their two young pianists. To start the ball rolling, Tante Krummel and Bernhard would have to take the train from Adna to Tacoma. After an overnight stay at our house, both mothers and budding pianists would board the early boat for Seattle where an appointment of no mean proportions had been made. I would say that within both mothers' hearts lurked the prospect of possibly squeezing in some shopping on the side.

Prime object of course was the gaining of an evaluation of their respective offspring's talents and future possibilities at the piano. Each mother had agreed on seeking this verdict from one whose judgment carried weight, and cost money. His name, Pierre McNeeley, the reigning impresario of matters musical (piano of course) in the Northwest. It's flattering now to realize the heighth of their aims. As for the two performers, neither of us seemed to rate the upcoming judgment on the same monster level as recitals. Cold fear on our part might have been warmed by the anticipation of the roundtrip cruise and what might await our eyes and stomach at a restaurant! Our individual merits as pianists was reliable debate material, done with utmost parental modesty. The classic countering never reached anything remotely resembling agreement.

"Aber Alma," mother's friend Adele would protest, after mother had extolled Bernhard's outstanding virtues, "just because he has control and excells in rapid fingering doesn't make him the most gifted." She politely neglected any mention of his being far ahead of normal piano-grade level, or his owning a technique and strength that nearly overpowered his teacher. Without fail mother would rally with:

"Aber Adele" (with lapses into German words here and there), "Bernhard plays with such unusual fine expression and feeling. His classics are so impressive. I'm sure *he* is going to be the concert pianist." But this was not the end.

"You are overlooking the fact," came the rebuttal, "that Ilse (my given German name) can memorize and also transpose. Why, she knew how to play before ever having a lesson." Innate social decency forbade their changing the formula. If they had only asked me, I'd have cast the tie-breaking vote. Bernhard was miles ahead of me. But they never did and so it just remained in static limbo.

At age eleven, red letter important days seem to take forever to dawn, which is probably why nothing was divulged until a week prior. This one dawned with a wide open sky of blue as four fluttering hearts managed to brush teeth and hair. We fairly floated over the three blocks to the 12th Street carline, dressed in our best for an event with all the earmarks of a momentous holiday. Of course there was the judgment element, but for the moment it was pushed aside, if not forgotten.

Bass-noted blasts spouting from the "Tacoma's" stacks bounced back and forth from docks and shore, mingling with the jostle and hubbub of ticketed passengers, all Seattle bound. Up tipped the gangplank and up went our heartbeats as the final blow of departure stunned our eardrums. A white frosted Mt. Tacoma (correct name in '23) rose behind the ship, seeing us off. Ahead lay the beautiful clear waters whose crossing was an hour and a half pleasant journey afloat. Not even a child intent on every nook and cranny, within limits of the entire ship, could fail to be struck by the sweeping views from each point on the decks. Artists with palette and brush, trying to capture snowy rows of the Olympic peaks, were a fairly common sight. It was a gentle ride on open water with an evening view of quiet green islands which briefly shared the privacy of their curved shorelines. On the return trip ringside seats were snatched quickly if conditions indicated a colorful sunset, which only glorified the panorama for many pairs of spellbound eyes. The trip always ended too soon.

"Just try and see all the way up to the top," urged Bernhard as both of us leaned against the deck rail, craning our necks to the very tip of the L. C. Smith Building. "It's the tallest building in the whole city, forty-two stories," we announced to each other in great awe. Suddenly other buildings and clock towers began to grow taller too as the steamer began to sidle into its moorage at Coleman Dock. It is entirely possible the two of us were the most unjaded visitors in Seattle that day.

With eager feet we joined the stream of passengers over a long elevated ramp suspended above the lower waterfront streets. Peering into the first enticing downtown store window we were shocked to see a black draped photo of President Harding in the center of a display! An ominous tone was in the morning air. Newstands were in a commotion, selling Extras with enormous black letters that shouted, "PRESIDENT HARDING IS DEAD. FOOD POISONING SUSPECTED"! Somehow we had missed it up to the moment, which was not all that hard to do in the '20's. Silent draped pictures met us at every turn as we continued our way to the McNeeley studio. Life and music seemed to be carrying on anyway. I remember the distraction of my inability to stop the clock. Like a dentist appointment, your die was cast and there was no turning back. It was forward march with the two properly suited and summer-hatted mothers firmly in the lead. Alas, the correct building was located immediately, and we were shot quickly to the fifth floor by an all-closed-in elevator.

Had we misread the main floor directory? Poised on the threshold, our sun-glazed eyes blinked uncertainly into a subdued lamp-lighted interior. Assured by a shadowy receptionist who seemed to come from nowhere, we were acknowledged and asked to make ourselves comfortable. Her graceful gesture had indicated a grouping of indistinct davenports and chairs and with our pavement oriented feet sinking deeply into thick Persian carpeting, we dispersed our bodies onto a long furry davenport. I believe even our mothers were quite unprepared for all the lush and velvety, the sculpted busts and the exquisitely beaded lampshades. Everything exuded a muted breath of assured superiority, and for an eleven year old it was pretty heady. Looming into view now in

35

the adjoining room a magnificently long Grand Piano stood bathed in a pool of soft light. Beside it an ornate oriental floorlamp heightened the mystique.

To my relief, Bernhard and his mother were ushered in to lead off our audience period. Anything was better than being first. He played very well and I was self informed enough to know his intricate timing and flying fingers were more than I would offer. I could hear him skittering easily through "Rustle of Spring" and another difficult and heavy chorded number and could almost see the thoughtful attention being given his performance. There ensued a great nodding of heads and low-spoken conferring. Now I could see Pierre McNeeley's face as it beamed compliments in the direction of his first assignment. He looked fancy and dapper like someone in a movie.

"Now let me hear what the young lady is going to play . . . your name is Ilse, I believe?" I lost no time in agreeing that it was while my mind asked wildly, "What will he think of *my* piece and will my fingers turn to wooden sticks as they did at most recitals?" Schwarwenka's "Polish Dance" received as much spirit as I could muster and I've forgotten the second offering but I do remember its finish. As I swung into my usual quick pivot from the piano bench I heard:

"Please don't leave the piano yet." His voice was as soft as the dreamy lamp next to me, which I could have easily collided with in my haste. "Now . . . sit down again. I understand you transpose readily. Please play any portion of your number again, but in the key changes as I call them to you. Let's begin by adding one sharp." Tension was easing as I was in more familiar territory with this being something I indulged in at home for the fun of it. Several variations later we ended with his rapid test for perfect pitch which I passed easily and without knowing it was anything out of the ordinary. More conversation ensued between McNeeley and mother, McNeeley with me and then all of us together, ending abruptly just as I began to feel the whole thing was not a terrifying experience. His verbal advice had been optimistic with definite counsel to continue our studies and work hard. Meanwhile our teachers would be alerted as to individual strong points via a series of notations he had entered into a written report. At least we had been worth the trip!

Later conversations over lunch between the mothers must have been a nonstop chattering bee, done in ladylike fashion in keeping with the dulcet tones of a strong ensemble just a few steps from our table. Their choice of a luncheon restaurant had likely been reached for this reason, but Bernhard and I were more engrossed in what Meeve's Cafeteria's white tiled counters had to offer than in the melodic bowings of violins and cellos. The supreme test of heeding a gentle reminder to not let eyes exceed the size of the tray required full concentration as we viewed the feast. Being taken out now and then for a sundae or ice cream soda was within our realm, but sitting down at white clothed tables to hot meals with plates, knives and forks was not. To be fair, we had lots of company as dining out was not in force during the '20's. It seemed there was nothing each lady presiding over her steamy territory would rather do than dip her ladle and serve you. But which ladle should you choose? A glass dish of red jewels sparkling up ahead quickly fixed choice of deserts, for in my mind it ranked as a rare elixir of the gods. The high estimation was brought on by mother still being doubtful about recognizing packaged Jello as a desirable item for her pantry shelves at home.

When normal lessons and life resumed in the fall, I failed to see any great change taking place in my teacher's attitude. Things went on just as before, test and qualification sheets from Seattle notwithstanding. I definitely was no more a privileged character than before our judgment day, whose drama and history were never to be forgotten. Subsequent trips to Meeve's Cafeteria, though still wonderful, were never quite the same. As for mother, the checks made out to the teachers continued to be written, perhaps signed and blotted now with greater conviction.

9

The Boy Next Door

Several metronomed months and books of cadences later, one of my secretly cherished wishes came true. Intangible as yet, the event became a first encounter at performing as an accompanist. None caused more of a goosepimpled uprising than this initial tryout—and it was due to mother's carefully reserved, but pleasant good neighbor policy.

Across the sideyard fence one spring day, after two housewives had snapped the last Turkish towel to their respective clotheslines, mother and Mrs. Evans had carried their usual brief pleasantries beyond the weather and the admiration of the rosebushes between the two homes. "Would your daughter," Mrs. Evans had ventured, "be able to accompany Theodore sometime soon?" "It would be of such help to him in learning a particular solo he is working on right now." The two families were not acquainted to the point of discussing music, and I rarely saw their one and only offspring Theodore (not to be confused with Ted). Nevertheless, the reedy notes of his saxophone must have mingled among the rosebeds with my inverted triads, and Mrs. Evans had just added two and two.

A saxophone was an unknown instrument to me then, but I would have agreed to anything having such a close proximity to Theodore. Because a college chemistry major and a gangly twelve year old girl had just as little in common then as they do now, Theodore fell into the class of "unapproachable and worship from afar." His mystique was sharpened upon listening to mother's incredulous surprise at first hearing of Theodore's dinner time priorities.

"I do think," she confided to my step-father during a meal, "they are indulging him even beyond the limits of doting parents . . . just imagine . . . they cut out the centers of their T-bone steaks for their son, while they eat the trimmings!"

Window-curtain peekings, and any other method I could get away with, disclosed Theodore to be the ultimate collegiate, complete with worldly airs. He only appeared in sporty cream colored cords, pullover sweaters and at all times, it seemed, a tennis racquet dangled from one hand in cool casualness. Would I accompany him? The question was not put to me directly, but I remember the prospect filling me with numb delight when mother gave me the word. What was more, I was to go over on my own as mother did not see this as a social call. The time was set for late afternoon.

Poised on the rack of the Evans' upright piano was the needed music, and quickly I noticed the denseness of black notes on the exposed page. Theodore, looking all natty and worldly-wise, stood at ease, saxophone in hand and peering around in his horn-rimmed glasses. We got right down to business, that of me lending his saxophone needed support, which was in my favor as words would have been hard to come by. The title looked back at me as if to say, "Yes, that's right . . . you read it straight, my title is "STRINGBEAN." Had Mother been present her neighborhood policy might have been tested.

Theodore centered the music, and up close the notes were crowded one on top of the other. With a sign of relief I saw these to be his notes, with the piano part printed below. Three staves were new business and I fervently hoped to not lose my place and thereby cause the great Theodore any agitation. However "STRINGBEAN" and its accompaniment proved well within my realm, thanks to tedious exercise drills within my studies. After page one was twiddled away I judged this much prettier and more fun to play than Hanon or Czerny. The saxophone tone was pleasing, as was the awesome thrill of being a duo with Theodore, who barely glanced my way. "Stringbean" became the first of its many counterparts, to be played in later years when novelty music, held together by froth and bubbles, was quite popular.

My second fling as accompanist, to take place just two houses beyond the Evans', was in the wings. This one was destined to raise an entirely new variety of goosebumps.

How the second accompanist trial came about, I do not know, but mother was saying to me one day, "Mr. and Mrs. Rae would like you to come to their home this evening . . . Marjorie's elder sister, they tell me, has a lovely voice, and they would so much like to hear her sing along with the piano. Setting it for an evening hour was to accommodate Mr. Rae, who of course worked during the day.

I adored Marjorie, my Junior High schoolmate and peer, and would have played for her sister under *any* circumstances. And circumstances there were . . . vague, unveiled and undiscussed, for Marjorie's sister was mentally retarded. In these years people merely sensed, and silently assumed, and at my age of twelve, felt a fright within their presence. Evening time came and I skipped down the sidewalk towards the Rae's neat brown and white bungalow in what must have been an apprehensive skip. How would Eileen act? I had not been face to face with her up to this time and any experience along this line was a vast unknown. Like all the other kids, I gasped at the gory rumors and weird tales of goings on at Steilacoom, the State Mental Hospital, then thought to be a considerable distance from Tacoma. Majorie never spoke to me of her sister, which was correct procedure in the '20's, and

Eileen remained a closeted mystic being as far as I could comprehend. The Rae family was one hundred percent Scotch, with fascinating burrs that intrigued me—such a far cry from the accustomed German accents of many of our friends. Mother spoke excellent English only tinged with an accent, having been tutored during boarding school years in Germany.

Mrs. Rae, plump and courteous, was welcoming me into the living room. She always seemed to be all twinkly smiles and dimples. Mr. Rae, jovial and ruddy-cheeked in his Tartan plaid jacket, rose from his easy chair to greet me. Soon I was seated at their piano, a black upright model much like the one at Theodore's house. They had just introduced me to the elder daughter Eileen, who was peering at me in a most pleading way—like one who wished only to please.

The word compassion was not in my vocabulary then, but I remember feeling my fears just melt away when I caught her expression. She was not pretty like Marjorie, who always reminded me of one of my favorite paper dolls with her dark curly hair, pink complexion and laughing eyes. Eileen's face, at one fleeting glance, looked like it had been tightly squeezed together, forcing her eyes to squint in order to see, but she smiled right at me. I only hope I smiled back. All was in readiness. The sheetmusic stood on the rack, plain white with straight black letters that read "D-U-N-A." A question quickly formed in my mind. Where in the world or what in the world was "D-U-N-A"? The answer was not immediate but came later, and from my old reliable source, Green Book. Here amongst the lovely lyrics of some ballads in the Scotch section, my eye stopped at the word Duna only to learn it represented a very beloved scenic area in the Scottish Highlands. But back to the piano bench of the Rae's, where after the front cover of the music was turned, sharply printed black notes stood out starkly. I can see them yet. The ballad was of a slow tempo and easy reading, allowing time for my eyes to veer from the accompaniment line to the printed words above the notes.

Definitely, this song was not light fare but charged with emotional sentiments which poured out an undying devotion for the spot called "Duna." What did it all mean? "Angels often pausing there, nae thot Eden half so fair." The heavy lyrics went on as Scotch and Irish ballads do, and the quiver was leaving the voice of the child-like yet older faced sister. As we reached the final bars, a strange and warm feeling came over me as I sensed we were doing something special for Marjorie's parents. Instead of the quick twirl from the piano, brought on by years of speedy exits at recitals, I was unable to leave my post. Mr. Rae was standing close beside me, his one arm around Eileen and his other resting on my shoulder. As I timidly peered upward I witnessed a transformation. His face now was hardly recognizable from the cheery and jaunty expression that had glowed so brightly just a short time ago. Big dripping tears were sliding down his rosy cheeks, and his jaw and chin were atremble. Over and over I heard him chant softly but almost passionately, "Duna . . . Duna . . . my lovely Duna." I can now understand his letting go so completely and unashamedly at hearing this dovelike and blameless daughter singing away in her heart-rending fashion of a place so very dear to him. Had it been in my more mature years, I would have joined him. By the very quirk of musical circumstance, we did in later years play for the dance portion of the annually observed "Bobbie Burns' Birthday Concert." When I was exposed then to the onrush of joyful yet sad tears at the first throb of the proudly performing Bagpipers, I really understood, and was for the first moment transported right back on the piano bench at the Rae's home. And so went my initial invitation to sit down and accompany a voice. I believe it served as a first touching of heart and also was the first time in my life I had seen a grown man cry. Neither were forgotten.

10

Steinway Overture

Our oaken Kimball now faced a front room wall with only a high oblong window above its tall top available for looking elsewhere than the printed page. We had moved. A routine tuning had been droned away by our faithful Mr. Gruetter almost immediately to help ease any moving trauma of the piano. Actually it was just as well to lack any distracting windows as the new teacher's regime was to preclude much peering into the outside world.

Enrolling in the new and yet unfinished Jason Lee Junior High, finding a new girl friend on the block and all the other facets of getting your feet wet in a new neighborhood, were not as complex as facing up to a different music instructor. With my step-father's urging and full approval, mother really went to the top this time. The first meeting clearly underlined the obvious fact as well as gaining her approval of my acceptance. She was, among other attributes, such as the revered accompanist of Tacoma's Orpheus Club singers, the most polished, technically trained, highly ranked and highly priced. Her name, Rose Schlarb, and her fee, $5.00 per concentrated half hour session. Nothing to trifle with in the '20's. Consequently and in kind, the pages of my assignment notebook, written in her crisp hand, were not filled with compassion. At least not for the likes of someone who now was listing strongly toward easier and more entertaining routes among the keys by improvising and playing what came naturally.

Added to the leather music case now were exacting rulers and special pencils. All the better to construct columns and mark division lines between melodic fifths and minor harmonics. Once again exercise time necessitated the reappearance atop our piano of a relentless metronome . . . in fact my step-father went so far as to purchase a new one with a more dependable spring. What ensued was a forced and difficult test of my co-ordination. With eyes glued to the graph's columns, and brain translating the messages while my heart endeavored to match the ruthless metronome, I was not in a state of euphoria. It didn't take long for me to awaken and find I was expected to grasp much more than a general diagnosis of a piano's general health.

Rose Schlarb's methods, like a jet plane, shot right up to higher altitudes where a minute study of all eighty-eight keys and their intimate anatomy could thrive. Almost without warning I was foundering in deep waters teeming with such creatures as "overlaps," "elastics," "leaners" and a whole new kettle of fish known as the "Cadences." The water became icy when my already weak reading of complicated timing (opting to feel or hear the same), was now exposed to a pair of blue X-ray eyes. There was no dodging the fact, she *expected* my comprehension of "two against three" readings and interval fractions reduced to thirty-second powers. Why oh why did music have to be so complicated and perplexing? Not only that, but the key signatures preceding these blockbusters were anything but the homey one or two sharp or flat variety. They matched the whole devious plan by soaring off into the higher echelons of five and even six! I used to put off my dislike for them by thinking they were like a flock of blackbirds all huddled up against the staff and crowding for perches. However, the blackbirds helped promote a more aggressive friendship with the piano's black keys, who in turn proved to be not so stiff-necked and unapproachable after all.

Strangely enough I was not unhappy or distraught with the new approach. Fascination and challenge took away some of the inadequate feeling and every now and then I could perceive an important point enough to keep me afloat. The refined atmosphere of the Schlarb home (also her studio) was not lost upon me either, for I was nearing the impressionable age of twelve. To make the turn off the sidewalk into a tree sheltered yard and then trip down a winding and flower-bordered flagstone walk leading to a charming home was definitely enjoyable. After pushing a doorbell and hearing Mrs. Schlarb's lyrical "Come i-n-n-n," and she managed to enunciate the word "in" in two syllables, and on two different tone levels. I loved this part of my session which was such a far cry from the barrenness of former office building studios. Also included in my love was the elongated gleaming Grand piano where all the exacting took place, always graced by artful vases of fresh flowers. Just sitting there before that expanse of taut golden wires, facing silky draped French windows, made one wish to play and act like a lady, even if confused. Another love was Rose Schlarb's rosy-blonde hair, pulled into an elegant French twist. However, this elegance had no effect whatever on the plain facts of piano-lesson life. They never seemed to change and it seemed no teacher on this earth had the slightest interest in what was going around in my head.

In the midst of Cadences and class, the kids at Jason Lee were humming a different tune like "I'm Going to Mandalay" or "Charlie My Boy," both of which I considered pretty exciting stuff. Picking them out for myself on our Kimball was not hard but the occasions for doing so were. They had to be played to an empty house, which in those days was not a daily occurrence at all.

If I had known the Schlarb lessons were to end after one year in a way not in anyone's plans, I might have tried harder to overcome the sense of tedium and strain of assimilating what was to me a mountain of mumbojumbo. Her Spring Recital was to be the swan song of a long line of these affairs, and I at least bowed out in style in what looked like a true English tea party, and where her selected students wondered if they really might become "artistes" someday. I know I came away with a lot of respect for the finer points of music (and surroundings to go with it), but still not without the urge to play out some of the things I knew were all inside of me. The time was nearer than I thought.

A Personal Requiem

Open discussions and the revealing of projected plans did not float in our family air, so to speak. It never entered my head that they should. We had lived in the Anderson Street bungalow a year now and I had never paid any attention as to why we were only renters here. There was a forested acreage away out of Tacoma, which it seemed was in the process of becoming our next home. To me it was only a dim faraway thing that might never happen. In reality the site, southeast of Tacoma, was to my step-father the sum of all his hopes and dreams. He loved outdoor living and the labor that came with it, perhaps a compensation for his many years of eight-to-five bookkeeping. We had made a few high adventure trips out to this land of trees and quiet, not too recently vacated by rugged loggers. Standing in what still looked to us as a dense forest (and it was), it was not hard to imagine the Indians had only recently vacated the premises too.

With the friendly help of a nearby pioneer and his wife, the only folk for miles around, enormous brute stumps were dynamited and then parted from their ancient roots very unwillingly, by a hand-cranked stump puller. For our step-father it was exhilarating and challenging, though mother feared it to be too physically exhausting. My brother and I reveled in a Paul Bunyan atmosphere and our little sister was too young to care. Mother, who would have been happy anywhere our step-father was happy, went along with the new approach somehow and seemed to enjoy the raw beauty. Her main concern was her fear of his overtaxing himself, for he went on the attack full steam ahead. As for the dynamiting, it scared the daylights out of all of us.

Meanwhile city life went on much in its usual manner. One day my step-father came home earlier than his accustomed 5:30 arrival. He had not been feeling well of late and had left his office ahead of time. Mother was out somewhere, leaving me with one of my infrequent opportunities, namely, the chance to sit down at the piano and find out just what I could do with all the new tunes floating by me at school. Even Theodore was tootling some of them. Instead of hearing my usual fare when my step-father opened the door, the syncopated notes of "Charlie My Boy" were literally bounding off the wall. With my mind centered solely on the grand experiment and finding the tune to be easier to do than I'd thought, I heard nothing until he stood in the living room archway clearing his throat.

Ordinarily his way of dealing with my brother and me was never harsh or unreasonable, but today I could feel his shock of indignation come across the room. "Are you about finished with your practice?" I am going to lie down here on the sofa for a little while. By the way, what was the name of that song you were just playing?"

My fingers halted in mid-air at his first word. Everything seemed out of place and strange anyway. He never stretched out on the sofa, nor came home early. His question carried no threat, but a direct answer was due, and right now. When he heard my reply, the name of the silly little song sounded ridiculous to me now, he said, quietly and firmly, "I do not care for that song . . . and I don't believe your mother would either. Please do not play 'Charlie My Boy' (by now the title sounded repulsive) in this house again." And I didn't. It was as final as the end of the world. If ever I felt that what I found to be enjoyable, was of lowbrow taste, this was the time.

How would I know only about a month later would find me alone in the house again, and sitting down to the piano? Not in fun this time, but in utter remorse, seeking consolation in the only way I knew. Mother was at the hospital, waiting out the waning hours of life at my step-father's bedside. Sudden cancer had stricken. Hardly without thinking, I had turned to Green Book, quickly turning to the section of hymns within. I knew I needed something to fasten to. Sadly I sought out the one I felt would reach across the city into the hospital room and deliver strength and support. The hymn chosen was "Nearer My God To Thee," and I played it softly singing along repeating verse after verse until I heard our phone ring. Mother was on her way home with our neighbor, who had taken her to the hospital earlier. It was all over. His express wishes were followed. No services, just a quick cremation but somehow I felt a contact had been made with him in his last moments, one I deemed he deserved. Even in later years, I never told of this experience. For me it was an unforgettable and very personal memorial.

PART II

TRANSITION

Transition

I count it now as a major milestone of life—that age of twelve and a half, when life *and* music both underwent a dramatic change. The shocking and unexpected death of my step-father left mother broken of heart and bereft of finances. He had suffered severe investment losses in post-war (I) Germany's money market crash, the axe falling shortly before his sudden illness. Thus he was unable to carry out his enthusiastic plans for our projected move to the forty acres of woods he was leasing from the State. His drawn-up layout for removing the shell of a house, and the replacement plans for a family farmhouse for us, to be built by a competent carpenter, became merely sheets of paper. We were left with one choice—moving to the forty acres and becoming pioneers. All we had now was the long term lease, lots of thick woods and a crude pole and log house. It sat upon the two cleared acres, with barbed wire fences holding off thirty-eight more, all crowding forward with trees and rampant underbrush. At that time, certain acreage was state-designated as "School Land," with bid and buying options at a later date. That the lease fee was nominal, was one bright spot in our dismal picture.

Sad goodbyes were said to our comfortable city home on Anderson St. before rattling for hours over rough roads, the overloaded truck trundling in our wake. Any hello at the other end was bound to be dubious. We would be landing a good five miles south of Puyallup (closest town) in a sparsely settled and wooded region whose one and only landmark was Kupfer's corner (now The Willows Center). To label us as "pioneers," even in 1925, is entirely accurate—we qualified. Electricity hadn't probed that far from a main road yet, and neither had running water. And then there was the raw-boned structure called a house by the former lessee—living proof that moonshining came more natural to him than carpentering, for nothing was plumb, and gaping cracks were a dime a dozen. Besides that it lacked front porch, cupboards and any decor such as wall or floor coverings. The two nearest homes were acres away and the mailbox and the two-room schoolhouse were each a good two mile hike. And we were fresh from Tacoma!

Oddly enough, around two weeks covered my adjustment period, during which self pity at losing friends, leaving a new Junior High School and most of all, our loss of father, had me weeping into my pillow every night. After that the pure adventure of the woodsy and semi-primitive way of life in this undeveloped area just took over. I seemed ready and willing to enjoy country living. First misgivings at seeing our beautiful oak piano in such an unbefitting setting soon melted away. Strong backs and willing muscles had struggled to push it in place closeby a window. Here it took root and remained, too monstrous for any whimsical furniture changeabouts. I remember that first day, looking at its long front tilt-out panel all wood-sculpted in graceful acorn clusters, and feeling a sense of sorrow. How did this wonderful piano feel in this strange place? If it suffered any disorientation shock, the time was brief as I lost no time setting the glass-clawed feet of the stool upon the cold and unyielding linoleum. How it echoed against the cheerless surroundings!

I like to think Fate, or God's sense of timing, placed me at our piano during this difficult transition and what must have been, at first, a nightmare for mother who was now a bewildered widow. Somehow from between all the packed and unopened boxes of our things, Green Book had been snaked out and put on the music rack, to be played and re-played. Lessons were over now, weren't they? We didn't talk about having to leave them hanging, so to say, in midair; it was just an understood fact, physically and financially out of reach. We were, without a doubt, living out an emergency and with the finality of closing a self-locking door behind you and then losing the key; the book on over eight years of concentrated lesson time just snapped shut. The forward propelling music gears had quietly shifted themselves. I was on my own, musically speaking. How mother must have thanked the relatively contemporary composers such as Rudolph Friml, Sigmund Romberg, Victor Herbert and others, for I spent most of my now unrestricted piano time with as much of their material as my ever listening ear and willing hands could command. And then there were the happy and bubbly Viennese waltzes, familiar folksongs and last but not least, the lilting tunes of the day.

Before long our new Citizen's State Bank calendar with its caption of "Puyallup, Population 6000," announced Spring, as did the glossy white blossoms on a large inherited strawberry patch in the back clearing. We were carrying on as best we could, a new version of family living. Once in awhile now mother even whistled along as I played a favorite of hers. With the likes of "Rosemarie," "Naughty Marietta," "The Desert Song" and many more I just never ran out. For her they must have taken some of the sting from "Doodle De Doo," or "Brown Eyes Why Are You Blue." Also some of the newer hits were taking on Spanish and South American flavors and adding more worldly temperament. All was not lost—the piano fare was not going completely downhill after all! Added to this was what emanated from our radio's horn-like speaker. All in all, playing time far exceeded the former practice sessions. It was like at last being able to open Pandora's Box, with no penalties attached! And so the repertoire grew and grew.

However, nothing I could have played would have helped mother's facing of her two new abiding fears, fire and drowning. The lighting of our Coleman mantle lantern each night boded explosion and fire. My brother and I became the steady fingers guiding a lighted match toward the fragile mantles. For daily accidental drownings there was our deep well, topped with a lidded wooden cover over its boxlike and above ground frame. This entire area so close by our long back porch (for the sake of convenience) was strictly off limits for my two very young sisters. Again, my brother and I, who at first did not mind tugging up the full buckets from the water below, became the chief motivators. On every other front though, mother was tops, her German perseverance overcoming inexperience at every turn. Pioneers, yes—each one of us. Unfortunate or timely change of music direction? Who knows? Mother would have taken pleasure in hearing the classics bounce off the rough and furry walls of our unfinished house, but how could it continue? No teachers, no money and no transportation. Again propitious timing plotted a course. A live musician within the area we now called home was as rare as a $100 bill. If you played at any level you were SOME-BODY. And if you could play a whole lot of things at random besides, you were a STANDOUT. And you were to be heard.

At the tender age of fourteen (a year and a half into our hinterland living), I began my uncontested tenure as Community Pianist. Believe me, I earned the capital letters. If I had searched for the scarcest commodity to bring along to Firgrove, I couldn't have done any better. Unless I had brought money. Competition for the fictional title was absolutely non-existent, so all that remained to do was, sit down and play. The then two-roomed schoolhouse boasted a piano of sorts, but each successive set of teachers proved to be devoid of keyboard knowledge, beyond do-rae-mi. Strictly a setup for a large rock in a small pond!

Our Americana midwest type school (rightly named Firgrove) also served as the center for activities. Here it was that kids, parents and friends cast themselves briefly into the role of group participants and listeners. A great oneness prevailed for it was a fact of life in Firgrove. No stump-farmers were rich. And who would live here besides stump-farmers? The second great common denominator between the assemblage was the anticipation of refreshment time, which without fail followed all meetings or programs. Firgrove per se did not exist. The name loosely embraced isolated and scattered groups of acreages whose people were tenaciously held together by a do-or-die P.T.A. No magazine charm type of country living prettied up hacked out clearings, where naked platforms of former giant trees and makeshift houses often stood side by side. Tourists, had there been any, would not have been captivated by vistas of cleared and rolling fields, quaint buildings and Farmer Brown leaning against a rail fence. In atonement for its shortcomings, Firgrove gave recompense and gave it freely with few questions asked. It said welcome to those looking for some kind of a place to land. The acres were there in abundance, available for a price that now would scandalize the entire real estate industry. The many who were unable to purchase even in small payments, rented, leased or just squatted in a spot hopefully remote enough to escape attention for awhile. For anyone fortunate enough to buy and gather acres, and lived to see it, Firgrove promised a bonanza. Very few achieved or reached this manna from Heaven, but it was there and waiting. The other attribute was what now is in such great demand—unbounded privacy.

And so it was. Firgrove was ready for a pianist, or a "Py-ano player" as some termed it. Up till now the old upright school piano had served only as a whipping post for endless thumpings of "Chopsticks." The exercise to this day, which I looked upon then as a mindless way to belittle a piano, still raises my hackles. Quite naturally whenever I was playing a program, my ears caught all audible remarks from the audience. I became as accustomed to them as the fresh barn aroma that forced its way into each gathering. I often overheard, "Look, she don't need no music," or "she must play just by ear" or, "she don't even watch her fingers," and so on. Luckily it did not go to my head. In fact sometimes, I felt myself to be some kind of an oddity, like someone who could read or spell backwards.

One night after the reading of the P.T.A. minutes had doggedly been read to one and all, followed by the treasurer's single digit report, and just who would serve on the next kitchen committee, a startling fact presented itself to me. I could, just me, make people dance! The evening's meeting was over in our chicken-coop style building known as "The Playshed." An accurate description of our "multi-purpose" facility can be narrowed down by calling it a stone-age version of today's creations. As mouthwatering cakes and hand-crafted pies were sized and pre-cut in concordance with the night's headcount, an aproned lady said to me: "Why don't you just sit down and play the piano for awhile. Our coffee ain't boiled yet." Whether it took much coaxing, I don't remember. At first nothing happened. People either listened from their bench perches, or continued to visit. Kids ran hither and thither, diving and sliding across the floor. This was a lively practice engaged in after soap flakes had been sprinkled onto the rough surface, should some games be played, and often ended with surreptitious sliver picking and assorted bruises. I kept on as faces waxed into smiles while the hearty aroma of brewing coffee began to fill the Playshed.

The next time I chanced to look up and around, two couples were up on the floor in self-conscious but actual dancing positions. This was a first for me, and I hardly knew what to do about it. So I kept on playing. I don't believe I had ever seen this form of dancing, having only been taken to ballet recitals up to this time. And did I know how to play a Circle Two-Step? They had a caller. Of course I did, for trusty Green Book had pages of Two-steps, all memorized much earlier than this. I was off, using "The Girl I Left Behind Me" for a starter. The unique performance was brief, as serving time was announced shortly. But it was not forgotten by them, or me. The feeling of putting a beat into people's feet was new, exciting and fun. The whole lengthy period as resident pianist flourished from Coleman lanterns to electric wiring. From outdoor walk-ins to indoor plumbing. From wooden schoolhouse to new brick building. From teachers to still other musically unequipped teachers. From program, to program, to program. One thing was certain. I was not the unfortunate piano player who lacked an audience!

During these early years, Sundays wove themselves a pattern. We expected and received hardly any company from the city. Few friends owned cars and would not have ventured way out over narrow dirt roads to a place lacking even an address, if they had. Now and then local company paid a call, or else the reverse. Some Sunday afternoons found me over at the Wright's loghouse, our closest neighbor. Theirs was chinked together with logs, instead of the peeled poles of ours. This industrious Mormon family was "working" their forty acres, having preceded us by several years. Their piano had been shipped out from their former Utah home, along with ten of the twelve children and two work horses. After the main noontime Sunday meal had been cleared away (no mean feat), they often migrated to the seldom used front room. In this room Mrs. Wright had thumbed her nose at all the rustic shortcomings of her existence. The walls rebloomed annually in a wallpapered series of flowered garlands and bowers, resolutely pasted over last year's crop. Mr. Wright would seat his well over two hundred pounds into the Morris chair, celebrating his honestly won seventh day of rest. Radios and TV's were unborn as yet, leaving the airwaves of this homey scene free and clear. A creditable piano stood against one wall awaiting someone to put music into this downhome scene. Once again the slot was open.

All I had to do was flit down the tree and stump bordered narrow dirt road. In those days it ended abruptly at the thick fencepost corner of the Wright place. Next I would turn myself through their unique gate (every stump rancher had his own version), brush by two of Mrs. Wright's thriving Lilac bushes, trip down a worn and grassy path to the main porch, always bedecked with woodboxes, milk pails and such, be let in the door by two of the girls close my own age, walk into the parlor . . . and sit down and play.

For them it was supreme contentment to hum along with "Beautiful Ohio," "My Isle of Golden Dreams," or "Memories." Jazzier tunes were left for other days, this was Sunday. Soon one of the elder sons would appear, guitar in hand and strum along. A new experience for me as I hadn't played in company with a stringed instrument as yet. My insistence on a correct blending of chords began right here, nice looking son or no. The music had to be right—and harmonious. The pleasant sessions usually concluded with the indisputable fact that it was "time to milk."

Boredom and budding teenage restlesness, though it came very close at times, never claimed me. I longed for listening audiences while seated alone at our piano, experimenting with what I heard as provocative and tantalizing music. And more often than not, an almost barbaric crowd of thick trees just beyond our clearing was my audience. Blessed with my share of girlish imagination, I found ways to atone for the remoteness of anything and everything so dazzlingly pictured on sheet-music covers or the few movies we saw. In a way I think I gained a few points. I could romanticize to an appropriate background of music, played by me of course. That is exactly what I did, by adapting love-struck lyrics and customizing them all for myself. Whenever a "he" appeared in the words, I could insert the name of a boy. For starters I had all the three teenage Wright boys names at my disposal! This way I could voice phrases which otherwise would not have left my lips. So for now, and of course I thought it was for forever, the romantic world of flappers, sheiks, rumble-seated roadsters, silk stockings and garters had to come to me via piano dreaming. I was smart enough to realize the utter improbability of a sporty roadster wheeling by on our two-lane gravel road which ended at the Wright house, and I was very sure Sheiks rarely took to stump farming.

The first song I really remember working over quite hard was "Yes Sir That's My Baby." I had noticed its way of waking people up and putting them into a happy mood. Or better yet, on their feet. The effect was the same everytime, and one could improvise at great length with the catchy phrasing. A new light seemed to shine, lighting up all eighty-eight keys. Improvising or "playing around with a melody," as it is sometimes called, came upon my little musical scene. A perfect cure for music monotony! And then there was syncopation, and perfecting a breezy "tá-da," little knowing that in later years I would avoid any semblance of a "tá-da" in my playing!

Next came the revving up of the already rapid bass pattern of "Yes Sir That's My Baby," until my skinny left arm groaned from all the switching between lower bass note and upper chord. With it all came a feeling of pleasant alarm. This was really quite jazzy wasn't it? But where to go with it or where to play it? Would all the wonderment ever lead to anything? The first "Talkies" were giving life to the movie screens and I knew it was too late for my first suppressed desire of becoming a movie pianist or organist. What would be left now? As much as I liked reading, and I did a great deal of it through every source possible and a five mile distant library, I wanted music to be in first place. All the Agatha Christie mysteries, English novels and unblushing romance stories were great, but there had to be music, somewhere and somehow.

Preceding the jazzy revelations of "Yes Sir That's My Baby," another significant fact of sadder substance had been faced. A persistent ear infection soon after our big move to the country had led to an emergency operation at The Tacoma General Hospital. It was serious surgery, demanding in those days a stay of ten days. A sizable piano-less gap was already developing when family friends in Tacoma arranged with mother for me to stay with them during a two week post-surgery period of frequent check-ups. The whole affair for me was a double crisis, for their home was without a piano. It was a warm May in the city and daily walks were taken, during which I kept an open ear for any stray notes coming out into the air from any of the houses I passsed. One day the sound I had been waiting for, tinkling piano notes, came out an open door! Each day thereafter I'd stand out on the sidewalk on the same spot, torn between my timidity and my overwhelming desire to go knock on that door and ask if I could come in and play their piano. I rode it out, but one more week of doctor visits and timidity would have been waived.

55

13

The Adolescent Pianist

"Now why don't you just sit down and play for us?" It was among the easiest of orders to take when we were having company. "We'll help clear the table and dry dishes. The job will go faster with some music. How about starting out with "In a Little Gypsy Tearoom"? They didn't have to ask me twice. Soon our for-real country kitchen would be abuzz with chatter, humming as the soapy water sloshed and the silverware clanked. All to the music of a piano. Mother's embroidered and snowy-white dishtowels flapped away while the pianist sat in the next room happily filling a series of requests. It was the one time I could, without qualm, escape the cleanup process.

A first romance generally enters an early teen's life at this point. That mine should make its bow by way of music goes without saying. All my important events seemed to emanate from the same source. During the past year I had secretly and romantically been sizing up all the available Wright boys. Of course it was a lopsided endeavor that failed to produce any returns. However, each of them dearly loved music so I saw them frequently, either in their home at the piano, or at ours. Only the eldest was fortunate enough to own an instrument, and played quite well on a guitar. While I knew he was too old for me, it didn't stop me from sitting on the barnyard fence at twilight, entranced as he milked the cows. Had he shown a spark of interest, the age barrier would have been waived. The next brother down the line was pleasant, soft-voiced and also without any romantic leaning in my direction. Then came the third. Like Goldilocks with her choice of three, he was just right, a choice he knew nothing about. The owner of a most happy-go-lucky disposition, with a singing voice to match, he literally sang morning, noon and night. His amazing collection of lyrics were all memorized, with proper inflections borrowed from family Victrola records brought along from Utah. His sisters along with so many others were currently stuck on "The Letter Edged in Black" and "The Prisoner's Song," whose morbid verses had no appeal for me, either to sing or to play. At last we had something in common, for the happy singing brother refused to spend any time learning them either. Up to now the biggest detriment to any romance had been his unmerciful teasing of me, often to my tearful distress. I stayed with it, forgiving his roguish manners and awaiting his next appearance, wherever it was. How could he be so cute and so mean? At what stage or why the worm turned, I don't remember. For all I know, his whole act could have just been a cover-up. Whichever way it was, he soon began to come to our house at other times than when we gathered as a group. Preceding him up our long driveway, and timed with his bouncy walk, I would hear "I'm Looking at the World Through Rose-colored Glasses" filling the country air. The song was made to order for him.

Our two hearts really began to beat as one, after one particular evening at our house. Six or eight of us were singing, playing pinochle, bantering and enjoying a new music addition. Mother was always in attendance—her presence acknowledged rather than frowned upon. She must have been happy to have us at home; the two little sisters were, after a certain hour, tucked away in their beds. This night "he" had arrived with a medium-sized instrument case in hand. Not long after coats had been hung, the shiny case was opened, revealing a brand-new "Banjo-Uke," with attached instructions. Somehow, enough hard-earned money had been saved to allow such a purchase, for the instrument was of a good quality—definitely a step up from the tinny Ukes so popular then. Later, after a few chords had been tried and it was evident that, in order to play anything at all, their number would have to increase, I heard, "I'd like to come over *tomorrow* night. Maybe you could help and teach me a few things. What time could I walk over?" As calmly as possible I answered, "Oh, anytime after seven would be fine."

The next evening finally came to pass, and for some reason the dinner dishes and cleanup were behind our regular schedule. I could hear the strains of "Rose-colored Glasses," coming up the porch steps. Soon he was breezily opening the kitchen screen, only to find his instructor with dishtowel in hand. He was fresh from milking and barn duties, a fact that was never noticeable and added more points in his favor.

"Got another dishtowel?" he smiled, "I'll help you finish these." Thereafter, to assure repeat performances, the time for his evening musical advice was coyly set a bit ahead of the dishwashing chore period. He always showed up, received the proffered dishtowel and dried *all* the dishes. A womanly wiles set-up for sure. He knew it, and I knew it, and no one seemed to mind. Well, perhaps mother, who had a horror of anyone with possibly unclean hands making contact with the dishtowels. She may have reasoned nothing too drastic could have happened during the few acres between the Wright's place and ours.

We practiced, and practiced, using the little square box symbols shown in the instruction book. To branch out from these confines and into impromptu playing of pop songs was another story. He did well, but only when I was physically near to prompt him on correct chord changes—and correct our music had to be, romance or no. How to fill in

57

his lack of basic know-how was out of my patience range, but at least I kept him from playing klunkers. For the rest of the summer and fall, we were a twosome, with the music and without. In our frequent playing for others, he had to sit very close to the piano, where I could keep him posted, and for all anyone knew, he wasn't dependent on the pianist. To keep working ahead of the batter, I learned to foresee upcoming chord changes and deliver them, sotto voce, several beats in advance, which prevented a breaking of the rhythm. This maneuver was to pay off in later years. One could say he was shot down without my cueing—and just how his male psyche handled the obvious fact that I was his musical "Svengali" never came to light. To regard it as my chance to even up his former relentless teasing, never occurred to me. We were too engrossed in chords . . . and choruses . . . and harmony. . . . . and heartbeats.

The following spring he graduated from high school and soon found work, through his elder brothers who all worked in Tacoma now. The rhythm of the homey little musical romance was broken, leaving me with two more years of high school to finish and no one to coach . . . or dry the dishes. If my music brought forth a first boyfriend, what else might be in view? Like a slowly developing photo negative, the beginnings of a shape were taking form. Clearly the music indicator was pointing out the advantages of only recently completed years of instruction as an asset. It was a start on what my erstwhile romantic figure sang with such heart: "I'm Looking at the World Through Rose-colored Glasses." A musical world of course.

14

Saturday Nights
Before They Became Saturday Nights

Most of America during the Twenties and Thirties, it is said, was steeped in the great Saturday Night Syndrome. It simply was THE night and the tradition even seeped its way into the pores of our small and remote Firgrove area. We too shared the belief of this being the night to get out, go somewhere or at least do something different. Unfortunately, all our Saturday eves did not reach this standard. When all else failed and bleakness seemed imminent, we did have Horace Heidt's evening radio show with good danceband music. And The Lucky Strike Hit Parade's revelation of the top pop tunes. Daytime Saturdays for those like me who definitely lived at home, Saturday's dusting flew faster as thoughts of the evening's prospects shot about in your mind. Naturally we cleaned house on Saturdays, along with the rest of the nation. The day gained further import by late afternoon, as many laborers enjoyed the Saturday grant of a seven hour day. It was like a buildup to an occasion when home arrival still left a whole bonus hour at the workers' disposal. All this if you were lucky enough to have a wage earner in your family unit.

As I think back on our pole-house days, it was actually exciting to see our brother Hans bring the old car up the driveway at 4:30 instead of 5:30. He was beginning his long tenure with the Northern Pacific Railroad, a big hefty plus that prevented our family from going under. To be sure, his white broadcloth shirt and blue serge trousers were already pressed and ready. Almost without fail Hans would be "tripping the light fantastic" (as he termed it) that night. Conversely and by some form of animal telepathy, Saturday nights were even transmitted to our milk-cow "Susie." Instead of being docilely at the ready, or reasonably close by, her whereabouts on this night, as Hans set forth for the barn, were shrouded in mystery. "Just like a woman," Hans would wail when most of his bonus hour had to be spent thrashing about amid our dense underbrush, pleadingly calling her name.

A Saturday movie was not entirely out of the question, provided we had the admission price and someone's old jalopy was operative. There were no guilt qualms about admission for such outstanding films as "The Covered Wagon," any picture starring Richard Dix or one of mother's favorites, Reginald Denny. As if to prevent the onset of a serious dilemma, the proprietor of our closest area grocery store suddenly became a partner in the newly constructed large dancehall. This edifice, sitting catty-corner on the well-known landmark of the Willows Corner, was only about two and a half miles from our door! Of course we would still need the necessary ticket price and transportation, but our hopes were high.

Music, always my angel, assisted in fulfilling the wishful hopes, if in an indirect fashion. The grocer and local friend to all had often expressed gratitude for my community music work. Evidently he reasoned a "Pass" ticket to the new Willows dance hall would be turnabout and fair play. I don't remember arguing his point. Marvelous opportunities now were ahead. At last I would see and hear live dance music and get to watch real musicians putting their notes together. All of this in front of my eyes and ears. I could hardly wait. The way was further paved when he included the two Wright girls in the gesture. Even Mother had to allow the three of us together could not cut too wide a path. This plus the fact of the grocer and his wife both being present in the hall during the whole evening. Luckily, the Willows then was still too new to have gained any kind of reputation, and we were saved by the infancy of a probable stumbling block. It was by this fortunate chain of events that our all important Saturday nights were filled for about six months. Not with dates, but with wide-eyed enthusiasm and no cash outlay.

During the happy induction period, we fought as best we could to avoid the dreaded stigma of becoming wallflowers. We so wanted to do everything right. Every little move and nuance of our attractive and polished role models, the girls who were continually sought after as dancing partners, was eyed and noted. To feign nonchalance, while sitting on the taupe velour davenports lining the wall and desperately hoping for a partner, seemed to be a first lesson. If sitting and wishing failed (and it often did), the next maneuver was to take courage in hand and join the groups standing along the raised edges of the floor. At least this put you closer to the action, though at first one felt oneself to be exposing a brazen kind of determination. Like a horse with blinders on, you looked straight ahead, with careful sideglances only when you couldn't stand it any longer. The game was played in groups who stood in line, changing places as to who was at the head in the most advantageous position. Fairness ruled or else friendships could end. Other maneuvers such as control of facial muscles kept us engrossed instead of heartbroken. We tried our best to avoid a dropped jaw when an oncoming likely prospect, who seemingly was bound in your direction, kept right on going as if you didn't exist. And when it did happen and this male body paused directly before you with a mumbled "May I have this dance please?'' it was almost too much to remember what we thought we had learned. If you had done your reconnoitering well, the fellow had already been screened as to whether this was a bargain or a lemon. To be honest, I'm sure we projected our true images of just plain silly girls, dying to dance and romance, but not entirely sure how to accomplish it. The combined exuding between the three of us of any Clara Bow "It" was imperceptible. "It" in the Thirties was that indefinable feminine attribute capable of wreaking havoc. Unlike the term "sexy" to come later, "It" was a milder version with just a touch of mystery. Perhaps the cruel term of local hayseeds might have described our trio better, and had anyone named us so aloud, we'd have retreated to our respective log and pole homes, badly crushed. We probably rationalized our adventures with the philosophy of one of Mother's oft-used sayings, "Even a Cat Can Look at a King."

As Fate would have it the Willows suddenly zoomed into popularity, pulling in huge milling crowds to dance away on its spacious and excellent floor. A strong current of public fancy was stamping it not with the brand of a boondocks country dancehall, but as an out-of-town sophisticated place to go dancing. The very mention of the name "Willows" or "Willows Corner," served as a geographical locater, bestowing a status of sorts to our wooded corner. Opposing factions sprung up and depending on whom you spoke with, the Willows was either a modern and wicked place, or a well-run and good place to go. Of course I belonged to the latter group, but had we roamed about in the big parking areas outside, the opinion might have been revised. Inside however, very little escaped our attention or scrutiny. The flirtations from coy to not so coy, the smart repartee in latest catchy slang and the obvious superior dancing couples, and the clicking spike heels, latest hairbobs and dancing dresses. And of course, boys . . . boys . . . boys, some as old and worldly as twenty-two. For me the whole thing was hung together with the music of THE DANCE BAND. At that age they were like creatures from Mars, unattainable and terribly exciting. Would I ever ever in this world be a part of one?

With great remorse we awoke one day to discover that our lovely floating balloon was about to be punctured. The jig, so to say, was up. Our beneficent grocer friend and donor of the free passes fell prey to the sudden gush of green-backed receipts. He had, in our way of thinking, gone off the deep end, thereby leaving us in the lurch. Actually we did not blame him, for he and his wife had worked long and hard with the grocery and gas station prior to joining a partnership as owners of the dancehall. So off they purred in a manner befitting their advanced position, behind the wheel of a super-long and bright blue Buick Sedan, to the land of sunshine and affluency, Florida! And with him went our ticket connection which he evidently had forgotten to establish with his partners before setting off. Perhaps it was just as well. Due to persistent rumors and publicity, home approval of the Willows had definitely swung to the negative. The verdict was, no more unescorted Saturday nights, and who had an escort!

For awhile life went into a terrible slump. I remember fully equating the heyday's finale with a world tragedy. It just didn't seem fair. Whatever would we *do* now? Only in looking back can you pick out the markers separating the chapters of your own particular days and years. Therefore it's easy now to see how once more a needed musical divider was waiting in the wings. Not right away, but in the offing.

15

And The Meek Shall Inherit No Solos

"I have invited the Depot Agent's son to come and hear you play." For historic purposes the time was in my fifteenth year and the place again was Adna, a few summers removed from water wings and dog-paddling in the Chehalis river. My great fondness for my German Auntie closest to my heart, Tante Krummel, was often coupled with astonishment. You never knew what her spur of the moment ideas were going to be. From what many would have considered barren material, she created social occasions where before none had flourished and somehow people felt better about themselves for it. However, the keeping of these imaginative if not imposing events, sandwiched in between whatever impeded them, made for something less than a humdrum atmosphere at home. With my own flair for expanding a growing backlog of well liked tunes and then playing them at the drop of a hat, I fit into the scheme of things "extraordinaire." Most of them clicked.

"He is here now visiting with his parents, but he lives in Seattle," Tante Krummel continued while whirring her whisk beater through a bowl of fluffy prune whip. "I understand he plays . . . what is it? I believe it is called a Saxophone. You know, he participates in a JAZZ band there." No one I ever knew could say the word "Jazz" quite like Tante Krummel, for her years in England as a private tutor left her with b-r-o-a-d A's and a precise enunciation. This lent a portentous dignity all of a sudden to the form of music so downgraded in my home circle.

My listening immediately became acute. I knew nothing of all these dazzling facts. I didn't even know Adna's Depot Agent had a son, let alone a musical one. To me Mr. Wood was a green-eye-shaded individual whose home quarters directly above the depot I considered to be a most delightful place to live. The plan went on, "I thought perhaps the two of you could strike up some music together." I was used to my Tante's frequent use of "strike" as a verb, but "the two of you" phrase struck fear into my soul. "Wouldn't that be interesting?" was her innocent question. Interesting: It was earthshaking. But this was no time to plead my fear. And what did I really know of Jazz? Nothing, technically speaking. For me it just pleased my ears, my mind and my fingers. Possibly I knew it as variations upon a theme that transferred themselves from whatever popped into your head, and then into your hands. Or was it a series of phrases for filling up empty measures crying out for help? One thing I knew it was for sure—off limits at home. What to play at this little tête-à-tête was, at the moment, a moot question.

Like his father's trains, the Depot Agent's son, an older man all of possibly twenty-five, arrived as scheduled. I was summoned from somewhere outside, for as the time grew near I had lost any desire to be in the front room. My heart, already aflutter as I came into the room, did somersaults when I glimpsed the other half of our musical twosome. There he stood. Tall, slim, blonde wavy hair, smooth-faced and one hundred percent—suave. A sporty plaid vest set off his camel-tan attire, rendering him the human embodiment of what every young girl ogled over in the fancy magazines. The term then was "debonair." And I was FIFTEEN!

Introductions were made, at which point Tante Krummel had to return herself to the store on a special errand. Bernhard was nowhere to be seen, visibly at least, for he was a great one to secrete himself when it so pleased him. "I understand you're doing a lot of piano work on your own, and that you like jazz," was the opening remark from my learned superior. "I've been hearing about you from Mrs. Krummel."

The last statement of information had a plausible foundation. The Krummel's store also housed the U.S. Post Office for the entire rural area. Twice daily the sturdy blue and white striped mailbag was toted from store to train depot, a distance of about two or three blocks. The officious ritual, complete with securing the locking device atop the bag was an impressive event. When the metal lock clicked with a snap, you felt the awesome responsibility of the whole act. I loved skipping alongside and was extra careful not to collide with the important canvas sack and its important contents. At train time everything from the worn wooden platform to the blistered paint in the starkly basic waiting room became charged with an electrical magic beyond compare. The incessant rat-a-tattings of the telegraph were about to be swallowed up in the thunderous roar of oncoming churning wheels, screeching brakeshoes, circles of smoke and strange clanks and spasmodic hisses. The bracing of this monster of fury and speed to a complete halt caused open mouthed amazement. While the mighty monster cooled its heels in a deserved breather, the Adna mailbag was swung aboard into the waiting arms of a mail-car attendant, in exchange for a lumpy bag of new mail. After all the noise and clatter had subsided into a diminishing series of chugs, the platform and depot's innards slowly shuddered back to normal. I always stretched my eyes down the track until the bluntbacked observation car looked like a toy train and disappeared around a bend of the Chehalis River. Short local bits of interest then flew back and forth between the agent and whoever was around, which had a lot to do with why I was now sitting down engulfed in a sea of self-conciousness, to the Krummel piano. To my dismay, but not a surprise, not one bright or responsive bit of small talk was at my command, much less upon my tongue. How did one start off such a thing as this? Would he be the one to just begin playing something, or what?

"We've been using this new little hit number in our band lately," he began mercifully. "Would you happen to know it . . . it's called 'Sweet Sue'?" "I don't believe there's a piano copy in my case." What a pity, this would have been an opportunity to see what Sweet Sue looked like on the cover. He continued, "The band really blows hot on it. Let's just play around with the melody for a bit." As yet I hadn't found an opening to inform him I was most familiar with the number. Inwardly I thanked him for his choice of an uncomplicated piece, containing holdover measures for fillips and fill-ins. He went right on without a pause to remark on my being so current and trouble-free with, "Do you have any key preferences?"

"Oh no," I answered most truthfully, "any key is all right with me," at which his eyebrows arched a trifle. What came forth from the Krummel piano, which I usually found most cooperative and willing, was a mediocre effort, all but wiped out by nervous intimidation. No one was around to spur me on with, "Oh come on now, we've heard you take off better than this." Anyone who remembers "Sweet Sue" at all would not blame me for soon becoming bored with its repetitive thirty-two bars with not a chance to add any input into the empty measures. However, the successive phrases were not getting to my cohort, who blew them all away in differing styles. Mine was to plug away and hold the melody.

I soon fell to watching the little key-lids of his saxophone flip open and shut, as I contemplated the greatness of this worldly creature. This even surpassed Theodore and the "Stringbean" solo episode.

Would I wax bold enough to suggest a number of my choice, one requiring more know-how. No I wouldn't. Instead, at the end of the chorus marathon he went on about "the Band" and how well they were doing and to add insult to injury, what a great pianist they had. I sighed. At no point had he shown any burning desire to hear me play anything on my own. And I had just recently mastered all the intricate chord changes in "Tea For Two"! What's more, I could click it off in a perfect soft-shoe beat. One time as he shuffled among the sheets in his case, I strained my eyes to catch sight of some enticing sheet music. There was none to be seen.

As I recall, Mr. Debonair was quite a proficient saxophonist and I certainly remember how let down I was over the outcome of our little session. At first I suspicioned it, and later I knew I had merely served as straight man for as many take-offs of "Sweet Sue" as he had been able to devise. I had met and unsuccessfully dealt with one of the rare species of the music world. He was the one you come note to note with somewhere along the way, whose only true happiness lies in tootling his own horn. Luckily, the Agent's son left on the next train back to the big city. The incident, beyond what I chose to relay to my Tante in less than true fashion, was closed.

16

Exhibit "A"

I don't believe young people were so attuned to self-analysis or preferable lifestyles in the Twenties and Thirties. The choices just were not there. This is not to say we didn't spend time wondering where we fit into the scheme of things. To match up with those who seemed better off than you had all the urgency of today, but it seemed the better offs were truly a select few. My personal idea of reaching a sought-after goal was that of tripping about in an office, à la the attractive "Fritzi Ritz" in a popular comic strip. This embodied my ideal of being gainfully employed. Noon hour or after five would see me, the vivacious flapper, prancing down the avenue in my high heels and attractively neat outfit. I would be salaried and a vital necessity to the whole office scene. By this time, of course, my music would be floating about in the rarified air of an established hotel's lobby or dining room. Possibly only on a Saturday afternoon or evening.

Maybe all the foregoing accounts for why I really liked to play "Five Foot-Two" with so much bounciness and joy. After zipping off the racy words, and more so after my first glance at Miss Five Foot-Two on the sheetmusic cover, I knew within my heart she and I were not even vaguely related. I was taller, less curvaceous, had eyes of green, and when I sang out, "turned up nose, turned down hose," the game was really over. But the last specification was within physical reach, and by making various observations I could turn out a fair job with rolling my hose. Flaunting it was short-lived.

"I think, Ilse, you might like trying to wear a garter belt." The voice was my dear Tante Krummel's at her tactful best. We were both standing in the Krummel guestroom for I was in Adna again on a summer visit. Slipping out of the dress worn on the train, the rolled down hose had stood out in all their rash glory. "Do you remember," she asked in her even keel voice, "how well turned out the teachers who boarded here always looked? And how very much you admired them?"

It was true, I had. She went on, "I always considered them to be the very ESSENCE of neatness." The evidence was glaringly clear. They wore garterbelts, no doubt about it. However I really credit my Tante's lingering English accent from London Governess days with striking the message right into my inner soul. When she leveled out the phrase "the essence of neatness," my conscience took a nosedive. And as I desperately wished to resemble the highly attractive and garter-belted young teacher, I was quickly convinced. Later we crossed the street to the big

Krummel store, and from Tante's extensive Dry Goods Department came a pure white garter belt. At least a tiny, tiny pink flower was tacked at center front.

In the sunny afternoon of that same day, after moving into the spare bedroom, the same old joyous feeling came to me as in earlier childhood days. Evidently the anticipation, and then actually being in the Adna countryside with the Krummels, still sent my heart flying. Though I now saw myself as infinitely more mature, having closed the gap between fifteen and sixteen, my snail's pace maturing had not gathered much speed. I loved the pleasant well-kept farmlands, just far enough south from Tacoma to afford the sensation of having traveled to another clime. Here the sun shone warmer, the swimming water offered comforting warmth and the fruits tasted sweeter. I know now, had Grandma Moses emanated from this piece of rural Americana, her paintbrush would have stopped right here. Adna's lone and unpaved street suffered few incursions from its tranquility. Only an occasional car or feed truck rattled over the gravel, usually at a slow pace in preparation for a halt at the store. Lining the street, a row of modest homes presented trim flowerbeds, exuberant fruit trees and wooden fences with gates. In the back, the velvety dark brown loam of the Chehalis River basin shot forth gardens straight from the pages of a brilliant seed catalogue.

Bless the absence of any crystal ball. I did not know this visit was to bring the heydays of easy-go summers to an end. But they ended with a bang. My great wish to emit a flapper image and for having my music recognized within my own age group (away from home) had gone begging up to now. Thanks to Adna, my faithful piano and Bernhard, I was about to become a touring guest star. Bernhard, newly graduated from High School, took it upon himself to have me meet Adna's jet set. Altering his mother's format of "come over to our house and hear her play your songs," he would take me into *their* homes. The audience by necessity would be handpicked classmates whose homes contained a piano. The odds of my scoring a success on this road trip were quite favorable as Adna, at that time, was not overburdened with a lot of home jazz talent. Included would be a bit of social chit-chat, interspersed with the latest new hits and then requests, all to be performed by me. As the presenter he calculated to bend ears, raise eyebrows and enliven a lazy Sunday afternoon. Underneath it all was the devious hope of creating date material for me, which in turn would clear the path for double dating along with him and his girl friend.

To persuade me was not difficult. Having been accustomed to playing the game of catch-up to his two year seniority, I couldn't frown on the chance to not only catch up but ascend to the upper level of his fellow graduates! Never even a stray thought was given to Aunt Lottie's "wholecheese" admonition. After all, it hadn't been my idea. Adna's town vicinity was to be forsaken in favor of the open countryside and the prosperous farms of some of his classmates, necessitating the use of the Krummel family car—a fairly new and proper closed Sedan, glass windows and all. This show was going on the road.

Off we went on a deadly quiet Sunday afternoon, Bernhard executing enough deft maneuvers to make the unwieldly and box-shaped Dodge seem to zap into the trip like a graceful deer. His acute left turn at the nether end of the Chehalis River bridge was a work of art, for I had done enough driving myself now to know expertise when I saw it. Away from the two-laned paved highway, the Dodge's rugged tires sent gravel and pebbles flying in our wake as we sped eastward. Fenced acres of velvet green pastures hosting fat and contented cows blurred by in rapid succession with here and there a roomy and tall barn whose lee sides still claimed remnants of Barnum & Bailey circus posters. A quick look at the speedometer recorded our speed to be 45 miles per hour, and why not for it befitted the whole racy idea. I gave an ear to the jaunty driver as he advised, "Now be sure and play your real jazziest numbers. I told all the kids you were a whiz and they're chomping at the bit to hear you take off." So far nerves or concern had not filled my mind, but when the Dodge began to slow down for a turn into a hedged lane uncertainty started up within my heart as to whether I could fill the bill as a demonstrator. Bernhard tootled us to a respectable halt, causing only a few khaki swirls of dust to rise behind the rear bumper before settling gently on the car's surface. Like the clincher to a coach's peptalk I was hearing, "And don't forget the 'Twelfth Street Rag,' the faster the better. Boy they'll think that's hot stuff." We prepared to disembark and I almost wished I was back where we'd started from.

Straight ahead, looking us right in the eye, was a rather gaunt and narrow shaped farmhouse of a Puritan design. A bannistered porch angled from the front and continued across one entire side of the home and it looked like neatness and austerity prevailed. Immediately we were received through the screen door and lead into an almost Victorian parlor. Hardly a setting for red hot jazz. In keeping with the mood, no one was occupying the parlor furniture, but sat instead upon pulled up dining table chairs which stood in a kind of ring as for a program. That almost did it. What had Bernhard projected this drop-by to be? As always my eyes quickly zeroed in on the object of prime importance to me and there it stood—an old curlicued and scrolled upright piano. One could just about tell nothing other than a polishing cloth had made contact with it for years. During the small talk which to my surprise sprang up immediately, it was laughingly mentioned how much fun it was going to be hearing the old piano played as hardly anything had ever been played on it! Silent prayers formed in my mind, all addressed to the eighty-eight keys not to be frightened at such an abrupt attack. Experience had taught the fact of ballads or waltzes with sustained notes being easier to "cover up" on stiff keys, provided some pedal leaning was applied. But, to bring off even a shred of verve with "Twelfth Street Rag" or "Doll Dance" on a crotchety old keyboard would spell sheer frustration.

I don't remember what I started off with, but I had enough sense to make a pleasing rather than splashy beginning, even if not acquainted with a term such as icebreaker. Just as much a relief to me as the relatively friendly keys was the lack of any awkwardness or social ineptness among our group. Everything flowed along in a most comfortable manner and when it came to "The Twelfth Street Rag," I almost broke my own speed record and managed to not go overboard into sloppiness, giving my nth degree of effort. In the middle of the prancing syncopation, an elder brother descended the steep stairway at my right, silently finding himself another dining room chair. Perhaps the steady beat brought him down into the parlor to see what was going on. Though I'm sure neither Bernhard nor I had been aware of the old show-biz axiom, "leave 'em wanting more," we did just that, once more proving innocence is bliss. We must have sensed the wiseness of terminating an act while it was still warm. Graciously served homemade cake and red jello, served on glass plates, put a fancy trim on what now was taking on a party air. The old parlor waxed from stiff to ambient as appreciation, quick talk and summer warmth enlivened the air. Couldn't we stay a bit longer? But we took our leave, not hurriedly but with a hint of purpose. After all, another presentation loomed on our schedule a few farms, barns, and dusty turns down the road.

The second performance does not stand out in my mind. Anything else after the first flush of success must not have registered with any impact. Both programs had been well peppered with spontaneous requests, with Bernhard quickly reminding each person, "Didn't I tell you—you can't think of one she doesn't know." Luckily for me they didn't and in my favor again, I was not touring a heavy music-performing territory. Had other musicians materialized out of the listeners, pianists in the main, I would have shrunk into the nearest corner. Where competitive spirit was required, I was a mouse. So far I hadn't been caught.

Tootling back to Adna over bridge creeks and late afternoon slanting sun rays, the two of us must have beamed in satisfaction. All had gone as planned and more. An alternate objective, tossed in by Bernhard, had hit its target. The target, who was unaware of his role in the play, was to meet and hear me and find himself unable to let me leave without trying to make a date. At this point Bernhard would step into the picture and suggest a double date with him and his new girl friend, Florence, for starters. If it worked, then my entertainment while in Adna would not rest so heavily on his shoulders. As if rehearsed, the scene ran pretty true to the plot, which sounds much more devious than it really was. He was a good friend of Bernhard and he was also all cut and dried beforehand. I had ogled him in early teen admiration when he was one of Adna's star basketball players. His other qualifications included being a good solid product, rooted in the fertile soil of a landmark farm owned by a landmark family. As I think of it now, I can't remember any double-dating taking place. It might have been waived daringly for a movie for two in Chehalis, to be followed by an ice cream treat at the St. Helens' Hotel lovely marble fountain.

At the present the new date material was enrolled at W.S.U. in Pullman, and was only in Adna during the summer months. This lent impetus to getting a foundation established. Graduation was his preamble to taking over the reins from aging parents. His collegiate and rah-rah-rah status had put the gleam on his armor so to speak, as my contact with these racy fellows had been nil. Be that as is may, the glamor was not sufficient to rule out my dismay in discovering later that he knew a great deal more about cows and tractors than he did about music. It was the old music vs boyfriends situation again. His customary response whenever I played the piano came forth in the drawling and popular phrase of the day, "Yow-zah . . . Yowzah," a byproduct of weekly tune-ins to Ben Bernie's Saturday night band program. Somehow this appreciative phrase didn't suffice and it seemed it was going to be the extent of his critique. Otherwise the romance bumped along in a hit and miss fashion of dating when I was in Adna, and the relaying of letters.

His one visit to our home, though pleasant, hastened the affair into a state of lukewarm friendship. The arrival in his parent's blue Buick, a car I considered straight from heaven, had been exciting. Accompanying me to my Saturday night playing job was not. How it came about for him to have to be with me on a Saturday, I know not, except for the fact of Saturday being the night for anything of consequence. The whole evening gave a clear indication that taking a girl to a dance where she was one of the musicians was not fun, and never would be.

Later, Tante Krummel and mother confessed to sharing a great holding of breaths when the romance appeared to catch fire, and then a great sigh when the few flames flickered into embers. They saw our twosome as too much youth on both parts and an unlikely pairing of interests. I wasn't so analytical, but I did know the whole thing didn't click when it came to music. We didn't share that language too well, beyond Ben Bernie.

Never one to sit back and evaluate, I still must have noticed now the advantages of owning an on-call repertoire. The music was there, loads of it, "Out Of Nowhere," "Blue Skies," "April in Paris," "Stardust," "Strike Up The Band," "Lover Come Back To Me," "Embraceable You," and on and on. There didn't seem to be an end to the lovely, spirited and beautiful melodies floating about. I didn't know this was a golden era of creative and listenable and danceable music. To claim them for your own, play them for yourself and for others, was like catching colorful butterflies to examine their brilliance, and then releasing them back into the air.

17

Pianos vs Boyfriends

Nine times out of ten, romance and music belong together like a perfectly matched pair. The busy working musician will add a clause to this pleasant euphemism with, "except when the *music* of this lovely phrase is a *musician*." When he attempts to combine music (or his playing thereof) with romance, he sadly discovers before too long they're as unwilling to blend as vinegar and oil. His active music playing can and often does loom as a stumbling block, or the noted third party of "Two's Company, Three's a Crowd." This little axiom, like all its kin, makes reasonable reading, but is unreasonable to live by. And so everybody gives it a try and every now and then makes it work.

The earliest indication of the annoying triangle became my testing ground before I suspected any conflict. Or had enough sense to put a name to it. After sadly believing no more dancing nights at the Willows would come to pass, one did. Very little dating or dancing had transpired during the interim following the Wright girls and my debut there about a year before. My long-delayed escort for the upcoming tremendous evening had been attracted to my music during a visit at the home of mutual family friends. These often served as forerunners to social contacts. For most of the boys I met in this fashion, the piano and I weighed about even on the attention scale, with the piano usually being the novel attraction. As for the ones I managed to fall in and out of love with, it must have been a 50-50 situation. I think they all toyed with the idea of the pianist possibly being as jazzy a companion as her rendition of "Some of These Days." She wasn't.

At last, I was going to a dance with a boy. Mother, left without too solid a reason to object, given the sketchy family tie-in, gave half-hearted assent. Perhaps she saw it as a major unloosening of the last strings. I viewed it somewhere between a significant victory and a perfect solution for a return to the Willows. Imagine, I would be hearing the brand new eight piece orchestra everyone was talking up as being real hot and snappy. "Wait 'till you hear their One-Steps, they really sizzle," I had been told. One-Steps were invariably placed onto an evening's dance roster immediately after Intermission, and for good reason. Everyone, both the band members and the dancers, needed all their renewed strength for this racehorse exhibition. The unwritten rule prevailed, "Don't get out on the floor unless you can MOVE."

Like mose girls, I had my make-believe heroes. Movie stars like Richard Arlen and Buddy Rogers and the phantom millionaire's son who would somehow come into your life via some miracle. When it came to real life heart throbs, I was drawn like a magnet to cute college boys and dance band musicians, neither of which were at my disposal in great numbers. And now I was on the brink of a dancing date with a built-in partner. No more insecure standing along the sidelines playing the pretense game, and what's more, another exciting prospect lay in the view for the evening—one I had lost no time in recognizing. For this paradisical night, I would have the wonderful fun of beholding and evaluating eight live and masculine musicians. Truly, my little cup was running over.

As we stepped from his Ford roadster into the Willows parking area, a trumpet's high brassy notes soared out into the cool evening air, from within. It seemed to light a fire under all feet strolling towards the entrance. In fact, for me throughout the many many years, this same magical sound has never lost its allure. Now we stood before the ticket window. No more a giggling girl was I, awaiting the all-important recognition and nod from the ticket person, as when we three singles had presented our pass. Suddenly the whole Willows assumed an entirely different character. The arched top of the little window was still the same, and soon we joined the ingoing throng of eager dancers in company with Evening in Paris perfume, bright red lipstick and unmistakable Brilliantine. Nothing had changed from when I had last seen it. There stood the taupe plush davenports, grouped against the wall. There was the red-bricked large fireplace, the three-sided refreshment bar and best of all, the bandstand with the trellis work at the edges. All of this was just the trimming for the large and glossy-smooth dancefloor awaiting the oncoming rush. Distraction and uncertainty almost overtook me as my date and I paused on the promenade walkway. Would I be able to summon up any bright remarks and cute gestures I had so minutely observed on previous evenings here?

Getting away had been a bit wrenching, with mother suggesting more than one ground rule as she stood at the ironing board. My date, who must have compared the list to a driver's license test, remarked later as he settled into his car, "Your mother is really concerned about your going to a dance with me isn't she? I don't think that's so bad either." I nodded silently in the dark, but only in partial agreement.

To not resemble hillbillies had been a primary concern of the Wright girls and me, but tonight my confidence was upheld by a skyblue dotted silk dress. Sturdy German trunks at home still held lovely fabrics and items of more affluent days. This dress had been handsewn, with a low sash in a reverse dotted white and blue, placed at the hipline in accepted style. Advice for the accessories had come from my brother Hans. Like me, he loved dancing and was, in my estimation, a most reliable source. "With a pair of peach colored silk stockings," he had offered, "and some black patent leather shoes, you might look like a real dame." It was followed to the letter. And yet, despite all the prepping and the primping, music was destined to put a crimp in tonight's story!

The marvelous new band was clipping off "Sweet Annabel Lee" in the stacatto style required for "toddling," and though no brilliant conversation had taken place between dater and datee, we had warily joined the others out on the floor who were wheeling and rotating around the springy surface. Good dancehalls prided themselves in maintaining their expertly layed, hard-maple surfaces. The correct amount of give, projected to reduce leg and foot fatigue, was an important feature. Though my partner was not an Arthur Murray, he could at least do the toddle, which incidentally was the first of the bouncing along side-by-side dances.

It had been my custom and privately savored indulgence at the earlier dances to spend a good portion of the time ogling the boys in the band. Nothing too unusual, for lots of girls had the same weakness. Truthfully, I probably gave them a double ogle. Once for being young men and once again for being musicians. And a third time if they were particularly good on their instrument! By this time I was becoming critical and had a fair idea of what sounded to me like unusual talent. My searching and beseeching looks brought no returns, other than a casual wink and I was too shy to progress beyond visual admiration. Female aggressiveness was not the mode of that day.

The habit must have been ingrained, for here I was on my first date, doing the same thing again, ogling. In fact I was reveling and rolling in a whole new field of players, all nattily dressed alike, brandishing wailing saxes, brassy trumpets and one sliding trombone. With the clownish antics of leader pianist, Harry Foley, thrown in, I was all but carried away. During intermission, and to my blushing shock as my date and I sipped at our Green River pop, one of the ogled musicians sought me out and sat himself down on the empty stool at my left side. He hadn't taken a gamble, not one bit, as I had been far from unobtrusive in admiring his flashy sytle and his dark curly locks. Lacking the necessary feminine finesse to include my escort in the conversation at my left, I kept turned toward the player as we talked about music, current hits and such. My mind was busy floating above a high "C" at this unprecedented event. My date was left to stare into his Green River soda as I chatted on, dumbly committing such a faux pas. When the musician excused himself to return to the bandstand, I knew right away something was amiss. While my evening's escort was not visibly angered, he was far from happiness. With moderate annoyance he determined, "You're sure crazy about dance music aren't you?" This followed with the suggestion of my rather being up there on the bandstand than out on the floor dancing with him, which was not true. I wanted both. A definite pall hung over the remaining hour and the fun of the evening was on a downhill slide. Though I saw and heard of him off and on afterwards, any further nights of him taking me dancing appeared to be a pleasure he could do without. Now how would I get to the Willows? Music had the answer to that one too, but was opting to hold it in abeyance for awhile yet.

Meanwhile the dream continued in the undaunted custom of young girls pursuing romance. There would be other times, other boys. So said mother. I tried to imagine that music and love would come together to make the happy ending. Until then there would be various launchings of trial balloons, some destined to burst at the hands of music. To wit:

I was gazing into a pair of remarkably pale blue eyes, while noting the creamy curls of a tall young fellow seated upon another bandstand. Even in another city! His very occupation, learned through mutual friends attending this evening's dance in Seattle, had already created a high degree of romantic interest. When he left the bandstand to dance with me (arranged by the friends beforehand), the balloon soared aloft again. I had been taken to this Government Employees Costume Ball to enjoy hearing a band put together by musical members of the local Customs Office. The volunteer group of about ten had no strict rules as to members leaving their post, or taking to the floor. By the end of this exciting evening, he had been given detailed instructions for finding our wooded home and I was on cloud nine. To think of it! He would be driving all the way from Seattle, bringing along his violin so we could "collaborate," as he termed it, on some music.

To be sure, our home front was given a proper warmup for the event. Colorful potentials filled the air of our pole house, with me taking wild guesses as to his position with the agency. His only pounding a type-writer or working at books never crossed my mind. Instead I had him enveloped in a black cloak of mystique à la radio's "Thin Man," uncovering smuggled dope and contraband material. All this and music too, painted an eligible picture.

A few questions disturbed my optimistic outlook. What would he think of our pioneer-like house (upgraded now but still highly un-citified)? Would I be able to hold my own with his possible violin novelties, such as the popular "Hot Canary"? Did I know *all* of it? The fetching little tune soon began to work itself out in my head. I don't know why, perhaps it was personal pride, but the thought of not coming up close to 100% when asked to do a certain number, represented failure on my part, or a discredit to how I wished to come across. It certainly sharpened my listening ears from these years on. The fortunate combination of birthright, my memory bank and sometimes pure luck wasted no time in becoming magnetized into the needed action. But back to day dreaming. Perhaps this tall, blonde adventure-filled fellow would be effecting the jazzy Rubinoff style (an immensely popular violinist of these radio-filled days). In that case our twosome would really click.

The facts of musical dating were learned early and as I was at this time playing in a dance orchestra, I knew what not to do. The forbearance of several boyfriends had already been strained. Taking me to a dance where I promptly had to leave them, and join the music-makers on a stage, did not a happy evening make. As one of them phrased it succinctly, "It sure makes you feel like a dunce." Never could I imagine the Custom's Agent in such a role. That could, if necessary, be dealt with later.

A driving northwest rainstorm did its best to remove some of the dazzle from his entree. I had opened our backdoor, which led indoors from our large and covered backporch, only to see my Nordic sleuth leaning on an outer support post to remove a pair of heavy black rubbers. "Oh, don't bother to take them off out there," Mother had wailed, "come on up to the door and leave them." That he did and then I could not help but note the magnitude of this pair of rainy-day footwear. Undoubtedly they were the largest I had seen up to now. After hanging up his impressive and dripping raincoat of sooty black, and his black brimmed hat, I introduced him to mother and my two little sisters. The very next thing he did, before making small talk or noting his surroundings, was to tenderly open the red velvet lined violin case, which up to now had never left his side. As he did so, I made note of a definite pause given to bestowing a loving gaze upon the instrument inside. My mind, working a mile-a-minute now, raised a whole new likelihood. "What if he turns out to be a concert violinist?" He had, I remembered, dropped the word "symphony" during our dancing. If so, mother would enjoy a lovely evening, while I, well out of classical practice now, would be hard put to hold up my end.

Thirty minutes later his violin had answered my doubts and confirmed several new fears. He had brought along his own music, every page of it as bland as an ulcer diet. Where he collected such a bundle of wishy-washy music I knew not. Every sheet was sparsely printed in either a slow tuneless waltz or a plodding fox-trot. How had he fit himself into that danceband? Added to the dismay of the pianist, was the performance of his much admired pale blue eyes. Whenever he bowed one of the higher notes, they rolled alarmingly upward as if in distress. This act now made mother one of the dismayed persons in the room, for she decried out uncivilized and rough ceilings! However, I felt and told her later that his mind was totally in musical channels. We played on . . . and on, mother and the girls dutifully sitting on the sofa. Whatever were they thinking, I wondered, as his violin droned us into yet another hum-drum melody, his glamor steadily paling before my eyes. What a dull evening this had turned into with the soulful eyerolling being almost more than I could bear. I dared not catch the eyes of either of my little sisters. Well mannered as they were, I knew both must be having thoughts of their own. And pray tell, where was all the very obvious insistence and pursuance of just a week ago?

Refreshments later went beyond the usual cake, salvaging some of the disappointment, and the visiting back and forth was rather pleasant. The subject of just what his position might be was tactfully avoided. I was thankful for that, as I wanted something left intact of his former image. When time came for his departure, I was diplomatically left to escort him from the backporch. However, it wasn't at all like the lines of

"Last Night On The Backporch, I loved her most of all." As he bent to tug at the flopping large rubbers, I breathed a sigh. He *was* nice. He *was* tall. He *was* rather handsome and his work was still mysterious. Could I at some later time guide him to more expressive music? As he carefully picked up the black violin case, my assumption became a certainty. He was not going to try to kiss me goodnight. How could he with those cumbersome overshoes, and one hand clasping that precious case? Instead he held my hand at some length (with his free one), pressing it warmly while expressing his gratitude for the visit. All in all, quite a departure from the norm.

Peering through the dark night's rain, I watched him stride toward his car, unseen by me as yet, but pre-pictured as a racy model befitting his calling. The first amazement was seeing him sort out a key and *unlock* the cardoor, an act unheard of in our parts. The second letdown was the very ordinary sedan, rivered in coursing water, and just as inky black as the night air surrounding it. As black as his raincoat, and his brimmed hat, and his suit, and the cumbersome galoshes. Things were not measuring up.

The next contact made, was by mail. I tore open his letter to find a proper and carefully written "thank you," including mother and my sisters. Try as I might I could find no hidden meanings or implications. Perhaps the disappointment had been mutual! Music had enticingly led the way to this encounter so rife with romance, and then had, without visible violence, killed it dead.

18

Strike a Piano—Strike a Match

Fate linked up with the piano again in plotting my romantic future. Or should I say Fate, the piano and a calculating mother? As I have said, our German friends often drew my brother and me into their social circles. Among them there was often someone who remembered our father as their family doctor. It was a warm touchstone for us. Mother, in her resolute fashion after their divorce and his subsequent leaving of the United States, had firmly closed that chapter of her life. The whole subject was off limits, leaving Hans and me uninformed as to his whereabouts or destiny. It was like an erasure of his whole being, and one he evidently chose to keep that way. Ours was not to question.

Naturally with several younger fellows in these later German groups, a particular one took my eye. And once more, no like message came from the other side, for I was just another voice in the Alto section of the German singing society known as the "Saengerbund." He was not an instrumentalist, but qualified to a degree with his husky and pleasing voice that charmed others as well as me. Before long my brother and he became both singing and imbibing buddies, and for some reason made an arrangement for their respective mothers to meet. Their plan included the two mothers exchanging experiences of earlier years in Germany, while I played the piano and accompanied this fellow (her son) in some pop songs he liked to sing. I saw it all as a golden evening wherein my light would at last come forth from under that bushel, leaving him in utter astonishment. Maybe even to the point where drinking large quantities of beer would just be boring!

His mother sent previous word that she would bring some German "gabaek" (cake or pastry). We elected to augment with salad and coffee. We were ready, but not really. Up to now I had not seen his mother, since they lived about ten miles distant and she had not attended any Saengerbund Concerts. Their attractive home, pointed out to us by my brother whenever we drove up North Hill, was painted in candy-store pink and white—this in the days when hardly anyone ventured beyond white, yellow or grey. It should have told us something.

"And this is my mother," he was saying to us as mother and I had let them in our backdoor, which served as main entrance and exit. One look and I was aghast. If anyone had searched in a great effort to pick out the one least like mother, she would have been the choice. Her hair was short, bleached to an alarming blonde and topped with a crown of precise ringlets. Mother's was long, straight and pulled into an unvarying topknot bun. His mother's ampleness ran at large, spilling over the restraints of a gold belt at the waist. Mother still clung to the proper confines of a corset. Our visitor's dress vibrated in shades of purple, with perfume to match. Mother, who doted on soft blue colors and only occasionally dabbed from her gift bottles of Yardley's Old Lavender, looked washed out by comparison. When our guest opened her shiny lipsticked mouth, which required no priming, the antithesis was complete.

Despite the blatant contrasts, the evening was not a failure. We were a willing audience to her outflow of colorful stories. It was better than a movie. She only allowed herself a break when her son sang, whereupon the subject changed to his potential talent and how this particular period of his life, as she saw it, was the first stop on his rise to ultimate stardom. He would of course need proper management. Noting my ease at picking up on any number he wished to sing, and putting him in proper key range all without benefit of written music, fairly made her blue eyes glitter. The visit ended with her still in good voice, and the rest of us in humble defeat.

In about a month, an invitation was issued for a return visit to be held at her home. Mother tried for an out and out refusal, but knew she had better go. "But I've heard all about her house with the eighty-eight French window panes, and the parquet solid oak floors, over and over. I shouldn't have to go and *see* them too," was her weak defense. The evening was to be more than reciprocal, for it was in honor of her son's birthday, with other people present, even younger folk.

With my brother at the wheel of our old Dodge, the three of us headed down South Hill, skimmed the valley floor and circled up North Hill. The evening was lighted up with a full moon and my mind foresaw a romantic party ahead. Hans parked the car. There was no doubt about it, this was the place. All eighty-eight squares of the French windows sparkled the indoor lights out into the evening. People moved about inside and all appeared festive and exciting. We were ushered into the hallway and taken upstairs over satin smooth oak steps, into a chintz flowered sitting room. After depositing our wraps it was back down the stairs and meet other guests. I had high hopes of being claimed by the son very soon and being made sort of his silent partner for the party. One sweeping glance revealed the prized piano, shining ever so brightly, but so was everything else. To me it seemed a quite ordinary upright and I fervently hoped it would surprise me with unseen qualities. The voice of our hostess could be heard, explaining at large: "You haff to vatch your step . . . I don't like to cuffer up the hard vork of my husbandt, und so I shust place a little rug here and dere." The issued

79

warning referred to the solid oak floors handlaid by her husband, which were as brilliant as they were hazardous.

The party progressed with no indications of a paired off couple. Lots of people drank lots of beer, the bottles of which bobbed within a washtub on a sea of ice. The piano had already been played and the man of the hour had favored the party-goers with smoothly sung solos, to much adoration and applause. "Isn't it vunderful," his mother was beaming at everyone, "he iss going to be a radio star, I know it. Und my piano iss being played again, 'chust listen to the tone of it . . . undt she can play a-n-y-z-i-n-g."

Later I saw mother ascending the stairs, in the wake of the other mother. And what was *this* all about? I looked around, my brother was nowhere in sight and I hadn't seen my make believe escort since his last solo. To my mounting chagrin I overheard that the two missing fellows were down in the basement! My look down below from the top basement step was enough to confirm all doubts. There they were, carrying on a duo beerbust, singing away lustily at German folksongs, without benefit of accompaniment. My heart sunk into my shoes; I wasn't even in the running. However, my brother remained true to his pre-party statement: "Whenever you two (mother and me) are ready to shove off, just say the word. Whatever the Mater says, goes." The word was given and he kept his promise, leaving the birthday boy alone for the time being. His not even seeing me off was not total heartbreak since his image was deteriorating by the minute.

As soon as the three of us were underway, with my brother safely executing the sharp curves of North Hill that were mother's undoing each trip, I felt something was in the air. Though I'd been driving everywhere since age fifteen, I made no offer to take over. We were dong fine, real fine I thought, as mother seemed to be breaking out into suppressed chuckles for no apparent reason I could see. Her humor was not aired too often, but when released it was contagious for she could enact the parts with great mimicry. It took awhile before I could track down the source, as each time she would start out with, "Well, Ilse, you'll never guess what's in store for you," only to break up again at the thought of it. The old Dodge was now grinding away in second gear as it crept upward towards the Willows Corner, the tall trees and home. Finally it all came out and I sat in a bemused state of shock as I heard:

"The piano, believe it or not, is going to be *your* piano, every key of it. Not now, but you will get it later when you become of age . . . and become . . . a part of the family! A part of the family . . . how could she assume such a thing as that? She was even ahead of me! I was still agape as mother explained my future in more detail. "It's all quite plain," mother continued in a mocking tone, "she has you scheduled for her daughter-in-law. That would make you a big help in promoting her son's singing career, while also becoming owner of the piano, all at the same time." There was more. "She isn't content with killing just two birds with one stone, she wants three." Bird number three was the daughter. A legally processed agreement, to be signed immediately after our nuptials, would put complete control and ownership of said piano into the newlywed's names. With this paper, the grasping hands of her daughter would forever be stayed from any claim on the instrument. "Well," laughed Mother, "what do you think of such a clever plan?"

I can well remember what I thought—disillusion, disappointment and dismay. Oh where was romance? I had met the daughter at the party and thought her both beautiful and charming. However, her mother had confided to my mother's startled ears while upstairs in the sitting room, "My daughter vill neffer get that piano. Her husbandt makes fine money, let him buy her vun. I payed for dis vun with hard, hard vork. I eefen soldt apples on the street ven vee first came to Tacoma. Let's see her do such a ting as dot, with all her fine clothes."

By the next morning I could at least smile about it—it *was* funny. And it became even funnier when my imagination took a voice in the matter. In the jargon of the day I was going around exclaiming, "Yee gods," am I ever lucky this whole set-up didn't occur a hundred years ago, instead of the enlightened Thirties." In those days marital choices were handled by parents with few questions asked. Perhaps the stakes attached to the deal were of greater proportions than a polished piano, but who knows? Years later I found the whole little episode classified as a case in point. Innocent pianos can often become a sore point in family relations.

19

From Graduation to a Domestic . . .
With Fringe Benefits

A royal blue, leather encased High School Diploma was now proudly on display upon our library table at home, dated June of 1930. Just viewing it lent an added dignity to my person, earnestly pressing me into seeking a higher status of summer work than previous berrypicking seasons. Hopefully if I found anything, enough time would be left before September for my usual trip to Adna. Tante Krummel had graciously offered a Fall term at a Tacoma Business College to the graduate . . . bestowed in honor of her and mother's great and abiding friendship. Pride had to absorb this velvet lined blow . . . . Mother was not a good receiver. Of course, she assured herself, post-Depression days would take care of this gesture.

I enjoy thinking back on my first real job—that of a live-in babysitter. The whole venture loomed like a step into the beyond. I had been away from home many times, visiting and having summer fun, but away from home and working—never. How could I have known a surrender into a quixotic way of life was to occur? Or that the job would render me a prize victim of "cultural shock," a terminology out of my sphere at that age? Or that my piano playing would cause an extraordinary link to form—one between the menial and the musical?

Dodging mother's qualms, a newspaper ad had been answered via letter. We had no phone. Our mail soon brought a prompt reply to please come in person and discuss the particulars. Fairly simple so far, except for us this meant a fifteen mile trip to Tacoma and back, a serious consideration in our case. A few days later, mother and I stood outside an imposing four-storied brick building, about six blocks from Tacoma's busy downtown. I had set down my small satchel (packed in case I stayed) in a recessed entryway. A fancily scrolled metal plate above read, "Cambridge Apts."

"This has to be the right place," we agreed as we studied printed instructions for admittance through the locked double doors. The leaded glass panes reflected only deeply shirred folds of opaque fabric. I dialed the apartment number given from the entrance wall phone as directed, and like magic several tiny clicks from the direction of the doors signalled its locks to be freed. We proceeded. Fascination at such a beginning to an interview began to set in. Once inside, all was mellowed carpeting, backgrounded by walls scrolled in swirls of beige plaster. Brass emblems of English crests with crossed swords hung with aristocratic bearing. Here and there dimly lighted floorlamps indicated opulence. I don't know about mother, but I expected to see Carole Lombard come slinking down the hall any minute. What a description was gathering up for later telling to the Wright girls who were always receptive to anything glamorous. Though only five years removed from city living myself, our sudden plunge into pioneer life had well begun to reshape a lot of my thinking and being.

Again we pressed a button and the solid door to Apt. No. 106 opened immediately, but not for us. A well dressed lady was stepping through, closing her purse as she passed us by. We waited. "Come in . . . come in," said a voice from inside, and as we complied we found ourselves confronting a harried looking woman, bent over a Windsor desk. Her cotton dress looked like she had just pulled it over her head, disarranging her hair in the haste. "Excuse me," said the voice, "I just have to enter this payment into the books before I lose track of it . . . things get lost in a hurry around here." All the while we exchanged necessary and brief facts, her whole being was breathing off waves of frustration. Mother was instantly sympathetic to a situation so rife with plight. Just seeing the two of us together, sharing the details of my first job, sent the lady into memories of her own departed mother and tears sprang to her eyes. As mother comforted her, I wondered what we were doing here. It was soon settled—all provisions were agreeable. Primarily, I was to keep an eye on two year old Georgie, any housework or other incidentals would be secondary. Going home to Puyallup would be possible every weekend and the salary was five dollars per week. My acceptance of the terms was hastened by the handsome, darkwooded immense Grand piano, occupying an entire corner of the spacious living room. Other discreet glances had revealed two young girls sitting on the floor carelessly scissoring at pages of paper dolls. They seemed to echo the temper of their mother, jumping up and down erratically, fighting over the scissors as scraps and cuttings trailed behind them.

Before mother could tell me goodbye, I had already been dispatched on my first assignment. "Where's Georgie . . . now where has he gone," the lady wailed "Hurry and run outside (meaning me) and see if he's gotten out on the sidewalk . . . he's only a little over two and shouldn't be out there alone for a minute. Girls, did you let Georgie get out the apartment door?" And thus began the first of the long series of searching for what I soon learned was a gregarious Georgie. And I hadn't yet unpacked my satchel!

After several taxing weeks I still had not found any kind of a pattern to live by in this household. Hectic was a way of life here. With Mrs.

Johnson as manager of the apartments, and her husband co-owner, the family apartment unit became hard pressed in exuding any homey atmosphere. I soon found my erstwhile bailiwick to be the nerve center of this 64 unit building. As for Mr. Johnson's schedule—it was something I failed to understand. He could pop off on sudden departures to California, necessitating wild suitcase packings and last minute searching for mates to stray socks and an ironed shirt. Sometimes he'd arrive home at proper dinner time in very ordinary fashion, enjoying the children and lounging in his easy chair. There were vague connections involving the operation of Tacoma's Western League Baseball Club, borne out by several pairs of new uniforms hanging in the long wardrobe closet. For his daily work, it developed, he was a second generation owner of an established Paint & Wallpaper company downtown.

Quite naturally (but unnatural to the new babysitter), each day promised adventure, most of which was undefined, unconventional highly irregular. Explanations of the episodes, which erupted daily and sometimes hourly on the hour, were brief. Fitting myself into the dizzy picture took time and a reconditioning of the customs and habits of my whole life. Before mastering my distrust of the Cambridge's automatic elevator, I raced up the back stairways at top speed, sometimes taking two at a time so as to complete my missions in about the same length of time had I used the elevator. It would have been much simpler to have confessed my fears. Though exposed to them regularly when a city dweller, or on city shopping trips, these had all been in the competent hands of a live operator. I can't say why but it took time to place trust in such a mechanical genie, which it seemed to me could go amiss sometime, causing who knew what to happen. The possibilities kept me stair leaping, and agile.

The one and only saving grace in this spasmodic existence was the beautiful Chickering Grand, a quality instrument from Mr. Johnson's family home. I soon loved it with increasing passion, for it stood out like an island of hope among all the hubbub, becoming my secret ally. When it ran afoul of proper respect I sprang to the Chickering's defense. Sometimes it was in horror, as on the second day when I came upon little Georgie actually attacking the fine ivory keys with his father's hammer. And grievously every time the ten year old daughter's brief skirmish with her practice left the keys all tacky. She sampled hard candy along the way, changing flavors at will. After a consoling cleanup and dusting over the glassy finish, I managed to find time to sit down and play, transporting myself from a domestic to a grandiose performer in some kind of penthouse. "Penthouse Serenade" was a very popular number then, and with my imagination I was right on scene. As always Green Book's ballads and my favorite Viennese waltzes were aired when time permitted. Each was a delight to feel and finger.

Coming as a complete surprise was the fact that I had unwittingly been entertaining Tacoma's Chief of Detectives and his wife, who occupied the apartment overhead. Their flattering comments to Mrs. Johnson, after asking to come in some evening and listen closer, was something I had not suspected. After that, one musical occasion begat another, and another. On one of them I was out in the kitchen clearing away the supper remnants, hoping to catch a glimpse of Mrs. Johnson's emergence as a socially dressed hostess. Instead she dashed into the kitchen, still adjusting her slip, with "Why don't you just sit down and play when our friends come this evening. I know they will enjoy hearing some of the songs they like. I'll see to getting Georgie to bed!" Not a bad trade and also affording a chance to wear my good dress, in truth my graduation dress. To my sorrow the Johnson's entertained infrequently, which was understandable.

One night after one of the rare suppers with the complete family all eating at the same time, Mr. Johnson had walked into the long front room and melted into his favorite roomy leather chair. It was a little space of quiet when the phone and the door buzzer were both silent. The girls were out in the summer evening with Georgie in tow and a precious serenity prevailed. From the living room I heard, "Elsa, please come in here and play a few nice tunes for me." Mrs. Johnson sent me from the narrow kitchen with, "I'll clear the table, it's crowded in here anyway with the two of us." I needed no coaxing as I was very fond of Mr. Johnson, who seemed a calm and collected balancer amid the disorder.

On the first of these little intervals I had lead off with some pretty and tuneful waltzes of the day such as "Diane," "Charmaine" and others. Suddenly the grand piano's clear tones were further ornamented by one of the most beautiful and thrilling whistling sounds I'd ever heard. And it was emanating from the leather chair. Although mother in her younger years possessed a similar talent, this surpassed it. The pitch was perfect and true and as I turned in amazement I noticed the look on his face of happy satisfaction. When we both reached the high note near the end of "Alice Blue Gown," the room was filled with glorious sound. Next thing I knew, the figure of Mrs. Johnson literally sailed through the air. She aimed her flying leap right into her husband's lap! Kisses and hugs followed and I kept my eyes pointed out the window as I knew her tears would follow soon. Emotional moments at the Cambridge were a daily occurrence, but nothing like this! Though the little duos of whistling and piano were too few and far between, they became moments to treasure.

Before the summer was out I had progressed to partially riding the everyday merry-go-round, without falling off. Periods of dreadful homesickness (my first) had almost overtaken me, but indulgence time for sinking into melancholia just was not available. With Georgie seated in his wicker buggy, I had wheeled a path into the sidewalks between the Cambridge and the green sanctuary of Wright's Park—a saner type of babysitting than chasing Georgie's favorite red-striped ball. He loved to play with it on the south side of the building, where two sets of steep side hills took anything round and set it rolling. Being young and agile, I could usually capture the runaway at the first landing on St. Helen's Avenue. To miss here presented the awful possibility of another steep hill before hitting Broadway with its streetcars and traffic, which happened only once. After that episode, Georgie's little tactics were not above suspicion anymore and ball rolling took place at the west entrance, on the level surface of Tacoma Avenue.

The two girls, though younger, were not immune to leaving me aghast either as on my first night in the apartment where I shared their bedroom. There they were, sitting in bed eating huge rounds of watermelon as if it were nothing out of the ordinary. When they took the rinds and buried them under the bed pillows, I had to get out of my bed and take action which was greatly resented. "We do it all the time," they giggled. "You don't have to tell us what to do." So many things happened the following day, there wasn't time to dwell on watermelon rinds and sassy remarks. I soon learned to check the waterglasses I had filled for the dinner table in case Georgie's little fingers might have experimented on them again with the salt and pepper shakers.

In all fairness, the Cambridge did have some redeeming qualities. I doubt the splendiferous piano alone could have offset all the liabilities. Mrs. Johnson's trust in me grew to the point of allowing me to use and carry (when necessary) the all-important passkey—the one that magically opened every lock on the premises. This valuable key, so perfect in operation, had one bad fault—that of coming up missing when needed. Thank heavens the frantic uproar that ensued when it was, was never the result of *my* carelessness. I couldn't have shouldered the responsibility. On the other hand, the utter joy and relief when the wayward key was tracked down was enough to put the rest of the day in a celebrative mood. Another plus directly due to my apartment months was a suggestion never taken seriously; it remains as one of the unanswered questions everyone has left hanging along the way.

One of Mrs. Johnson's close friends was to visit briefly on her way through from Chicago. She was involved in the management of a hotel in that city. Her enjoyment of hearing the Chickering played led her to seriously offer to take me back with her. I could hold my own, she felt confident, in being the house pianist in their dining room or lobby. Heaven knows why, but I didn't even flirt with the potentials. Perhaps Chicago sounded too remote, or too wicked . . . all those movie gangsters and mobs. Most of all, I was in no way ready or anxious to fly from the Northwest's nest as yet. The Johnsons both said, "Think on it . . . she'd take good care of you . . . it's a great opportunity . . . her hotel is lovely and reputable." All of that did not impress me sufficiently to discuss the preposterous idea at home. For the present, getting back to our woods, the family and a steadier balance of life was more important. And . . . one of my boyfriends had stopped by the Cambridge briefly with a piece of music he wished to sing for a program, and I was hoping the title, "We'd Make a Peach of a Pear," was an indirect message for his accompanist. Also Freda, the apartment caretaker's daughter, and I had made important plans to attend the following Friday night's dance at the downtown "Auditorium." Such were the priorities!

The night of the dance was the only time I traded on the name and prestige of the Cambridge. I must have reasoned it owed me something. Freda and I had asked her elder brother (who would be home that night) to listen for the door phone and push the button releasing the locks on the outside doors. While Freda and I left as a twosome, we did not return as such, having both recklessly said yes to separate escorts who would see us home. The whole evening was of a daring mood as it was, since I was wearing one of Mrs. Johnson's former party dresses. "Someone should be using it," she had said as I hesitated. The fun of floating in sophistication in a filmy, green-flowered chiffon, the jazzy dance band, and all the little glassy squares of light twirling from a crystal ball overhead, simply did not call for taking the streetcar back with Freda to a place where I was employed as a babysitter! Therefore, at the end of the ball, Cinderella directed her escort's roadster to her "home." "It isn't far," I blithely told him. "My apartment is quite close to downtown." As we stood in the arched doorway of the west entrance, he politely asking, "How do you like living here . . . it's sure a nice place," I had snatched the wallphone from its hook and immediately the big doors went click, click, click. Clutching the big brass handle, I yanked the door open and like a streak of lightning, I was inside throwing a "goodnight" and "thankyou" over a disappearing shoulder as he stood outside the glass door. He probably knew a frightened chicken when he saw one.

Summer ended and went out in a blaze of glory, so to speak. In early September I would be embarking on a nine months' Business College course and my mind was racing ahead as I gathered my belongings for the place I'd been wishing and hoping to be . . . home. From out of nowhere, as she often did, Mrs. Johnson had burst into her apartment, looking wild and distraught . . . only this time she *really* was headed for hysteria as she seized the phone and babbled, "FIRE . . . FIRE . . . FIRE!" From then on all was mayhem and I'll never forget it, for even the motive of this hand-set fire was high drama. The arsonist, a crippled and jealous wife, who with a handsome husband occupied a fourth floor apartment, had furtively set fire to the draperies. I had played for her before and felt an eerie strangeness come into the room each time. Evidently she had been driven to desperation and revenge over her condition. During the ensuing pandemonium of roaring fire trucks, flashing red lights and screaming sirens, each hubbub halting at our doors, her devious mind lashed out once more. While firemen uncoiled hoses and shocked tenants stood agape at their doors, she had slipped into the basement via the backstairs, and touched off blaze number two. This time it was the locker storage items. Both fires were later contained, but not without reams of choking smoke and tangles of soggy hoses snaking along the corridors.

As the neurotic wife's husband was a public figure of clout, she was left in his custody for the night. This act robbed a few people of a good night's rest. As for me, concern over the highly emotional Mrs. Johnson almost matched my own aftershock. And so, on this highly dramatic note, my only job as a domestic came to an end. Or as termed at the outset, my job as Georgie's babysitter.

Goodbyes at the Cambridge were not permanent. I was sincerely issued an open invitation for any needed overnight stays in the city. While the kind privilege was not overworked, we did see each other now and then and remained friends for many years. The beloved Chickering was not out of my life either as I was to play it again and again, once for an impressive large party the Johnson's had found time to host.

The irony of this last portion verges on the sinister. Some ten years later the whole Cambridge Apartment building burned to the ground, except for topping brick walls. All sixty-four units were charred and ruined beyond salvage by an unexplained fire. Fortunately there was no loss of lives. And sadly with it all went one great and Grand Piano.

PART III

CHORUS

20

The Lithuanian Connection

1931's stage was one of bleakness. Life's brightly shining stars such as Fame or Fortune had to cower in the wings and await a more favorable entrance. However, the currently running play, starring Disappointment and sometimes Hope, went on. Bread cost 5¢ a loaf and was practically tasteless and weightless. The effecting of optimistic moods was left to the young or the uninitiated. I was nineteen and ready to amaze the business world, through the training of a High School Business major, and a further year of Business College spent on legal secretarial skills. In my estimation this perfected me as the *compleat* stenographer, cool, smooth and the epitome of efficiency! Of course I had lots of company. Class after class of graduates in all fields had innocently timed themselves right into the great depression's ample lap. After countless rounds of self-presentation I was learning that professional people, especially attorneys it seemed, clung tenaciously to their iron-greyed and invincible secretaries. Or was it the other way around? Newer barristers could only hire girls on an unofficial "earn as you learn" program, where no matter how much you learned, the earning stayed about the same. Belittling as it was, I was glad to take part in the plan. My brother Hans agreed to make the daily detour, driving to and from his daily job with the Northern Pacific Railroad, to deposit me within walking distance of downtown Tacoma. Without this assistance the so-called job couldn't have taken place at all.

Meanwhile, the musical continuity thread was in need of reinforcement as well as something to signal a fresh chapter. If it was my lifeline (after a day at an office), my health was at a low ebb. Would the music angel hear my call? Again, she answered. An audition was forthcoming as the "piano player" (the term pianist was rarely used), in a small dance orchestra now consisting of three girls! Seems the angel appointed my brother as the appropriate channel. If I landed this (my pencil was flying) plus the wages from the pittance office work, the grand total would still be only a little better than nothing. Hans, whose job was supporting our family of five, had to count his "sheckles" (as he called them) quite carefully. In fact, he had fallen into this role during the years most fellows contemplated college and careers. Such were the times and the circumstances. In respect I will add he indulged in very little griping or complaining. So maybe now I could take care of a part of my own expenses.

The plot-changing audition, actually an informal gathering in the leader's family home, came to pass because of my brother's voluble appreciation of her obvious charms, of which she suffered no lack. Being vitally attractive was not all; Olga was also gainfully employed as chief bookkeeper for the large Ford agency of Tacoma, and breadwinner for the Kuzenski household of three. My brother Hans had met and heard her play the accordion at a "wing-ding" (pop word for parties then). Here it was that another amazing feature came to light. She could drink most men under the table and still remain in perfect control. I was to find out soon her 100% Lithuanian blood was something to reckon with musically too. During a party she had told my brother of her deep desire to lead and form a small dance band of all girls. Three had been collected so far, with Olga's accordion making up the fourth of a group. Now, she confided, if only a good all 'round and adaptable piano player could be found, her accordion could be put aside, except for Schottisches and Polkas. She preferred to be performing on her real love, the Saxophone. The table was set for my entrance.

Very soon thereafter we became a newly formed all-girl orchestra and an early Spring evening found us driving to our maiden engagement in a small city about an hour's drive from Tacoma. I believe it was either the Auburn Kiwanis or Rotary Club. The evening proved to be a series of "firsts" to remember. As the surprise job had materialized after only one rigorous midweek's practice, I was inducted into the group as speedily as a 1-A draftee into the Army. We embarked, all of us, in our leader's shiny Ford Coupe, the only self-owned car among the whole ensemble. The paved two-lane highway north was flying by at a pretty good clip I thought, considering the entire orchestra was wedged between two solid car doors. For anyone not sufficiently dated, a "Coupe" was an enclosed, two-doored, one-seated but roomy car. However, it was never meant to play the role we were forcing upon it, which today would be that of a touring band's functional Van. Three pairs of feet, though entangled, contrived to stay clear of brake pedal, gas pedal and gearshift and chances for alteration of our melded body positions were almost nil. A full set of drums jangled along behind our backs, frequently knocking heads with the spare tire in the trunk.

Wouldn't it be marvelous, I had often thought to myself, if our group of girls could effect some of the velvety smooth class of the popular "Four Evelyns and their Violins"? We did have one willowy thin and symphony oriented violinist, and we also had her opposite in our bouncing drummer. On the other hand, we had all strained our budgets in buying the exact yardage for sewing our look-alike fancy dresses. The fabric was filmy sheer and abloom with large and demure pink roses, causing mother to air some seldom used German epithets during the sewing. Her reception of the whole venture was lukewarm to the point of showing little interest for the dressmaking. I don't remember how she relented. Maybe the fact of Olga's mother offering to make mine, which of course would not measure up to standard. To be sure, when all the dresses were finished with their rippling flared and calf-length hemlines, mine was the only one that did not dangle or twitch.

As we continued onward toward Auburn, it soon became apparent that the dozens of identical pink roses were the strongest similarity between us. Being the youngest and lightest, I became the necessary lap-sitter, which did little to separate me from the flurry of words within the car. To add to my alienation they were speaking a tongue known as "girl-talk," a language quite foreign to me. Unsophisticated or not, I was essential to them as pianists then were generally the crux of any group. Musically speaking, I outranked them and in time became an equal-reckoning member and settler of any music technicalities, despite my unworldliness. Any foolish or romantic moves on my part were well scrutinized by three pairs of eyes, for which I was not always grateful.

"It's a good thing we left early," the girls were repeating as the miles stretched on over several sets of railroad tracks. A mild lurching was now taking place as the drummer suddenly felt the need of her purse. With much jostling and elbowing into my side, she finally located her evening bag, a deep bottomed affair I had noted at our departure. "That was a helluva struggle, but I found it," she panted as I waited to see what she needed so badly from the bag. Within the semi-darkness of the Coupe I saw her hand extract a bottle considerably larger than a perfume container. I tried not to gasp when the shape became recognizable as that of a flask! "Who's ready for a little swig outa this?" she queried. "We need a lift and I wanna play some razz-a-ma-tazz at this joint, if we ever get there." The flask was passed around to identically pursed lips and sharp indrawn breaths. My lips were not pursed, they were ajar. I knew booze was consumed in cars, but girls carrying their very own whisky bottles? Not to mention, hiding them inside beaded evening bags! Why did mothers always have to be right? Back when I had first chosen to make a definite turn from the classical path, mother had coined an adage I thought to be a most biased opinion: "Jazz and respectability do not grow on the same bush."

"Oh, oh," came a warning, "we could get in trouble for sure now . . . we've got a minor in the car." "Oh well, do you want a little sip anyway?" this last addressed to the lap-sitter. Before I could utter a "no thankyou," it was decided I did not drink. Within the sardined proximity, the fumes alone were sufficient unto me.

Evelyn and her famous violinists could not have received a warmer welcome when we were taken inside a brick building once housing a movie theater. Their dinner was nearly over and then we could go into the main room and set up. This left time for the drummer and violinist to backtrack to the alley-parked car for reinforcements. It also left Olga to squire me around for I knew no one. Already feeling like Little Bo-peep, I trailed along in her shadow as she spoke brightly with various people. If only all that shiny polish were mine, and the flashing white teeth too.

Memories as to how well we played are dim. I imagine we trotted out Olga's wailing sax chorus on "All of Me," followed by me on the third chorus. At least we were able to air more swooshy ballads than at Grange dances. Our program must have included the violinist's standy of "Always," which she always rendered. Later, as the all important check was placed in our leader's hand, the committee was all smiles. Evidently we had provided good danceable fare. Now for the return trip in the Coupe, which differed little from the outgoing one, except for a common state of hunger between us. Highways then were not peppered with choices of fast-food outlets, and mile after mile of darkened buildings went by. The little car's steady hum was almost blotted out by giggling and silly jargon, and thrown together as we were, I was still viewing them from afar. However, I joined in the happy shout when a place to eat was found. "There's a light on, it must be open," screeched the drummer. For some reason the Coupe did not pause but slipped right on by. Olga was explaining, "I didn't think it looked good enough, we might find a better one, just be patient." The drummer then, in her own colorful choice of words, issued an ultimatum. The car was turned about quickly on an immediate backtrack. The snappy drummer had promised without a doubt, each one of us would become a victim of the Johnstown flood, were she not delivered to a restroom right now. Would I ever understand this type of "girl-talk," or much less, speak it? We all rushed in, the drummer in the lead and a bathroom was hastily sighted, while the rest of us read and priced the wall-printed menu. The place was on the fringes of dingy, but by now no one cared. With careful arithmetic we found our flat purses could afford at least one item apiece. Come Monday when Olga cashed the evening's check, we'd all be rich . . . by 1931's standards!

After the initiation night of traveling with the girls, our musical calendar practically grew moss. The rose bedecked gowns languished in our closets as the month of May and then all of June went by the board. Undaunted, Olga still insisted on regular practices just in case something popped. Her saxophone, which she played quite well, could not be denied blowing the notes of all the good songs now coming out. And so we laid claim on everything currently popular. Each workout bolstered our self-rating and we became quite sure all the people who were passing us by would be sorry someday. What they were missing was hearing Olga tootle out a song she virtually personified, "Smile Darn 'Ya Smile," and a slender violinist confidently bowing out the sweeter tunes, plus a mop-haired drummer whose jaws and drumsticks never missed a beat, and a reserved but fairly jazzy pianist. Put it all together you could say we flashed to some degree. In fact when our leader switched to her accordion for a Polka, we dazzled. I would watch ruefully as I noted the matchup between her row of sparkling white teeth and the even row of shiny accordion keys. To smile while playing was still out of my sphere of co-ordination.

It's really funny as I think back on it now. On designated practice nights the relationship between leader and piano player carried a strong resemblance to a business man's stewardship of the out-of-town client. "You'd just better stay overnight with me" became the answer to the whole distance problem. There was no point going home from my little steno job in Tacoma, coming back in to practice and then back out to Firgrove again. Besides the time involved, it also meant buying extra gasoline. And so on these nights, by right of prudence and good sense, I was awarded the deferences and courtesies due an overnight guest. After locking the attorney's office I walked the six or eight blocks to uptown automobile row and the Ford agency. Then we'd get into the Coupe, ride out to Portland Avenue and sit down to one of her Lithuanian mother's home cooked meals, always a delight of simple but pungent and tasty dishes, the likes of which I haven't tasted since. Following our session with new pieces, notes and chords, I was bedded down in a large square bedroom till wakened and breakfasted in the morning. From here it was a ride back downtown again in the Coupe. In return, I will say I caused her little grief. Other than a few infractions where the girls tried to correct by naive notions about weaving romance into the business of playing a dance job, I caused no ripples. Girl pianists were not plentiful, especially those who could waive most written copies, kept a good beat and could improvise their own chorus when needed (which was often). Sometimes (in later years) I used to wonder if Olga's custody of her pianist ever caused her to ask, "What price a good pianist?"

As for me, playing in the all girl band was yet another valuable lesson in flexibility and acceptance of other styles and interpretations besides my own. Without this experience one could become like a headstrong horse, making integration into a band either difficult or impossible. It seemed at this time the arrow to the future was pointing in the direction of dance band work. Be it bad times or not, people danced. An observation not to be overlooked.

21

Anchors Aweigh!

Early July the city of Tacoma was in an unusual hubbub, and so were our girl musicians. With its fine harbor to offer, Tacoma's Fourth of July celebration often included the anchoring of several U.S. Battleships just offshore. The town was now swaggering with bell-bottomed trousers, jaunty white caps and flocks of feminine playmates. Sailor-smitten girls literally sprang from the woodwork and the resulting combination ignited enough sparks to set off the city-planned Fireworks Show.

A local entrepreneur had made contact with our intrepid leader—or was it vice versa? Who cared. We had a music job—landing the playing plum of providing the dance music for the big "Fleet's In, All Sailors Welcome" dance! A large downtown hall at 13th & Fawcett, known as the Auditorium, (the selfsame place I had danced while working at the Cambridge) was all in readiness for a swashbuckling evening. The all-girl orchestra was not all that prepared—we needed two more musicians. By hook and crook they were searched out and an emergency practice was held to test the new blend. It just had to work for we were already hired. Truthfully, I'm sure each one of us counted heavily on our individual and combined onslaught of femininity to outweigh any Naval criticism.

The holiday evening arrived and our rose-flowered dresses were atwitch as we scurried and pranced across the stage with our gear—the stage large enough to accommodate a whole Navy band. "Let's not bunch up in the corner like frightened chicks," our leader was advising us. "We'll scatter the stands and use the grand piano to fill one end of the stage." The thing that stands out most in my memory of that evening was how physically hard we worked, trying to pump out enough volume to fill all the densely populated space out front. No halls were equipped with sound systems as yet. Our version of "Anchors Aweigh," devoid of one single brass instrument, must have lacked any sign of authority, but we played our hearts out on it *each* time. We feared one of the new girls—a violinist (in fact she was a teacher)— would not last the evening as this galloping music was out of her realm. This was the night of discovering the value of playing service songs for service men, at the right moment. You could hardly go wrong. They loved our playing of them, violin or no, and we felt as high as the flags placed throughout the large ballroom. For once I was happy with my geographical location on the stand, *and* the piano on hand (a singular double stroke of good fortune). From here my eyes enjoyed free grazing rights across the expanse of the grand piano and down onto a swirling mixture of tight navy uniforms, flirty skirts and prancing spike heels. The whirling and rotating scene, with modes altered only by time and fashion, was to play before my eyes for many many years and rarely did I tire of looking down into a groundswell of moving bodies, each translating your music from brain to feet. At the time I was not aware that the soul-satisfying piano now before me was to become an intimate friend, and like a good friend offer itself through good and bad times, and even lend its shoulder to weep on now and then. This was still to come.

By the end of the dance we knew we had not flopped. We had made it. Visiting city dignitaries and Navy brass, who exchanged goodwill messages up on the stage during the evening, smilingly included us in the credits for the successful dance. No one seemed displeased or unhappy. Yet each of us in the band could not ignore the little pangs of personal chagrin nudging our egos. Our colorful vision of dealing a real physical impact from stage to dancefloor just did not take place. Prior to the job we had mentally prepared ourselves for handsome cocky sailors who would attempt leaping onto the bandstand, disrupting our music while we vainly clutched to our instruments. How would we handle such a delightful rout? We should not have worried. Other than some breezy remarks and winks that floated upward into our midst, not one of us had been snatched away. Not even a hastily scribbled phone number had been wrenched from our lips.

As we launched into our closing "Goodnight Sweetheart," with our willowy violinist bowing the sustained notes, we could view the results of the evening as it swished before our eyes. Earlier flirtations had now waxed into heads on shoulders and cheek to cheeking. And here we were, six unattached girls, sitting up on the stage providing the mood! It was a bit demeaning.

As instrument caselocks were snapping shut and the drum set broken down for packing, we came to a sort of mutual agreement as to our combined lack of enticement. The stage was of theater height with no visible steps upward in view. One approached the stand through almost un-noticeable doors placed at either end, which then led up the steps into a backstage area. Evidently no one was prompted to figure this out. And so, darn it, each one of us in our filmy, rose-petaled gowns had just been unreachable and inaccessible!

I'll confess to fully enjoying being "one of the girls" in an all girl band that night. I also knew it wouldn't last. How often would hundreds of young sailors be, so to say, dancing at our feet?

22

Local Gunmolls Invade the Country Side

Bearing out the old phrase, "Nothing changes more than a woman's mind," our little group of girl musicians did not remain intact very long. First to drop out was the snappy, bouncy drummer. Another interest or perhaps greener pastures had caused her to seek a change. "We're going to try out a new drummer," our leader was explaining to me one noon over our ten-cents-a-bowl soup lunch. "She's supposed to be real good and boy is she a kick." I wondered if all girl drummers answered to the same description. The answer, revealed during this period of music making, was yes. The combined drive and energy of the three who worked within our little group was quite astounding, young blood and desire to work notwithstanding. As we neared the bottom of our soup bowls, another revelation came forth. I felt the weight of this new situation, for having to make changes from what had become a good balance of talents loomed as a distraction. The mix of their erratic tactics (save for our level-headed leader) and my greenness had managed to blend somehow.

"The big news is," my ears were standing on end now, "the Clover Creek Grange is looking for a good peppy band. I have a lead on it." My mind quickly recognized the wooded, yet prairie-like area south of Tacoma. She went on, "It'd be a nifty job for us. One of their members bought a new truck from our Agency yesterday and just happened to bring up the subject while he was in the office!" She certainly had not let any time go by," was my thought. "As far as I know," the story continued, "the head man on the Committee (a term soon to be laden with clout), will try and get over to my house so he can hear us play. If he likes our orchestra, he'll recommend us." What welcome news and if one dared to look ahead and envision possible steady Saturday nights and a reliable organization to work for besides, the future of the all-girl band looked rosy. And how much would they be paying us?

"And so I've decided," we were both now peering into our vanity case mirrors to check rouge, shiny noses and the red bow of our lips, "it's a good time to make some changes. As long as we're getting a new drummer, we'll add another musician while we're at it. We need something livelier than a violin anyway and she's been wanting to go into steady teaching and probably wouldn't like playing out in the country. Now if we get this Grange job, it'd be pretty nice to have a guy in our orchestra. The place is really out in the sticks." What was she leading up to, not that I objected to her reasoning? On it went, "I know someone who's heard about a fellow who's real hot on the Banjo so I'm going to try and get in touch with him and ask him to come to the try-out. Don't know too much about him except he's going through a divorce right now and can probably use the extra money." And who couldn't, I thought to myself, trying to sort out all these unknown characters I soon would have to face—and play music with.

The waiting time between the momentous news and evaluation was short. Soon I would know the answer to the questions burning within me. How would the chords of this banjo player match up with mine (whose correctness I never doubted)? How would you handle such a situation diplomatically, assuming our chords did not click? Would he be as my mind pictured him . . . "fast"? And what of the new drummer billed as a "real kick"? Just how zany would she turn out to be? But on the other hand, our leader was far from making dumb decisions. Banjos were a hot item now with Eddie Peabody's great popularity catching everyone's fancy.

My brother had willingly offered to make the drive back into town on the audition night. In fact he was more than willing. For one thing he dearly loved all music and with the fringe benefits of Polish goodies and exposure to our attractive leader thrown in, it was a good deal. When we walked into the large old two-storied house on Portland Avenue, her efficiency was already apparent. Drums were already set up, two spindly tripod music stands teetered upon the rug, and a heavy air of expectancy, tinged with the unmistakable pungency of Polish sausage, hung in the immaculately clean front room. Introductions were made.

99

Our leader's straight white teeth were radiant with hospitality. Not only was she the wage earner in her parent's home, she exuded confidence and charm, and when she picked up her accordion the white keys and her perfect teeth flashed in unison. I envied her. The kind looking gentleman seated on the sofa had to be the Grange Man. The smiling young man in a brown suit to match brown eyes and dark wavy hair, the banjo player. And over in the corner, pressed up against the tan kalsomined wall, the new drummer. Her Orphan Annie head of curls popped up behind an array of cymbals in acknowledgment of the introduction. The whole maneuver was in rythmic cadence with her Doublemint gum. "Yeah, I'm Babs," she chomped, "looks like you don't get any music to read either"—this after glancing at the piano's empty music rack. "Well, kid, we'll get along slick 'cause I can play in any key too." This brought on another toss of her moppy hair. In fact everything on her person twitched as if she had just received a jolt of electricity. "Don't tell me you play by ear" (there was that unloved term again)? When I replied I played either way she seemed impressed, while I wondered if the non-stop gum went the duration of an entire dance.

As always with new people, my melting point was low and having no smart reply at hand, I began to study our leader's list of music. All were familiar regulars such as "Around the Corner," "I Can't Give You Anything But Love," "Just One More Chance," and others currently in favor. Having made it my point to know the latest by bent ear and wits, I was quite sure in my role as back-up or leaning post for other instruments. Now let's see what the banjo player would do, who had been presented as "Kenny." Where would he stand with modulating chords and such trimmings I had up till this time been able to originate and throw in at will. Having only a lead saxophone to deal with had left the harmonic field wide open.

"Let's get going with an old standard we all know." Our leader was taking charge. "Then we can tell where we're at. One, two three . . . "

By the end of the session several facts had made themselves known. First of all, the banjo player knew all the old standbys, read music easily when necessary, and his twangy, strident banjo strings did add a lively quality. Thank heavens, we seemed to match up fairly well so far. The drummer registered absolutely no sign of fatigue with fast tempos. She would certainly remain plugged in for a four hour job. "Yeah, I'm married," she had quipped, "but I'm not workin' at it." Her beat was good and steady with only a slight bent towards some drummer's dilemma, the runaway horse acceleration. To me she represented a two word rhyme. Gum and drum.

The Grange delegate's face registered approval. Even more so after joining in the partaking of volatile Polish snacks and the hearty "house-brew" afterwards. I suppose something was found for me to eat and drink, who besides shunning any kind of brew, had little stomach for even their solid fare. It's not hard to see why I often felt on the outside of a circle, looking in. Our employer-to-be (we hoped) made his exit assuring us he would phone in the committee's verdict by the end of that week.

As soon as the door closed behind him, Olga (our leader) was ready to deal out the next hand. "Now," she was thinking outloud, "If he calls and says 'yes,' we'll have to make some transportation plans, and she was looking directly at me. It made no sense to have me come into town and then go right back out somewhat in the same direction to the Grange at Clover Creek. "If I can work it out with the Committee (the all-important word), I'll ask them if your brother could have a permanent admission pass in exchange for bringing you out to the hall." My brother, as before, found absolutely no fault with this logic. And so the audition evening ended on a tentative but hopeful major chord.

Within the week we were hired and the important pass privilege had been granted. To my surprise mother did not put up too stiff a resistance. Though the new job lacked specific details as yet, the homespun Grange label seemed to register some kind of a level on her respectability scale. To add further insurance to what mother hoped would be a safe evening package, my brother was deputized to watch out for me *beyond* the role of chauffeur.

After several Saturday nites had played themselves away, one thing became clear. My brother was failing to attach much authority to his assignment. But I cannot blame him for the one and only time our leader Olga became very annoyed with her piano player. As a bonus to musicians, the Grange saw no reason why each member of the band, one at a time of course, could not leave the bandstand and enjoy a dance. Had it not been for Olga filling in for me on her accordion, I would have missed this privilege. Each Saturday, as soon as I got up from my post, the Grange Master's son appeared to claim me for this token dance. He was my junior but I thought him awfully cute and he was a most excellent dancer. On the particular evening of my faux pas, we had slipped outside during intermission into a moonlighted parking area, hoping to avoid the prying eyes of all the Grangers. I for one wanted something straightened out. Was it me or was it my piano playing that kept him within close range a good part of the evening. To determine this took an extra four or five minutes beyond allotted intermission time. Meanwhile our leader was pacing the tiny stage. Where was her trusty pianist? Would she be forced to begin a set playing her accordion and was I in any kind of trouble?

When I showed up there was no doubt about it. I had transgressed in all directions. Even the committee lost no time in letting their thoughts be known after the dance. Olga told me later words such as "cradle snatcher" and "leading him astray" were used by them. Mortal embarrassment was mine. I was unaware as yet of the stigma attached to a girl danceband member. She was one that beared watching! My short lecture was concluded with, "It could have cost us our job." But it didn't and the incident soon passed into oblivion. My deputized brother was wholly unaware of anything wrong that night. He had "tripped the light fantastic" and met some "real dames." Consequently, mother missed the whole episode too.

23

To Be Or Not To Be

"The Racketeers" were being removed from their territory, by request. Not only our hold at Clover Creek Grange was crumbling, but the Racketeers themselves. Babs had fallen in love with a new man and followed him to another area. Olga's soon-to-be husband was only lukewarm towards her musical ambitions, leaving Kenny and the piano player with nowhere in particular to go. We did not float in limbo very long. A couple whom neither of us knew, by the name of Mr. & Mrs. Eaton, and who had danced at the Grange once or twice, had learned of our all being at large quite soon. They quickly added the two leftovers, Kenny and myself, to the three musicians already self-contained within their family unit, and came up with a five piece orchestra! They lost no time in contacting us and explaining how our two instruments would nicely round out the project they had in view. Before long plans were set for a trial run of the new orchestra, to be held at their Tacoma home.

My reactions ran from pleased to apprehensive. Pleased to be looking at what was becoming so vital, a music job. According to the sketchy details, "the boys" had already begun playing at the proposed hall which had been contracted by the parents. A rather steady crowd was becoming established and hopes were set on keeping them coming. Then as now, "crowds" was an important word in every musician's vocabulary. The apprehensiveness was sensing that everything was not out in the open as far as the pianist's post was concerned. Not yet.

"And this is our eldest son." It was a week later and we were all seated in the front wing of a many-roomed older home. Mrs. Eaton was definitely the family spokeswoman. "He plays saxophone and slide trombone. Over here is our youngest." I followed her fond gaze. "He's been drumming since he was only ten—his feet could hardly reach the pedals then." The missing and in-between son appeared after we had begun playing, a timing which turned out to be a chronic condition. He was the violinist.

The banjo player Kenny, whom of course I already knew, was due any minute. The thought of seeing his familiar and friendly face within this room of strangers, give me a lift. Geared to a slow approach in meeting new people, I felt a little edgy. I looked about the room. A fine dark-wood Grand piano kitty-cornered a large portion of the area, forcing the slight sized drummer into the dining space. A blazing South Seas sunset flamed across the face of his big bass drum, with the name "Eaton Bros." floating above. Would people mistake me for yet another family member of this musical brood?

As we clattered ourselves closer with much scraping of chairs and makedo stands I couldn't keep down the question that kept popping up in my mind. By now I knew I was a replacement for whoever had played before this, while Kenny was an out and out addition. The why of things seemed to throw their conversation into cautious remarks and veiled implications. Sheets of music sprawled across the piano now and we were to begin. It was to be a Schottische. The bespectacled drummer struck his woodblocks smartly to set the tempo and off we went stomping along in a one-two-three and thump beat. Next up was a hopping fast Polka and my mind said, "Is this what we'll be playing most of the time?" Thankfully it was not. The whole idea was a discreet test as to holding an even tempo, which I soon learned placed ace-high on their appraisal meter. Other music was tried with every one looking pleased, especially the parents. In between a break was taken in order for me to accompany the elder brother, who was noticeably short on words, on a novelty saxophone solo. If I had been startled at the "String Bean" title of Theodore's ragtime solo years ago, this one gave proof in the fact of aesthetic titles not fronting this type of music. The title: "The Dill Pickle Rag"! A faint but appreciative wry smile was his thankyou as a respectable silence filled the room.

As I had suspected, banjo-playing Kenny fit in like a glove, holding a dominant steady beat and adding the lively tempo they so desired. Would he be interested in every Saturday night was a question addressed only to him. And on a percentage basis, was the ensuing query.

The splitting of profits before the advent of our Musician's Union was a prevailing custom. Lots of dancers, better wages. Poor crowd, too bad. But why was I excluded from the discussion? Something was amiss, I knew it all along. The brothers had filled me in on "The Hall," a term always emphasized in the manner of an important person. It was somewhere out in logger country by a little town known as South Prairie. I had never heard of it.

His banjo in hand, Kenny was bidding all a goodnight. I nodded back a bit ruefully, since I felt he had not been as cheered by my presence tonight as I had been with his. Oh well, what of it? Our chords were compatible and that was what really mattered. Mrs. Eaton was now addressing me. It was going to be my turn. "Would you be willing?" . . . a pause and she began again. "Would you be willing to play the first night?" . . . another pause. What appeared to be painful for her was equally twitchy for me. Finally the matter boiled down as to whether I might agree to play the first Saturday on a temporary basis, pending the outcome of the night's happenings. While I could talk music, this bartering and answering of iffy conditions had me up a tree. And then when I heard the "possibles" I was torn between grabbing my hat and flying, or staying to hear the rest of the story.

"It's possible," I was being reassured, "that nothing at all will happen. We're just going to call his bluff." By now I must have looked stricken, but the story unraveled anyway. It came out in the exact replica of a "B" Western movie, in which my role was that of the pure and innocent victim. The burly logger musician (?) whom I was to replace had been fired for various and personal reasons, to which he had answered in a bellowing tone, "I'm staying and what's more I'll be back next Saturday night to prove it!"

"My dear," Mrs. Eaton was consoling me, "he's nothing but a big bully. If he does show up he'll soon see his job has been taken." Still I didn't take my leave. I can't remember ever giving them a yes or a no.

By the time next Saturday rolled around my mind had done yeoman duty as to what type of eruption could take place. Material for doing so was not lacking, as one more facet had been added by the boys at the close of our practice session. "Boy Curley (he now was called by name) sure has one short fuse. Especially when some guy dares to ask his black-haired girl friend to dance. We think she's part Indian." Had they not added the next statement I might have decided to back out right then and there. "After we get over this one Saturday dance everything should straighten out and we can get down to good regular dances. The crowds are picking up and we know for sure they'll be glad to hear a good piano player like you." It works every time!

The new job was not discussed in great detail at home. All the hidden and dubious parts remained undisclosed. Nevertheless, mother came up with a cause for concern. How would I be getting to this place and of equal importance, what kind of people were these new so-called employers? Nothing would suffice but a visual confrontation, for mother prided herself on snap judgments. Somehow the meeting fell into place easily. The Eatons had reason to drive out to The Hall before Saturday.

"Now don't you worry," the parents were placating mother who had opened our backdoor a bit earlier and received them into our farmhouse. "It'll be very convenient for us to pick her up right here at the house. This is about halfway and won't be but a mile or so off our regular route. We'll just cut down over the hill and swing into Orting." The entire package for them added up to nearly a ninety mile roundtrip. I was to be ready no later than seven o'clock that Saturday.

"And we'll bring her back right to the door too." This assurance was offered with one foot on the running board of their car, as we saw them off.

No use to explain how safe and socially acceptable it was in the country to drop a passenger off out in front of the cumbersome gates barring acreages from straying cattle. We watched Mr. Eaton back the side-curtained car down our long driveway. Mother's impressions for the moment must have been sitting on the fence, for she said little.

A brand new dress, not from the sewing machine but selected from the third floor of Rhodes Bros. Dep't. Store, was ready for the portentous evening. To date playing attire had gone from fluttering pink roses to the racy lean look of our so-to-say gun moll outfits, to the black satin bias cut long gown now awaiting a wearing. My figure was a doubtful accomplice for revealing its obviously designed clinging and slinky qualities. Slight hips and mediocre bustline gave revelations less than astonishing. But it provided a very important accessory to my personality, sophistication. Being the only girl in the orchestra, surrounded by white-shirted and black-suited boys, was not at all unpleasant to contemplate.

Again the rangy touring car, packed to its gills now, was slowly pulling up our lane. It looked like an overloaded tourbus. The time was seven o'clock and Saturday night. Soon the long radiator pointed eastward in the lingering light of a Fall evening. Darkness would close in before we reached South Prairie. I needed no gypsy fortune teller to forecast the night to be a turning point as I felt a foreboding taking root in my mind. After wheeling through the last little town of Orting, we were into foothill and sparsely settled country. Sometimes the car crept between rocky sidewalls or dipped into abrupt valleys and the roads grew narrower. Creek and river bridges and surprising railroad crossings were clattered over and left behind in the dusk. Hardly a dull trip to precede whatever would come next. I remember feeling grateful mother had not seen the roadmap to South Prairie as we snaked carefully around what now would be marked a hazardous sharp turn, and then almost threaded the car through a side-shaving viaduct before climbing up a sudden rise with zero vision. "Been lots of crack-ups here," the boys added appropriately, "especially on foggy nights." Hardly time to concentrate on whether Curley, when denied admission to the hall, might peek through some opening and spy a GIRL sitting in his spot and then proceed to tear up the place. I still wasn't ready for it.

Arrival was pulling up at a large and white barnlike building, bordered on one side by a pasture, all in evening shadows now with a look of pastoral charm and peace. The parents sprung into action, quickly making their way up a series of porch steps, with the motor nervously holding fast to an unraveling roll of tickets as her husband jangled the keys to the doors. I did not know yet that the whole evening's output was to be a family maneuver. The boys swung right into action too, unloading the hard-cornered instrument cases, which held priority over passenger seating and comfort. In they trooped, slamming their loads onto a slightly raised bandstand at one end of a long dancefloor. The mother, ensconced atop a high stool back in the entryway, was now fronted by a homemade ticket window. They all looked as if they'd done this a hundred times before. If anyone besides me was nervous, it didn't show.

"Just hang your coat in here dear," the mother was pointing at a row of dangling wire hangers in an adjoining cubicle. "You won't need to check yours, I'll keep it separate from the others." I had noticed the sign to the Women's Rest Room and was on my way there as the ride had been long and I wanted to check over my satin gown carefully for any wrinkles, etc. Beaming rays from incoming cars' headlights were now casting a glow into oncoming darkness, most all of them turning into the pastured parking lot. The restroom, a tribute to expediency, was one of the most unusual I had ever seen. Someone had simply pushed the frame of an empty outhouse up against the outside wall of the Grange hall and placed a short slatted walkway between the two. I walked in gingerly, fully expecting the usual country plumbing fare, only to be surprised by a new and white fixture that flushed like a rushing river. This ended the amenities as the bare lightbulb hanging from above revealed no sink or mirror, just splintery walls. So I smoothed the body-hugging satin dress and stepped out. Nothing to do now but join the others on the square bandstand, come what may. What kind of posture should I assume? Should I keep eyes focused on the blank panel of a very plain old upright, or should I casually cast an eye through the incoming crowd?

A general nervousness generated in concert between the five of us, as often is the case with a newly formed group. The added twitch was of course the anticipation of all the "possibles." Clickety-clack went the drummer wood blocks and saxophone, violin, banjo and piano notes hit the unfilled air. Due to the uncertainty of the moment, our first few numbers literally flew at an over eager clip as dancers took to the floor. Letting those first notes loose upon a virgin dancefloor requires fortitude until any professional polish comes to your rescue. We were totally unacquainted with the latter and it was fortunate for us the South Prairie ilk of dancers found no quarrel with jumping right into the action.

Within the first hour of bouncing Foxtrots and a Schottische, the back of my neck began to loosen up. I had been diverted thankfully by the likes of girl Schottische dancers I had not seen before on any dance floor. Here they spun themselves around like whirling dervishes, while maintaining the basic steps usually performed in a straight forward style. Round and round and round went the twirling. How could they keep it up I wondered. Later when we whizzed along with a Polka, I could see the Schottische had only been a preliminary!

Shortly before intermission the Western movie commenced, lacking only a few six-shooters for authenticity. The violin player had hissed in my ear, "He's here, I just saw Curley come through the door!" Of course I turned to look, and just then he and his Pocahontas lady-love became one with the revolving crowd.

The horn, violin and banjo chords suddenly ceased to make any sound and I was left to "Shuffle Off to Buffalo" with only a weakened beat of a drum to sustain me. The others on the stand raptly sized up the situation, preparing to stand guard if necessary. I think now I should have been in my black gown prostrate upon a railroad track as the villain came ever closer! "He's gonna want to get up on the stand and play with us," one of them muttered. From the cocky drummer came, "Well, we just aren't about to have *that* happen." The saxophonist built up the pressure with, "Look at all his buddies he brought along. They're all down there hanging around the stove, waiting to make trouble!" Couples were now dancing by with eyes flung back across their shoulders. We came perilously close to an alternate disaster, grinding down to a halt, which is a musical no-no. Somehow we kept the cardinal rule of "keep the music going whenever any kind of trouble erupts." The timing of the next scene could have come from Hollywood.

Just as the much-watched couple neared the bandstand, enter the Sheriff and his Posse. The fight scene was going to be cut. Voices were rising and I could see Curley's flushed face towering above the crowd. The next minute his powerful hulk was being briskly steered towards the door, but I had time to pull in my breath at his size, and his wild unruly curls of black hair that continued down his ruddy cheeks into wooly sideburns. I had imagined him well! His henchmen trailed along in a sullen parade of red suspenders and shuffling logger boots. "I'll be back, just you wait and see," was Curley's parting cry. Meanwhile, back on the bandstand, though hearts were doing their own fast Polka, the music played on. "Thank heavens for Sheriffs," I told myself thankfully. Who knows what might have happened? Another question was also on my mind. How would mother equate all this with the assurance given her only hours earlier: "You don't have a thing to worry about, we always insist on running a respectable dance"? They really did, with a little help from the Law.

Needless to say, the remaining hours at South Prairie paled in comparison. Going home even the former menacing curves and blind crossings seemed to have made their peace with the automobile world. A faint yellow moonpath stretched across quiet rivers and streams as we bridged and re-bridged. During intermission time I had been amazed to see the "folks" as kitchen staff. The mother, glasses still atremble (but not from fright), shakily speared steaming hot dogs from kettle to bun. She was indignant, all five-feet-one of her, as she was recounting Curley's complete disregard of their restrictions. They had put in an immediate call for the Sheriff, who luckily was close by. "Curley will never set foot in this hall again, as long as we are in charge," was her flat statement to all as she tapped a second vat of hot coffee.

How to whitewash an account of the evening come tomorrow morning? Mother and my two sisters would be ready to hear everything. I just could not tell all, for it would jeopardize what now looked like a good steady Saturday night job. The banjoist Kenny and I had been paid our percentage in cash before leaving. The amount was something like three wrinkled dollar bills and some loose coins! "And it's surely going to pick up now. Everyone commented on the good music," we were told. Considering the times, our take was modicum but not menial. At least we could earn as much playing for a dance as some men were being paid for an entire day's work.

So went night one as pianist with this tightly knit family group. As my premonitions had implied, it led straight into another music cycle. However, feminine intuition did not foresee a time span of eleven whole years, a thousand "Put Your Little Foot Right Theres," and not enough of what I considered jazz. Nor did it go so far as to pick the one from this initial clan of musicmakers who was to become my husband!

24

The Thirties vs a Serious Romance

Music for the time being was in a static condition. We played hit and miss dances here and there, which were fitted between the steady Saturday dates. The pianist and the banjo player, Kenny, had a rare conversation together one night in which we agreed the patterned music might be the Eaton's forte, but it was not ours. One thing led to another and all of a sudden we enjoyed talking with each other and taking longer looks at the person we hadn't really known up to now. While the country's time-clock was not set for any poetic or serious romancing, it somehow stole an appearance into our lives. I think both of us were equally unprepared, but did nothing to impede what was happening. We gave living proof of love not being synonymous with good sense.

One summer evening found us standing together beside a calm and moonlit lake. It was intermission time at a lakeside dancehall. He was offering me his brown suitcoat, to put over my bare shoulders. The selfsame brown coat I had seen so often now magically became Sir Walter Raleigh's velvet coat. From out of the starlit sky, or wherever such gathering emotions emanate from, we had much more to say to each other than throughout our whole two years of acquaintance. Phrases had always been, "Hello, looks like a good crowd tonight," or "that's a G seventh chord there," or the regular "Goodnight, see you at the next dance" had been sufficient. Now, when the dam broke, it really broke. But only for the length of intermission time! I invited him out the very next day (Sunday). One of mother's good homey dinners seemed a most natural step to take. Depression or no, we had home butchered meats and garden vegetables, which I knew would be welcome to a city fellow. Of course I hoped he'd bring along a bag of his French doughnuts, as mother doted on good pastries. He did. He was currently pursuing a baking venture so I knew it would pose no strain. Many revelations now came to light, such as his wishing to forsake a professional baking career, a trade he considered most unhealthy. Though he did not often dwell on the subject. I heard more of his early and unhappy attempt at a marriage within a strong Catholic family, and of his young son now being cared for by the maternal grandparents. While I knew these facts to be the very ones I had stacked up against becoming over friendly, their importance now began to diminish. Instead I hearkened back to my very first impressions of his quick and engaging smile, his sense of humor and always, those slender but strong and sensitive hands I had admired at first sight.

A new necessity was arising. It was our great desire now to drive together while going to our dance work. In order to bring this about he had to resurrect (literally) his father's old car. That the car was an old Essex (the Edsel of the '30's) still did not squelch the flame. If I didn't recognize the fact then, I do now: A romance able to survive the ignominy of an Essex stood an excellent chance for survival! Gone were my former attributes to exciting dating such as a father's blue Buick sedan or a Ford Model A roadster, complete with a rakish rumbleseat!

After our momentous lakeside discovery, other facets of each other's personality came into focus. I noted his honesty, goodness and great pride in his pioneer forebears from Kansas. Most of all, I was touched by the love and respect for his mother. Among his surprises were my preferences for our type of country living and the contentment with what we had. Up to now he had only seen me as a dressed up pianist. And so we had a lot of catching up to do. Only years later did he confess why he had never tried too hard in two years to engage me in a conversation. "How in the world," he asked, "did a fellow communicate with a girl whose nose was permanently tilted upward?" Evidently my reaction to "those" who carried liquor and smoked cigarettes had been more apparent than I realized.

Without warning now I was wanting to iron his white broadcloth shirts, so needed for playing nights. I'd be sure to take extra pains to smooth every wrinkle in those tricky-to-iron collars. I was wanting to cook good meals for him, to set up housekeeping with him. In short, I wanted to be with him and become a most wonderful wife. We would exemplify the happy couple of "My blue Heaven" who, though penniless, made it all work out somehow. All the lyrics of lovestruck ballads now sprang into first person as I hummed, "I Don't Know Why I Love You Like I Do," the pop song other people were singing so casually. Without a doubt, we would marry and play music happily ever after.

Dinners were exchanged and I met his family. Wishing to exude a warm and friendly attitude at the first dinner (not easy for me at that time), I offered to assist in the kitchen. Here his elder sister stood at the sink, a puzzled look on her face as she nervously contemplated a dark green avocado in her hand. We were all bent on suitable impressions. She handed it to me with, "You probably know—do you peel these or what?" I was of little help, for avocados were just as foreign in our kitchen at home. We often laughed about it in later years.

Another fall and another winter's months were torn from our romantic calendar that showed no circled wedding day. I had turned twenty-two and he was nearing twenty-five. Both of us had been playing odd jobs with the family orchestra; those nights had to serve as dating nights too. We had the cake, but no icing. Storybook romancing was tough in the Thirties. As for mother, I suppose she hoped it would all blow over as my many former fascinations had. She found no fault with my choice but failed to see a remote chance for considering marriage. We had nothing, she cautioned, except obvious reasons for even added responsibilities. There was no need to have the flaws pointed out, we knew them. Along with thousands of other wistful couples we sang, "Honey What I Couldn't Do, With Plenty of Money and You." It wouldn't last forever would it?

25

A Crescent Moon

The Thirties bore on. President Hoover, Rudy Vallee, "Life is Just a Bowl of Cherries," thirty-five cent movies (with free dishes), the Dionne Quintuplets, the Chicago World's Fair (for those who could afford it), and a general condition of flat pocketbooks. When would that cute little cartooned character named "Prosperity" actually peek beyond the corner and come into our midst? If not prosperity, something was beckoning to us from the corner, and it was Music. The ever watchful parents of our present music group were leaving no stone unturned. Crowds were failing out in the country. The mother, when counting out our meager wages, was almost sure to say, "Well, kids, you know . . . we always have to take the bitter with the sweet." And so we accepted our bitters—a few careworn dollar bills and assorted change, and hoped for the sweet.

A change was definitely necessary. An opportunity within the city would have to be uncovered to help save transportation costs, among other things. The parents felt sure the family orchestra, with myself and banjoist tacked on, and known as the "Eaton Bros.," had something to offer the dancing public. Our first year had tightened the loose knit and we were in command of what they deemed of such importance—a good steady beat. Now was the time to angle for a long-term situation, since there was a chance the two added members might be diverted elsewhere.

While the pie in the sky for most musicians then, as now, was to get the big break and be discovered, we were all happy to get the news of our new job, and a good one too, even if it was in Tacoma and not California. The more fortunate musical success stories were enviously referred to as, "Oh yes, he made it. He's playing somewhere down south (California)." To which our laconic sax player would drawl, "Yeah . . . he went south alright . . . South Tacoma!"

"The Hall," the Eatons were explaining, "is right in downtown Tacoma on the corner of 13th & Fawcett." How many times we had heard that all important noun used in a working musician's vocabulary. Coming right after "The Hall," in order of most constant usage, was "The Crowd." This last was a mythical entity whose preferences either made you or broke you. Evidently this new job was thought to be high on both counts. The building formerly known as the Auditorium had gained a spacious annex and undergone extensive refurbishing. Its large and excellent dance floor was the same one Freda and I had danced on during the Cambridge days. The new amenities offered a generous entry lobby, coat checking with hundreds of hangers, well furnished Ladies' Lounge and a big refreshment area, which with its swinging café doors and many tables more nearly resembled a Beer Garden. Whoever had landed the sizable painting contract must have fallen heir to an ocean of foam green paint, since every last inch of formerly varnished woodwork now shone forth in uniformed sea-green.

We would be working for a Mr. Ole Lund, who just happened to be searching for the right spark to light up his bold investment. Were we that spark? Evidently he had been convinced by the parents of our orchestra's ability to make his whole endeavor take shape and give forth life. To do so he must abide with a mixed dance policy and format, to which he agreed. Now all we had to do was prove it, as soon as the ads could get into print. With Ole Lund's theory of volume compensating for his planned low admission prices, the Crescent moon might rise again and shine in a new brilliance! The consensus of opinion was an awareness that these were yet hard times, but people still wanted and needed to dance.

For some reason, I cannot recall our opening night, except that it was not a smashing full house. However, word must have traveled quickly, since before long a steady crowd sent the ticket roll spinning and the orchestra into a concerted effort of measuring out enough correct accents and tempos to satisfy the most exacting oldtime dancer. In fact, within a year we danced them into three nights a week and the moon was waxing nicely, thank you.

26

Dancing . . . on Monday Nights?

Dancehall history may have been made during a portion of the Thirties at the Crescent Ballroom. Not by choice, however. One just didn't balk at a promoter whose ventures were currently increasing your operating cash. The fact was clear now, the Crescent was reblooming under the management of the enigmatic Mr. and Mrs. Ole Lund, a Scandinavian couple who had formerly and successfully operated the old "Oaks" on Steilacoom Lake. By day Ole Lund deftly controlled all train traffic in and out of Tacoma, as Chief Dispatcher for the Union Station. Nightime hours at the Crescent forced no breaking of character. The ballroom merely became his moonlight depot. He controlled, he regulated and he pushed all the buttons for keeping everything on track. Orchestra breaks were personally set as he consulted his accurate railroad watch. "Take your break from," and he'd zero in on the second hand, "from 10:07 to 10:17," He'd walk off and we set our watches, and complied. While we in the band seldom dealt with him personally, I'm certain some classic encounters took place between this aggressive hulk of a man and the barely five-foot-two mother of the boys, for she and her husband were always in our attendance.

"He must have been lying awake nights trying to come up with this one," was our cry of disbelief when our promoter presented his newest angle. Dancing on Monday nights! But you couldn't rule out Ole Lund; he was a cagey gambler who won most of his flings. Would he be able to turn blue Monday nights into anything but a flop? Would we be able to put ourselves into such a challenge and face the job of stirring up a dying fire?

The dancers appeared, we hardly could believe it. At first they dribbled through the double swinging doors as if they also felt this to be a strange set of affairs. Before too long their numbers became sufficient to keep the risk afloat. We termed them, not too affectionately I'm afraid, "the ones with their chins out," and even though I held them quite responsible for foisting such an unlovely night upon us, a small corner of my heart went out to them. I began to realize the degree of dependency they placed upon what the Crescent provided. Namely: a nominally priced, over-the-counter bottle of medicine to be taken as an antidote against loneliness, boredom or restlessness. Besides, in winter and the cold springs of Tacoma, the Ballroom held out free warmth of space and davenports that were soft and conversational. As a last-ditch seller, ladies were admitted free on Monday nights. By grit and determination, they held together, if tenuously, for about a year or more. During this begrudged stretch of time, we rightfully termed our evening address to be, 13th & Fawcett.

Unless you are a rare specimen, there is no way to remain musically fresh three nights a week at the same address—without artificial aid. For me it has remained an unmastered art. The task in these early Crescent years was even more acute, as the music was all but built-in. The resolute program of Pattern, Mixed or whatever title given to offbeat regular ballroom dancing, demanded a measured type of music, guaranteed to correspond identically with the various set of steps in each particular dance. Fun music, or improvising material, it was not. The primary concern was to not muddle up the feet of dancers.

The evening's roster for all three nights (and not to be tampered with) was displayed upon a tripod placed upon our large stage. Printed placards bearing the proper titles of each patterned dance were slipped into a tier of slots. The melodies befitting each one of them was about as colorless as the black and white printing upon the cards. They gave out information such as, "Two-Step," "Schottische," "Varsouvienne," "Spanish Waltz," "Three-Step" and so on down the list. You accented dips, swoops, hops and slides and began each one with the correctly metered tempo intro that had better not be too fast or too laggard, but j-u-s-t r-i-g-h-t. To do otherwise was taboo and would have thrown the dancers out of sync, and stamped us as a failure.

The pre-measured regimen gnawed at my ego, and though a stray Fox-trot or blues number sometimes found its way in between, they were not nearly enough. I practically anguished, after a new ballad I had copied off was played in the conforming "keep-it-peppy" style. To me it represented a flaunting or musical dignity and good taste. The mood carried on even so far as after midnight hours, after our drive home from Tacoma. While Kenny was unloading and packing away his things, I'd sit at our piano and try to atone for the injustice done to these lovely melodies. This time they were done in the manner befitting such pieces of music, and I'd sit and play just for my own satisfaction and by way of retaliating.

Green Book, bless it, came to the fore again. Every possible page was searched and divested for help in this case of oncoming claustrophobia. Innocent folksongs were hacked and sawed from their original tempos, and made to fit whatever steps I was working on. Almost like magic new Spanish Waltzes came forth as well as other pattern dances. The collected results were copied into our orchestra's music books and presto, we had something different and often recognizable. Then as now, people love to recognize a melody. Mother had a good laugh when one of her childhood folksongs emerged as a perfectly timed "Varsouvienne." Who wanted to grind out "Put Your Little Foot Right There" ad nauseam? The books are still in a packing box, should the dancing wheel make a complete revolution and come back to this style!

One night while gazing across scores of couples, each correctly stepping off the formula, my fingers and mind functioning by instinct now, I thought of a way to occupy myself. By keeping my eyes lowered I would not let them stray beyond anyone's shoetops and then see how many dancers I could identify. It worked for awhile as I peered over each pair of shuffling shoes sliding beneath my gaze at the piano. Wouldn't you know the old culprit "Depression" would cut short even such an innocent diversion as this? No one owned a closet full of shoes then, and after a few nights I had them all memorized.

27

Almost a Bluebird of Happiness

By the end of February we had been married in a very dignified and venerable Methodist parsonage in Tacoma. Just the two of us, with the well loved Reverend Henry Beach of Tacoma's First Church performing the ceremony. His gracious wife, and I shall never forget her, said I looked just like a bluebird of happiness and the promise of Spring in my new blue suit. At the end of the vows she gave me a "mother's kiss" and I all but melted away in a pool of tears. The happy bluebird image was only half true, even though the last payment had been made on the suit. Both of us shared mighty misgivings over going ahead on our own, daring to push the dire warning clouds aside. We decided to drive out home that afternoon and tell Mother. It wasn't easy.

Several months later a doctor pronounced me basically well, in need of gaining weight and strength, and quite newly pregnant. This last fact was more news to me than mother. However her concern for my new condition and her great abiding love for babies, born or unborn, soon won her over. With my brother Hans's dictum, "We really have to celebrate and have a big shindig," he and the community did just that. A large community hall was secured and an area-wide reception with all the trimmings took place. And of all things, with the two honored guests playing a portion of the music! Our local grocer provided the necessary commodities and the women took it from there. It was a night to remember and be talked of for some time to come. Mother swore she'd never seen such stacks of food disappear. Wedding showers were held soon thereafter and though many of the gifts came from Pohlman's Variety Store in Puyallup, (a 1930's dictate), we acquired what we deemed to be some imposing possessions. Everyone needed a green glass lemon squeezer, didn't they?

In comparison we were thunderstruck with the gift from our old farm neighbors, the owners of the cow named "Rio Rita." What did they do but give us a velvet-lined black folder which nestled rows of real silverware within. We knew of their second cousin relationship with Mahncke Jewelers in Tacoma, but never dreamed our owning a set of Gorham silver would be linked to the connection. The folder is gone, but the knives, forks and spoons go on and on.

Our first home had already fallen into our laps a month prior to the big day. The proprietors of our closest gas station on the Willows Corner (and former donors of the coveted Willows dance tickets) had recently opted to move into the back quarters of their newly acquired Willows Tavern, just across the highway (public drinking was newly legal). The white bungalow, trimmed in red, white and blue by the Standard Oil Company, was actually not for rent at all, but they would deal with us on a monthly basis while trying out the Tavern quarters. How about $10.00 per month and leaving all their furnishings, which they felt would be in good hands during the interim? The only drawback to the lenient arrangement was the high interest level of some of the tavern customers, indulgently promoted by the owners who would suggest, "Go on over to our house and see all the things those kids got." And they did—morning, noon, and evening.

In spite of living under the dictatorship of the Depression, fortune continued to smile upon the newlyweds. President Roosevelt's New Deal provided the groom with a road crew job and our provisioner-minded landlords had a line on an old piano someone wanted stored. This last boon cancelled out an upcoming acid test, whose first pangs were being felt. Could our love and marriage survive and prosper in a piano-less home? More news was unfolding; we would soon be finding ourselves playing three nights a week! Putting all the ingredients of this chapter into a bowl and cautiously stirring them produced a volatile mixture that alternately rose and sank during the oncoming months.

117

The Pregnant Pianist

Social custom and silly pride were now forcing me into the most difficult confrontation with a piano I had ever known. Without fail or mercy, the first features of pregnancy were pressing in, almost on my bridal heels. In the manner of the times, attempting secrecy was the name of the game. For me, a more difficult game would have been hard to find. Time after time I would ask myself this question. How could anyone who felt as wretched as I sit in front of a dancing crowd, depicting rhythmic joy several nights a week? In desperate moments I had visions of some eagle-eyed dancer noticing my plight and taking it upon himself to notify the Board of Health. Or when I sunk to the lowest ebb, the call became directed to the Humane Society!

Propriety set a mother-to-be's exit from the commercial world much earlier than nowadays. This meant I had only a few more months to conquer, if only I could hold out. Things were supposed to get better in time, weren't they? It was of utmost economic importance to keep playing and oh what a spot to be in for a pair of musicians. We were envied for being able to travel together to the same job, keeping it so to say, all in the family. What we kept "all in the family" amounted to multiplying our individual salaries of $3.30 per dance by two! Moreover my writing and finding new music and ideas contributed to the emergency of the moment.

As if to taunt me, the old reliable clock of pregnant tradition even reversed its tactics. Although breakfasts were often queasy, the alien activities in my middle somehow struck a knife's edge balance. But come the evening of dance nights, all the devils of prenatal nausea came out to romp and play. Morning sickness simply changed its act into evening sickness. On play nights any dinner was suspect, so by the time we had driven the thirty minute run to Tacoma, a weak and empty creature was slouching alongside a nervous driver husband, and slouching as carefully as possible to keep my long taffeta dress from resembling a nightgown. Kenny now found himself perfectly cast into the role of Simon Legree, and found no joy in the part. In a last ditch effort he would buy me a vanilla cone, demanding I at least give it a try. He knew better than to even suggest such a deadly descriptive flavor as strawberry or chocolate. Cautiously attacking this needed sustenance at less than an invalid's pace, necessitated taking the last blocks at a crawl and even re-running them before reaching 13th & Fawcett and the end of my cone.

Strange to say, each dance was played through without incident or accident. The urgency of the cover-up game must have pulled out all my stops. Actually, I could have skipped the whole charade. My present health and condition had already been accurately diagnosed by the whole orchestra! They played their little game too by not letting on or uttering one veiled remark. The three hours seemed divided into three sections. Part one was the period of shallow breathing and not allowing a mental picture of food into my brain. Part two became the iffy and wobbly time with no sudden moves beyond the necessary arm movement. Sometimes I would secretly (I thought) nibble on a soda cracker from my evening bag. As the third segment finally came into view, a tipsy victory seemed to be dawning. Later as we all straggled our way through two choruses of "I'll See You Again," with the parody I had written being sung to the departing dancers by our drummer, thankful relief took over. The dance had been played. The pianist had not up-chucked nor fainted across the keyboard. It seemed life would continue after all.

Once past the perilous nights, the remaining months before taking my leave were like a bed of roses. There was joy after all in my little secret condition. Talk about somebody wreathed in a cloud of deception, and mine was pink! Little did I know the pink would soon evolve into a garish green. At last the announcement was revealed, which was answered with, "Hope you can at least stay with us until we locate another musician. It won't be easy." Fate proved this statement wrong, and I found myself dismayed with the subsequent news a month hence that one had been found.

Indeed one had been found. One that was eager to have the job, able to do without completely written material and a good reader if necessary. And a fine sense of timing, they added happily. Then came the finale of this person's list of talents. The person was A GIRL! Twang went a whizzing arrow, aiming itself right into the center of my ego. That's when the pink cloud turned to green. The other qualifications I could endure, but a *girl?* Where in the world had she sprung from so suddenly? Playing music with other girls in the all-girl groups had stirred no jealousy pangs, but then none of them played piano and I felt no threat. In fact I had not as yet met another girl pianist. More of her statistics were to come and they were sufficient to give the sharp arrow a great big twist!

"She really plays quite well—she's real peppy. Though she's not as talented as you, she's real good, and boy is she ever *vivacious.*" This from my husband after an initial evening with my replacement. That almost did it. It was the adjective "vivacious" that set me off into long

119

pouts of self pity. "She's Irish you know," the report continued, which made sense as I had met her briefly and noted the dark curls, round face and invigorated smile, highlighted by a glowing complexion. Mine of late was more like an unbaked Pillsbury biscuit. Well, I would return and by then Miss Vivacious would be well tired of the regimentation of pattern dances. Her exuberance would be watered down to a trickle. Therefore when I bowed out in deference to motherhood, my disposition was suffering from the horrid combination of insecurity and jealousy. Any graciousness on my part was hard to come by. Time was to prove me not only poor at stepping aside, but also a poor forecaster of the new pianist's patience and endurance!

29

Intermission

Dancing at the Ballroom went merrily on, without their regular pianist (a bit too merrily in my estimation). Our Dodge touring car made its roundtrips to Tacoma with just the driver and his banjo inside. Not able to sustain a permanent pique level over being supplanted, I settled down to the summer months. More important things were on my mind now anyway. Up till now the reality of a first baby's existence had not been dwelt upon. All emphasis had centered on just weathering it through the immediate months. Now I was ready for that wonderful and calm halfway period when peace and goodwill seem to permeate and you and the world both gain a new dimension. Though we lived right on the Willows corner, it was still a novelty to watch occasional cars spin by from out our kitchen window. The setting was much akin to Firgrove and our polehouse acreage. Simple barns spoke of home-taught architecture, and several farmhouses, edged with pastures wrested from forest and underbrush, still held their own over the two-laned concrete highway. This marvelous paved road, which had already conquered South Hill's slope, halted abruptly at the Willow's Corner and took a wide bend westward to become Airport Road. I don't remember too many long or boring days. Not when my ambitious husband had a prolific garden going outback and there was always the bungalow piano to play—without an audience.

By late summer mother declared, "October will soon be here and we'd better get the *important* things ready." Cute bonnets, booties and frills had already gathered from modest showers. However, nothing posed a bigger crisis to mother than a baby's arrival without any diapers on tap. Her machine hummed out a good supply, all soft-napped flannel and hemmed to a gnat's eyebrow. My last purchase was at Tacoma's Rhodes Bros., in the infant's Dept. of course. I had always longed to march up to its satiny pink counter and seat myself on one of the revolving stools with other than gift buying in mind.

At last I could (with very apparent authority) ask to be shown their line of the important little "belly-bands" so rarely given at showers and now a definite item of the past.

Dr. Philip Kyle had pronounced a possible arrival date of "Maybe Halloween," on my last checkup. Our unpredictable daughter beat his estimate by ten days! Pure happiness presided over the whole family and for all of us the whole world resumed its turning again. The one and only grandchild was here and all was well. As for me, it was sudden euphoria. Mother was literally beside herself and the proud father cast all caution to the winds and purchased a new hat in celebration of the event. Mother, now cast in the role of grandmother, had left no doubt in Dr. Kyle's mind as to her ability to take over after my fourth day at the hospital. As long as all had gone well we welcomed the chance to cut the customary ten day length short. An outlay of $40.00 for Dr. Kyle's fee, which sounds historic now, had been met. With each day in the Tacoma General's eight-bed Maternity ward gong for $4.00, it was a saving to be grateful for. It is even hard now to realize the relativity of finances in the Thirties.

A more joyous and sharing experience I cannot remember. Even the new baby girl, whom we named Arlene Adele (the second name in honor of my dear Tante Krummel), joined in the wave of goodwill by being content to just eat, sleep and be ogled at. Mother beamed and whistled while deftly pinning diapers and tying the wiggly little side-tapes of the belly-binders. We all knew we had the prettiest dark-eyed and dark-haired baby in all this world. Any thoughts of playing dance music were on temporary suspension. The preponderance of motherhood was sufficient unto the day.

30

Vamp Till Ready

Nothing tangible stood in the way. Presumably I was ready to resume my post at the Crescent Ballroom. Details as to how our baby would be lovingly cared for had all been discussed. Two nights during the week she would be with our close neighbors who owned the Willows gas station just steps from our house. It was an expedient arrangement that seemed to please the childless couple. "I'd love to have her," Mrs. Annis had said with gathering enthusiasm. "I'll drive out to my brother's farm in Alderton and get out the old family cradle. Won't she look cute in that?" Saturday night's format, however, handed the baby over to her waiting grandmother, allowing us to sleep in Sunday mornings before going to pick her up. The pick-up often included a hearty Sunday dinner.

Musicwise, the plans were not at all cut and dried. Getting me reinstated stood at a mysterious impasse. Evidently the original changeover had lacked even a verbal mention of specific dates for my return, or whether I even wished to do so at this time. As a result, a sticky situation hung in the air. This was not the time for such threats as Kenny not playing unless I did, for jobs were still not growing on trees and no one was risking rocking the boat. Impatience almost overtook the waiting-out time, and then by ways I know not the whole thing became resolved and no boats were sunk in the process. Miss Vivacious went on later (with my blessings) to Seattle and became a popular pianist there.

The re-entry flight into the dance music world did not soar like a bird. Actually it touched down on flopping wings. I felt myself almost an intruder upon an established scene. I possessed no Irish smile and it would be too obvious to effect one now. In short, I was Miss Chicken again. The music I knew backwards; it was me I wasn't sure about. We unloaded as before, parking the car in lopsided fashion on the 13th Street side-hill. By this time my knees were beginning to quake. Once inside I quickly retreated to the restroom for hardly anyone was around yet and I could prolong my appearance on the bandstand. Would anyone be glad to see me back? Would some of the dancers remember me? I'll never forget the drummer's greeting as I began to advance toward the piano bench. He was the snappy young teaser among the three brothers. If ever I appreciated his quick wit, this was the time. With only a twinkling glance thrown in my direction, while busily fitting screws and brackets in place, he made his brief observation across his shoulder: "Well, I see it's *Amateur Night* tonight!" (Major Bowes radio program of that name was a hot item then, wherein aggressive amateurs were given free public exposure to humbly display their talents.) Though my laughter was in relief, we all enjoyed the humor before proceeding to settle ourselves in for three hours of music making. The taunting but good-natured remark had filled the embarrassing gap well, putting all of us at ease. While no ovations ensued during the dance, many smiles and a few sincere congratulations on motherhood came my way. It was enough.

All was roses for the time being. Kenny's months of tackling the world of carpentering in spare hours had produced a simple but solidly built five room house. However, with each load of lumber being paid for in cash, only two rooms were ready for occupancy at the time—the ample kitchen and a cedar-walled bedroom. A shiny new kitchen wood-stove and matched maple breakfast set and hutch stood almost mirrored in the freshly waxed blue checked linoleum, just waiting for the young family. We thought it was marvelous. We were fortunate in Kenny having a daytime job, plus both of us working together at music in what could have been termed "double moonlighting." Our baby was healthy with the best of dispositions and I could be home with her throughout the days and never worry over her care on the nights we were away.

But even velvety roses carry thorns, a few of which refused to be ignored. Though our marriage sailed on a fairly even keel, I sometimes sensed Kenny's awareness of his detachment from his first son's growing years. I should have been mature enough to initiate more open discussion, but I wasn't. Besides, his bitterness over religious binders and divorce legalities had done little towards his sharing the resentment. A blind spot evolved . . . and grew. Only oncoming years, coupled with "all things worketh together for good," was to adjust the clouded picture. The resultant clearness brought a relief of sorts to Kenny's resignation of his son's all inclusive Catholic upbringing, schooling and all. That Kenny Jr.'s entire future was destined to be within the Church was at this time only written in the stars.

Meanwhile there was another annoying thorn, one of a musical nature, slowly working its way beneath my skin. Reluctance at playing such a boring diet now began to take verbal form. To surrender to the temptation of not caring what I was playing, or just settling for making dollars, was against my principles. With no change in sight, the outlook began to look bleak. But who among us knew the most unhappy of world conditions, a war, was to change everyone's life pattern? Suddenly the public's vocabulary was alive with such words as "surprise attack," "Pearl Harbor" and the whole Japanese race. The whole effect was dizzying and hard to comprehend in its immediacy. Coastal dwellers from Washington to California could almost feel the hot breath of Hirohito blowing over their shoulders.

The first thing to directly affect our little setup of living, outside of keeping up with alien terms of "inductees," "curfews," "drafting" and clinging to radio news, was our dance work. With barely a stutter in the smooth operation of Ole Lund's empire, the whole Crescent Ballroom shifted gears from Old Time & Mixed Dancing, to Dancing Entertainment Center for as many new Fort Lewis soldiers as the hall's capacity laws could allow. Part One of the ballroom's emergence from disuse had succeeded as an expedience to the woes of the Thirties. Now a wholly unforeseen demand was knocking at the swinging green doors. Not only knocking but pushing through them like a huge order of Army Issue.

For us it seemed almost like mixed dancing had prevailed one night only to evaporate into thin air come the next dance. The venerable program tripod toppled and away went the Spanish Waltz, the Varsouvienne and all the other measured steps that had formed a pleasant dancing world of familiar security for our steady crowds. Their choice was either to be assimilated into the swarm of khaki uniforms and dance to their tune, or seek an alternate somewhere, for the Crescent was never to be the same again.

I'll never know whether Ole Lund ever had the time to consider searching out another orchestra more befitting the cause, or whether he just shrugged his massive shoulders and decided to let things ride.

Within weeks our trusted and spare-worded saxophone playing brother in the Eaton clan was drafted, and a new musician, just in from working at the Davenport Hotel in Spokane, was hired. He effected a more modern approach and in a way helped the others. I was copying and snatching up such innovations as "The Jersey Bounce," and I was also possibly pregnant, and World War Two was here—three weighty events not necessarily listed in order of importance.

31

The Jersey Blitz

The shocking blast heralding World War II had not even died away yet, and here we were at the Ballroom, suddenly looking down into unfamiliar khaki uniforms. Though an overnight appall and direness had seized everyone, the music and the dance went on. We too were caught with our defenses down, musically speaking. Now we had to come to the fore with the mood of the day, instead of recalling the bygone ones. To change our customary style without even a fitting was far from easy. For starters we relied heavily on "The Jersey Bounce," with the bounce steadily improving as deafening roars of applause urged us onward. "And the Caissons Go Rolling Along" became a singing and dancing ally and gradually we began to effect "swinging out" as best we could.

One night I remember in particular was when "The Jersey Bounce" had been noisily claimed for themselves by what looked like the whole state of New Jersey. They had gathered as a group at our end of the ballroom shouting "New Jersey" (in their own pronunciation) as they bounced and swung. It was hard to stem a rush of tears at the thought of what might lie ahead for them. While we had no "Over There" to bolster spirits, we had a Jersey Bounce. It often seemed like a reliving of all the World War I tearful movies. The Crescent lent itself well to the new emergency by holding out a welcome hand and greeting of, "Come on in, my prices will not break you, our beer garden takes no advantage of service men, the floor is large and your service busses will drop you off right at my entrance." It must have been a point of cheer for many, for the response to the Crescent's invitation was like an army of women rushing in on a huge department stores's annual sale. And there were enough girls to go around! While our orchestra was not Glenn Miller or the Dorseys, we worked hard and managed to fill the bill fairly well. New hits and good standards were mine to put on paper and for the first time in years I was happier with my lot at the piano. I could branch out and play what came more naturally. More than once a pro who had wound up in the Infantry Band or such would "sit in" with us and that was fun.

Like the old World War I movies, romance entered through the Crescent's doors, even to the point of reaching our family circle. With the grand piano now placed directly at the right boundary of the long stage, I was physically close to the dancers. One dancer in particular was destined to become a part of our family! For many weeks this dark, curly haired corporal had almost set up his headquarters under the far end of the long piano. Once during each evening he would politely request me to play a chorus on "Stardust" for him. Outside of this all I knew of him was his hailing from "Chi-cawgo," his love for music, and his ability to carry on a well-worded and mannerly conversation. I did not know the first night my now late-teenaged sisters attended a dance (somewhat in our care), and naturally posted themselves almost at my feet, he would be asking each one for a dance. As he paused before the elder one with his question, she glanced up at me for some sort of sign. With a quick affirmative nod from me they were off dancing amid the throng, as I tried in vain to follow their course. Only a few Saturdays later a romance was abloom, not without some sisterly pitfalls and skirmishes, but nonetheless thriving. Mother found herself about to prepare another serious Sunday dinner and Mr. Chicawgo made his brief entree into our lives, before shipping out to heaven knew where. The address and the heart of my elder sister were in his vest pocket. His re-entry came at the end of the war and their wedding followed soon thereafter.

Next up were what I like to think of as the smug months, and which I felt I richly deserved. In a complete turn-around of the seven years back trial, the Crescent's piano was now in the hands of a happily pregnant player. Kenny and I deemed it now or never if ever out little family were going to gain another member, war or no. Though classified for possible drafting of family men, Kenny was never called up. A temporary leave from the Northern Pacific was taken in order to fill in at the Todd Shipyards, where he soon became a leadman in the pipefitting department. No small job, it claimed seven full days a week. The seven year gap between pregnancies had not changed the same observance of the "no tell" tradition. No wonder I felt the smugness. My condition was confirmed, unannounced and much less, unsuspected.

32

Hello Son, Goodbye Old Crescent

Early in the cold January of 1944 our second child was born. A BOY! How lucky could we be? Instead of arriving on the projected February date, he chose to be an added attraction to our Christmas holidays. It was happiness revisited for a fair-haired and blue-eyed contrast to our daughter. The times however were still harried with the Second World War dragging along in its last stages. A general dissidence hung over everyone as to why it couldn't end right now without any further losses. We were having to burn coal and carefully place the baby's bassinet toward the warmth of our kitchen range. The proud father's seven days a week schedule left little time for wood cutting, or other needed work around our acreage. My shopping forays to town were laden with baby gear, ration stamps and nearby neighbors.

Some three of four months later I returned to the Ballroom again and this time without incident. Mother willingly became the perfect baby sitter for the second time. She had been scattering pointed remarks for some time as to our daughter's need for a brother or sister and now felt things were in a better balance. As before, playing music one or more nights a week still enabled me to be an at-home mother. I hope I took the time to be thankful for an arrangement so tailored to my wishes and needs.

One needed no crystal ball to foresee the downhill slide of the Crescent. Like the war, it too was in the tedium of fading away. Somewhere along all these months, Ole Lund had died suddenly from a massive heart attack, and there went the mainstay of it all. Possessed with more maturity and graciousness, I might have viewed the going under as the sad demise of a faithful and landmark ballroom. Twice before its curtain had been rung down, only to rise again to hosts of eager dancers. But this time it looked like THE END, with no encores in sight. Instead of a sympathetic tear dropping on the keys, I played out our last dance there with no regret. I imagine too many long and hard nights were still too fresh in my mind. The Eaton Bros. orchestra was, so to say, in a state of indecision, since we had told them we thought the time was right for striking out on our own. The same thing was about to happen again. That old musical divider tab was ready to be inserted between the pages—a major change was in the making as Kenny and I decided to wing away on a new musical flight.

I remember walking out toward the Crescent's doors on our final evening. Looking back over my shoulder into all that sea green woodwork, the long well-trodden walkway through the entrance lobby tiled in the same old black and white squares, and the rows of empty wire coathangers dangling in the checkroom. I issued what was perhaps my once in a lifetime historic statement: "I shall never enter this hall again." We were ready for flight—but to where?

33
Thankyou Ole Lund

Let no one believe our setting up musical housekeeping for eleven years at Ole Lund's Crescent Ballroom was all mopping and scrubbing. Again, it's the intangibles that only stand out with time and turn the whole period into interesting backthoughts. Not noticeable at the moment were such things as the amount of playing experience being logged off, recognizing crowd preferences and reactions, and trying to fit yourself into the musical pockets of fellow players' moods and talents. Beyond my wondering if ever a more plush and pleasant way to perform music would dawn on the horizon, I doubt I saw beyond the next month of dance nights. Like most long-together groups, we found ways to level off the mount of monotony that threatened to cast its shadow. And only rarely were we opposed to encore clapping and stomping. I must thank Ole Lund, however, for what has become one of the best and most lasting memories of all, if for nothing else than the sheer weight of musical impact.

As mercenary and enterprising as our employer was, he found it in his heart to waive all our ticket prices for every name band playing a one-night stand in the area. These were not passes to hear Joe McDuff and his Peoria Podunkers, but name bands whose list read like a Who's Who of the whole Swing Band Era. Casual as this act may have been for Ole Lund, for us it was a true bonanza. We didn't even have to stand in long lines of avid fans, and if ever we felt like the privileged few, this was it. Ours was to drink in the whole heady concoction of top-notch music as we danced to the finest, applauded and went a bit crazy. It was complete immersion into the joys of fine dance music and professional talent.

One of the early windfalls of this two to three year span was the Paul

Whiteman band which was one of the last to play in the old Oakes Ballroom on Steilacoom Lake, which wasn't bad for starters! And while we oohed and aahed at his "Rhapsody in Blue," my mind returns most often to how marvelous it felt to glide across the floor as they did a beautiful arrangement of "The Night Is Young and You're So Beautiful." That's the one that stayed with me. To write of the many we were able to see and hear would take pages. I remember the night Henry Busse filled the Century Ballroom and how it was the evening when *everybody* danced *all* the time to his irresistible shuffle rhythm that went straight to every pair of feet in the hall. Phil Harris held forth at our own Crescent Ballroom, his curly hair and infectious smile charming a whole front of fans who crowded close to the band stand. No one wanted to miss a single verse of "That's What I Like About the South" or "Woodman Spare That Tree," each done in his very own rapid-fire yet Southern drawl delivery. One of the nights that we actually stared in awe and amazement was the Jimmie Lunceford Crescent appearance. All those swaying bodies and horns in a show-type formation clipped off precisioned music that literally ignited sparks. After watching and hearing their unique arrangements we felt we had just about seen it all.

But more was to come. Shep Fields casually stepped in front of his band, dipped a soda straw into a glass of water and came up with his famous Rippling rhythm sound that sounded off their theme. The music bubbled and effervesced most of the time, making for a happy-type evening. For some strange reason, one of the playing leaders that touched my heart was Russ Morgan. It may have been his association with "Does Your Heart Beat For Me" or the cut of his Welsh features and dark brooding eyes, or my knowing his emergence from the hard childhood of a West Virginia coal-mining existence. He rarely waved his baton, since between wailing off a lot of trombone effects, snatching a violin for novelty work, slipping over to the piano where he ran over the entire keyboard, and standing at the mike singing soft ballads, he was a busy leader. He wasn't heavy with ingratiating stage presence, but who cared?

For glittering talent, but a detached manner in facing their army of admirers, I would say both Count Basie and Duke Ellington took first place.

Why I felt they played "down" to the packed crowd, I couldn't say but it was a definite impression. Perhaps their immense and secure success could have induced jadedness to creep in, or maybe the great Northwest was too distant from the East Coast. And then there were the Dorsey Bros. together and singly, and my almost doing a musical swoon when Tommy Dorsey's first glide on his trombone led the band into

"Getting Sentimental Over You." Seeing Ted FioRito's nimble fingers flitting across the keys of "my piano" during their Crescent appearance brought me up short. I did have a long way to go, but then he didn't have to grind out Schottisches and Two-Steps and the like!

All in all, each band carried out its particular image with enough talent and expertise to approach musical perfection, and I doubt that any couple among the throng of Northwesterners who came to see the splash was more grateful than we. All the adjectives and flowery phrases, now written almost in homage and respect for the demise of this high point on the public's musical taste scale, will never surpass the joy of having been there!

34
Test Flight with the Eagles

The first week of severance from the Crescent stood at Saturday night, a time when the new cut was most likely to smart a bit. After the years of steady grind, an open Saturday loomed like a bottomless pit. I had just put together the stray measures of "The Petite Waltz" and was at the piano trying it out. Though unvoiced, I know what each of us was thinking: "So this is what a no-job Saturday night is like." Somewhat hazily we both looked at each other and then put a rare claim on our davenport and easy chair.

"Sure feels odd to have the davenport over here now," I yawned across to Kenny as a well filled day had left me unusually depleted. The sofa had been rudely pushed to the wall by a brash newcomer, which was none other than a group of second-hand drums. These pearlized and sparkly components held the potential of paying for their existence before too long. Or so we hoped. Kenny's theory for branching out on our own was to work himself into drumming and then use his banjo and guitar as second instruments. With the addition of a horn we'd be set for combo work. Luckily the drums and Kenny were friends (up to a point) before all this took place. However, the casual friendship needed a good deal of rekindling. This meant the drum set had to be accessible at any hour for random practices and so they became a legal resident of our front room. Needless to say, the newcomer was soon fair game for family and eager visitors. They seemed irresistible to all. On one occasion even mother perched herself atop the pedestal drum stool, positioned her foot at the base drum pedal, grasped the sticks and let go!

While no one's efforts at aggressive practicing come under the heading of pleasant listening, I would rate drum practice the least bearable. Miles of rat-a-tats and thumps, along with a clashing cymbal and smashing high-hat within the confines of an ordinary room, breaks the tolerance barrier. But endured they had to be, if we were to fly alone.

We tried to feel confident about things; at least now after many years we were, so to say, legal. Back at the Crescent we had all become union members on a pay-as-you-go plan with our Musician's Local No. 117. Now we were adding another card into our billfolds, one called Social Security. This latest government venture bore our name, official number in the system, and listed Crescent Ballroom as employer. The two business-like cards were welcome and timely, in that it now seemed someone had sorted out working musicians as a definite species! I had hurriedly blotted my lipstick on my card one night for want of anything to fill the need of the moment, and it remained thus until we graduated to a plastic card. But back to our homey little evening at home.

"You'd make *some* piano player tonight," Kenny mused in surveyance of a disheveled and now reclining wife. Hardly said and mused over when our phone rang. Kenny slowly ambled into the kitchen and his staggered words floating into the frontroom were enough to raise me to a sitting position. "Less than an hour . . . well we can give it a try . . . only a piano player . . . ask for a Mr. who? . . . go on upstairs . . . O.K. I got it." Less than an hour and they were talking Tacoma? What were they thinking of? It was now almost 9:00 P.M. and Tacoma was always a thirty minute run.

Within an hour I was still wondering the same things. We were wheeling toward the city at a good clip while my mind took an audit of what I might have put on, or thrown on, I should say. The darkness within the car made inspections possible only by touch and feel. Though a tacit agreement existed between us about not playing separate jobs, Kenny ruled this late call as an exception to the rule, and I agreed it was an emergency. For top drama, a dispatching of needed musician to musical crisis has everything a mercy-bent ambulance possesses, except the wailing siren.

Hours later the Chevvy trundled back to Puyallup with a tired and disoriented pair inside. We had averted disaster, the crowd had held till our significant entrance and from then on the evening had clicked right along. It was the leavetaking that threw us. As we were picking things up a man came up and introduced himself as the Eagle's Activity

Manager, or some such title. During the rather short evening it had not been difficult to notice his appraisal and approval. When he spoke, however, his manner indicated so much indefiniteness we had to guess what was coming across to us. The best we could make of it was his inference of making us a duo in the lounge downstairs—three nights a week. Details were only in approximates—the length of our stay was vague. The salary was implied and to all intents and purposes we could foreseeably begin the following week. Actually, both Kenny and I were at fault in failing to get a clearer picture. We had not as yet learned to speak or understand Lodge talk! Without any visible qualm, Kenny said we would take the engagement, Lodge lingo and all.

You couldn't say our first flight terminated in mid-air since we lasted all of six weeks, four of which I would gladly have passed by. But it was long enough to prove the two of us could motivate a cocktail dancing crowd, and long enough to decide this format was not exactly our cup of tea. However all was not negative. Kenny's rhythmic background was of good style and familiar for me to work with, and the almost one hundred percent free choice of tunes was a holiday. A mood suggestive of playing hookey prevailed as set customs and patterned steps were left behind amid the newness of different surroundings. Like most story-book plots, a protagonist had to enter the scene. That is to say, the pianist, so newly liberated, now found herself flinging both hands at the keys in a fashion best described as perpetual motion. In these years a discernible melody was of importance, and musical coasting or orna-menting of another's musical output could only be indulged in when another body was carrying the tune. Alack and alas, there was no other body. I was the tune, not just now and then, but all the time! Six weeks of living and carrying out this realistic fact three nights a week put me somewhat in the category of the pitiful marathon dancers who com-peted in an almost sadistic craze during the Thirties. Only Kenny's assurance of "just a few more weeks and we can forget about the whole thing," kept me from seceding at the end of the first two weeks. Compliments from appreciative dancers and listeners gave sustenance too.

Foreign to us, but to our liking was the extended amount of time between dance sets. Heretofore we had barely tarried between dances as it just was not deemed to be good business. Now allowances were made for people to be reseated at their little toy tables, with additional time for reordering drinks from the bar. Cocktail practices were still a bit novel and my first amazement was the mountain of tinkling icecubes within each glass, as opposed to the liquid content. No one complained; it was all so new and daring. As for our dancers, they were not borrowed from the Crescent, though a few trickled across the street out of pure curiosity, and the differing profiles between the two soon became apparent.

Back now to our will-o-the-wisp employer. We saw him only on our opening night, where he exhibited moderate pleasure while popping in and out like a jackrabbit. From then on we heard vague reports as to whether he actually was in existence. His condition fluctuated between being hospitalized with acute pneumonia and being home taking it easy. Others expressed doubt as to either statement being the truth. At any rate he was not in evidence. Our checks were to be called for by us after the dance, at the bar no less. Even this act failed to shed any light and who was who and what was what. The waitress entrusted with the checks was always too weary to engage in any conversation as to whom we were dealing with. It was like doing business with spectral beings and not ever did we know if we were in favor, or out. One night in desperation we buttonholed the tired looking janitor as we trundled toward our car after midnight. "Of course . . . y'know," he mumbled, "There's lotsa different factions in this lodge." We agreed silently. *"Somebody's* always gonna be unhappy with the music."

Once more Kenny felt the old image of Simon Legree casting his shadow upon him. For me to keep the melody going all evening kept me far too occupied to worry about enhancing any stage presence I might possess. When I felt we were racing a beat to a danger point, how could I smile while hissing across the little stage, "You're picking up the tempo." And then when Kenny shot back with, "I am not," rat-a-tat-tat-, "you're dragging it down," my lips went rigid. Was this kind of sham going to be a necessary part of our new venture? Although he did it gently, it always caught me in the act when Kenny would remind, "Try not to scowl . . . they're happy, look, everybody's dancing." Other minor clashes were our selection of what I deemed an overabundance of fast beats and too few ballads. Kenny was acutely conscious about keeping a lively and peppy image, while I was the laggard who wished to dream on some prettier tunes. I couldn't see the crowd's champing at the bit as a continuing condition. If it hadn't been for Kenny's patience, we might have been the "Bickering Bakers' Duo." And playing for what seemed a bickering lodge committee.

Well, if not this, what kind of tea did we want? The need was to get started somewhere, somehow. We knew now the wishes and hopes were not pure daydreaming. One thing was certain, our group would number more than two, and please, we'd prefer a job with a substantial club, one not known for changing horses in midstream. And one with more than just a moderately playable upright piano. And one with more than cocktail-sized dancing area. Breathes there a musician with soul so dead, who never to himself has said, "I deserve to be playing in a better place than this"?

Our wishes were made known to our Musician's Local President, Grady Morehead, and while we knew the Union's primary function was not finding jobs for members, a report of your current condition was of mutual benefit. We had to cover every base possible in order to release a whole lot of vibrations into the waiting atmosphere.

Meanwhile out in the snug harbor of the Tacoma Yacht Club, a committee was belaboring which way to turn. Their long standing combo had recently chosen to bow out in retirement. Call it synchronization, or chance, or Divine Providence that caused the two sets of vibrations to intersect, for it happened. As I see it, they sent their uncertain query into the ozone at the precise time as we did and a perfect meeting took place. From there on telephone wires linked the airborne elements, which linked people to people. The first ring was placed from committee to Union office with inquiry into the name of Kenny Baker, which resulted in a go ahead nod. And so we all entered into the talking stage, sight unseen, just airwaved communication. Auditions in our day were uncommon. An employer could take himself to wherever you might be playing and from that form an opinion. Some of them took the trouble, but most went by word of mouth, your reputation, or similar means. Kenny's telephone conversation with a cautiously advancing Yacht Club Commodore was one wherein he confidently assured the man of our acceptability. Just like that the Kenny Baker Combo was hired, while in truth we actually did not exist as yet, beyond the drummer and a pianist!

From this rather fragile linkage came a most durable connection. One that was to wear throughout seventeen ensuing Commodores! Not to forget are the equal number of Shipmate presidents, in whose power it was to re-hire, approve and sign each yearly contract. In those days the Yacht Club danced away the hours on the upper floor of their old but charming clubhouse. In true dock-like fashion, the pavilion-shaped structure hugged the water's edge. Abundant windows allowed vistas of Commencement Bay fronted by a field of swaying masts. I was taken with the salty flavor and all the ship-shape brass and mahogany right from the first.

Our first ascent to the old upper deck of the Yacht Club is well remembered. Pitched in the steep risers of shipboard stairways, the royal blue carpeted steps led to the first glimpse of the dance floor. As we reached the top my spirits rose likewise. Kitty-cornering the bay-ward corner of a slightly raised bandstand stood a Baby Grand piano.

Now if it was in tune and had good touch and tone, my heart would hit high "C." High "C" it was and continued to be for over seventeen years, for this love-at-first-sight affair was one that never paled. I can only hope it was as happy with me as I was with its wonderfully bright and manageable keys that seemed to say, "Play me the very best you can, and I'll return in kind." Sometimes I swore the keys almost responded by themselves.

After these early and teetery beginnings, a bulk of years sailed by with Morrie Kenton, Al Meddaugh and the two of us on deck. A fifth dimension was added for needed depth and status whenever a more grandiose dance was scheduled. He would be in the person of John Joyce, if we could get him. For a few of the earlier seventeen seasons a bit of "Polka Dots and Moonbeams" joined us on the stand. In other words, we were meeting the prerequisite of any self respecting group by featuring an attractive girl vocalist. Everything just fell together as ordered. All college-going girls needed extra money; her voice was natural and true pitched, and she was our daughter Arlene. Not wishing to exceed the limits of parental bias, I will only say she was talented, charming and unaffected, and sang exactly on key! She had her share of fans who enjoyed such numbers as "Mood Indigo," "Aufwiedersehn," "Ballin' the Jack," and on and on. Apparently our other clubs and even the one night engagements all felt a certain warmness in the family touch, for it always brought forth comments and smiles. Maybe that's when I learned to smile while playing!

*A Valentine dance back in the Forties. Left to right:
Kenny Baker, Wayne Smith, Elsa Baker, Bud Smith.*

Play It Again, Elsa!

*Wedding reception at Blue Ridge Country Club in Seattle. Front
row: Art Doll, Al Meddaugh; back row, Kenny and Elsa Baker.*

Elsa Baker, seated at pump organ, waits for the bride's entrance at historic Oysterville Church in Oysterville, Wash.

The restored and precious Oysterville Church, dated 1854, where 3 o'clock Vespers are still held in the summer months.

Kenny Baker's big night to shine at "The Laurels" in Killarney, Ireland.

Here is a view of the strangest organ I ever attempted to play— in Kylemore Abbey, Connemara, Ireland. The bandana was the only head covering available at this spur of the moment "sit down and play" for a Catholic Mass.

My one and only appearance as strolling musician at an outdoor art exhibit.

Up in the choir loft at large pipe organ for a niece's wedding in Olympia, Wash.

PART IV

THE MUSIC MERCHANTS

35

Augmenting the Tonic Chord

Casting our lot with the Yacht Club way back in the late Forties was a literal casting of bread upon the waters. A regular begetting of other clubs followed in the wake. We didn't know it then, but the Fifties were to be the high notes upon our dance club scale. The resultant progeny of an attractive family of dance groups became sizable enough to keep us hopping. Actually you couldn't term it as hopping. Not when a lumbering set of drums was a part of your anatomy.

Club seasons ran from September until the following May or June. By virtue of each club's practice of setting up their calendar a year in advance, our date juggling was minimized. If you were lucky, exposed dates were filled with single or "casual" engagements. Somehow it jibed fairly well, and while we were not within the realm of those forced to farm out excess jobs, we felt we had our share. Especially pleasing was the luxury of grand pianos in our main three clubs. Add on experienced and congenial musicians to work with, and the complaint margin was quite narrow. However we never laid a claim on Utopia. The perpetual urge to improve, and the inevitable interference of everyday devilish situations took care of that.

Now I found myself seeking to play at a corresponding level with two skilled players, whom I hoped would consider me as a fellow musician. It kept my head and fingers on the alert. Keenly aware of the truth of my touch lacking the authority of male pianists, I tried all the harder to prove an identity by using imaginative ideas, being aware of trends and keeping a live tempo. The human condition, known as yearning for that pie in the sky, had dwindled down not to only occasional fits of unfulfillment. However, the longing to play dinner music in an established hotel, either solo or in a group, never went away. When dreaming of such I carried it a step further by making it an international clientele. Then Green Book's backlog could be used for the umpteenth time perhaps. Not that these songs were mouldering in the attic. They often found themselves pleasing the souls of ethnic lodge members or a nursing home resident still harking back to the songs from "the old country." "How is it you know these songs? They are so old—no one plays them anymore," or, "How can you remember all these tunes for such a long time? Why some of them are from *my* childhood," were questions that arose again and again. How to explain your personal attachment to a Green Book or your being able to memorize and maintain so much of it? My guess now is that it is equatable with learning the multiplication tables. You get a brain-fix.

Bit by bit Kenny was gaining the upper hand on subduing the unfinished rooms of our rustic house. Outside an oasis of semi-wild lawn, banked by fruit trees, berries and a prolific garden, gave off an erroneous air of casual country living. An army of trees and dense wild greenery, ever at the ready to charge, were positioned just beyond the perimeters, ready to cross the border and attack. Not exactly easy living, but long on privacy and the abundancy of nature. Like the postman's holiday, our vacations focused on family camping with tent, axe and a collection of survival gear. Our destination was *genuine* hinterland.

The dance clubs now comfortably filled most of our calendar and the family was taking on additional status too. Bruce, our blonde haired boy became Skippy Peanut Butter and baseball bat age. His brown-eyed, pig-tailed sister, Arlene (eight years his senior), had cast aside pinafores for a Junior Prom formal. Nearby in Tacoma, dark haired Kenny Jr., was no longer growing up with his Tacoma grandparents, having made an early but firm decision to enter a Novitiate school. This option came as a jumbled surprise to his father.

Relatively speaking, the Swinging Years were upon us now. While we were not big band size, we swung steadily forward not quite at full tilt, as music was still "moonlighting." My mind frequently dwelt on how to become a recognized musician, and still remain sensitive over not tipping the scale in what I saw as an unwise direction.

Now home and motherhood were counterbalancing each other fairly well against musical work and aspirations. With mother delighting in having the children as overnighters, or "Nacht-waechters" as she termed them (night watchers), my conscience was partially salved. Had greater opportunities come along, I may have capitulated. Who can say? My hand was never called and though frustration was known, it never really flourished. Always and ever was that desire to play better, improve my style and become more polished, no matter where I played. Euphorically speaking, we were basking in an era of the finest Pop composers, Broadway musicals and Hollywood theme songs. All offered a dazzling formula to work with and enjoy, in fact it was almost like having your cake and eating it too.

"And are you giving your children piano lessons?" was often asked of me by innocent people who evidently had never been in a like position. This endeavor is as fraught with potential disaster as a husband teaching his spouse how to drive the family car. Both kids weathered their way through several years of piano lessons and what I now see as an over abundance of motherly critique. No tears of sadness were shed by either when, in a mutual agreement, lessons were dropped during the teen years. At least a good foundation had been poured. Arlene tacked on a dozen or so vocal lessons, the better to sing with our combo during the money-demanding college years. She had a prodigious memory for lyrics, a good ear and pitch and attractive style, but never took the business seriously.

We naturally assumed Bruce to be endowed with a musical spark, which we would fan. He was so equipped and played his way through four or five years with very nimble fingers and sensitive style. However, teen-aged boys attached firmly to a piano are a rare commodity and was not to occur in our home either. The timing was unfavorable with his high school years coinciding right with the approach of Rock & Roll mania. As far as Bruce was concerned, it was goodbye piano and hello guitar. Not a difficult choice with a house full of guitars already. Before you could say Jack Robinson, he was thumping and strumming away with a pick-up combo at the University. Mom was again left to keep the home Spinet keys in motion.

One more significant event took place within these "fanning out years" as I like to call them. This one was prior to the demise of family piano lesson years. On a much remembered Palm Sunday we added another link to the long chain of Kenny's Methodist forebears. We became a church family. Kenny transferred via vows from an early Kansas baptism, while Arlene, Bruce and I received regular baptizing. To me it remains a day to remember right along with a wedding day and your firstborn. I must add the realism of where there's a church there's music to be played, was not long in becoming apparent. Not as apparent to us was the real fact of our family now falling into the category of an ecumenical household. Of course we realized Kenny Jr.'s Catholic commitment, but still failed to recognize this rather rare (then) classification. There never seemed to be a question of will this work and very likely is one of the reasons that it did.

These years were also leave-taking ones. We had waved a long four year farewell to Kenny Jr. as he flew off for a Theology stint in Innsbruck, Austria. Daughter Arlene's wedding bells were scheduled to ring in February. Before long we would be waving off the newlyweds for a first home in Washington, D.C. where the groom was to begin his career with the U.S. Treasury Dept. It was comforting to know Bruce would still be within striking and cookie-mailing distance, when he became a freshman at the University of Washington in Seattle. Like the proverbial worrying mother, Arlene's cross-country move carried possibilities of who knew what? Prior to becoming a bride she had worked

145

her way through a good portion of the higher learning years by holding numerous secretarial positions, plus singing with our group. Last but certainly not least, she had kept the wheel of romance spinning at all times. With Arlene not possessing a secretive nature, we all spun along with her.

If I could have sat down then as I can now, and assessed our little entity as a whole, I might have become smug. The discordant notes, as it were, seemed to be weeding themselves out. Kenny could now look ahead to retirement years without wondering if they'd ever happen. We had good club contracts, the kids were all three branching off towards dreams of their own, and ogre pianos seemed to be a thing of the past. But since this is real life drama, an unknown culprit was lurking in the shadows. We naturally could not see it as such. Off in a visible distance the first wave of rock music was just beginning to beat upon our musical shores. "Certainly," we hoped with all our hearts, "this isn't going to last." At this point our ears were only twinging in annoyance. What an indignity to music! And what would befall the many great tunes so dear to us and thousands of others—the listeners, the dancing crowds? Would our much loved music become discarded and put on a shelf marked, "Dated Material?" "It just cannot happen," many musicians told themselves. "This blight is but a fad . . . we're not ready to close the book on the Swinging Years yet!" Was pride preceding a fall?

36

Pianos I Have Known

I hope it is not too far fetched for anyone to believe that somewhere along my piano-strewn way I would get the notion of pianos being very similar to humans. From the very start our own Kimball was a trusted friend and a close companion of my little daily life. Sometimes I saw it as demanding after tedious practices, but by the next session, all was forgiven. Unconsciously I suppose I assumed this golden-veined oaken instrument felt the same about me. At about age twelve when the circle widened ever farther from familiar keyboards, a surprising discovery was made. *All* pianos were not nice! Though it was on another facet in growing up, this disillusionment was destined to haunt me from there to here. Would I could echo Will Rogers' charitable outlook on his fellowman: "I never met one I didn't like."

As sure as tomorrow's sunrise, the commercial pianists, who played here, there, and everywhere, were due for some emotional piano confrontations. I can testify to some kindling joy in the heart, while others generated only mute acceptance. Downright sorrow was never out of the realm of possibility either. As this is exactly what was going on for me during the early Thirties and Forties, I was to become well acquainted with the whole spectrum.

Is it any wonder, then, when a pianist has accepted a blind playing date, the suspense of what may befall his fingers, his good humor, and not to forget his ego, verges on the paranoid? Confidentially and if the situation warranted, I could maintain a thoroughly dissatisfied attitude throughout an entire dance job of struggling with a lesser than lovely piano. I remember one night in particular, where upon arrival in a handsome and well appointed hall, my eyes had beheld their "house piano." It stood in a corner and answered my look of horror by glowering back at me like an old brute. By the time the band was blowing the last number to the crowd that night, the fellows in our group were ready to push the guilty piano over the nearest cliff. With the pianist attached!

For me, and I know others will agree, the whole process carried all the perils of Russian Roulette. One of those pianos, yours not to know which, could be the one capable of delivering the bullet for an outright killing of our musical psyche. Bang . . . you were a dead duck. If on the other hand Lady Luck was smiling, causing the roulette wheel to pause on a winning number, it was Hallelujah. If it played well and was in tune, it was wonderful. If it was a good Grand you literally played your head off. In fact the whole world was a wonderful place. Feeling sufficiently qualified to do so, I've attempted a book, or a Picture Album of Pianos. If ever you've put fingers on keys, took appraising looks at various pianos, or perhaps wondered at their many styles and appearances, you may recognize a familiar face.

Before getting into the album, however, an obvious question needs to be answered: "Why in the world wouldn't a few prior phone calls have eased the suspense?" In our defense, many were placed to persons having to do with unseen halls, rooms and such. A lot of them went like this (and we are making the call now): "And would you happen to know anything about the piano on your premises?" The polite inquirer was usually Kenny as he took care of most of the groundwork. He would continue. "Is it in fairly good shape, would you know if it's been tuned recently?"

The first thing to float back on the wires was nothing, only the sound of silence. Then a bewildered, "Well . . . I guess it's all right." Upon further pursuance the voice became hedgy and sometimes even testy. The ultimate of all the answers was, "Well . . . IT PLAYS!" Along with this came an implication of "what more do you want?" Social decency and self reminding of who and what we were forbade a myriad of appropriate answers.

When speaking with managers of halls, we found the going a bit improved. "To tell you the truth, I've never paid that much attention to the piano." At least he confirmed your suspicions. Another statement issued as a closing remark was often, "Everybody uses it." So there you were.

As we became better established we applied more aggressiveness. Sometimes we won. In our long-standing stays with the various clubs, people listened and tuning or repairs came to pass. One time a whole new piano came to pass! The ones already blessed with Grand pianos were more concerned as good upkeep was just good business.

There is a way out of playing Russian, or Piano Roulette. Play only in places where the resident piano has already been met and checked out. Hard to do when starting out. After the Forties we did progress into the greener pastures of Grand piano land, or at least excellent Spinets. It had a lot to do with prolonging the music making years. But if you live and make music long enough and manage to remain in some kind of circulation, piano gambling still lurks in the shadows.

As a note of optimism I should tell of one time when disbelief turned into great satisfaction, proving that all was not lost. In despair at what kind of piano the roulette wheel had dealt me, I had taken pen in hand and described my frustration to the lessees of a particular building. We had just followed one of our steady dance clubs into their new address. Lo and behold the piano, prominently displayed on a stage, besides looking like a beggar at a ball, lacked any quality. The letter was later described to me as having been "written in blood." Their reply read (in part):

"At our last board meeting Mr. Smith was authorized to look into the matter of procuring a Baby Grand piano for the hall. I am so sorry things happened as they have, but my hands have been tied until your letter was received and could be read by all the board members. It seems this is the only way to get action."

The fairytale ending is my walking into this attractive facility at our next scheduled date and being almost overcome with emotion. There stood an almost new Kimball Baby Grand! We shook hands and became immediate friends and I played the dance in a tidal wave of gratitude and renewed faith. Another letter was dispatched, one dripping with tears of thankfulness.

And now to my version of the Piano Families.

37

A Family Album of Pianos

The Attractive But Dull Family

These are the good looking strain whose personalities have a lot to be desired. Like some women, their beauty is only skin deep. After a short acquaintance their true character is revealed. No heart and very little soul. To extract three of four hours of spirited music from such conceited creatures requires shrewd manipulation of both hands and feet. Namely, mustering up a semblance of striking touch in combination with an overbalance of pedal. Even with this technique, what comes forth neither leaps or charges, leaving a vexed pianist to contemplate building a fire under it.

The Ugly Frog Family

Here is a clan whose appearance is so drab you dread even saying hello, much less make a test run over its keyboard. While the rest of the band is busily setting up, you're still standing at a respectful distance, rooted at the sight of what is to be your ally for the next several hours. There's no hiding the fact. It's an old buffetted-about veteran, whose castors have long ceased to roll in *any* direction, inviting hernias upon anyone complying with your wish to please place it about right there on the stage. As for the exterior finish, all the furniture polish in the world would not faze it. Tobacco-stained teeth in an uneven row look up unashamedly as if to say, "We were once white and shiny keys, but neglect has brought us down to this." Nothing to do but join the old warhorse in a sigh of defeat. But wait. As grudging fingers do a few trial runs something happens. Like a kiss from the princess, the ugly frog magically issues forth good clear tone. He becomes more handsome each minute with keys pressing easily and springing back with enthusiasm. He only needed the kindness of human touch. After cleaning up the keyboard, offering your apologies as you whisk and dab, you can plan on settling down for a pleasant evening with a once proud aristocrat. You'll find its heart, though forced to beat in a rundown neighborhood, is made of gold. One piano such as this was mine to value as a friend during a seven year stint with a Latin dance club. First revulsion was replaced by respect and wonder. Though contrary to the fairy tale by not regaining an outer princely look it gave out an honest face each time paper towels and soap were applied. Removal of the front panel, when necessary, uncovered a still bright and shiny innerworks. Etched in an upper corner like an epitaph were the following words: "This Piano Was Manufactured by The Jacobs Co. It Is the Finest Instrument Possible To Make." To which I added a fervent AMEN.

The Insipid Family

What's frightening about this clan is their numbers and apparent disregard for planned parenthood. Like the proverbial bad penny, it keeps showing up. Upon outward glance it bodes neither evil nor good and can easily be walked by. To me theirs was a sorrowful lot, for I imagined few of the Insipids had ever known much loving care. One can only surmise the owners either inherited them as a piece of furniture, or bought during a full moon. A lack of breeding slyly unravels, a bit at a time. The keys are lacking in backbone, and fingers tend to linger on their putty-like surfaces of milky white. One thing is clear. Pride was not the manufacturer's aim, which is probably the primary cause of the whole product not giving a tinker's damn. Warning! This piano's "I-don't-care attitude" is contagious.

The Gargoyles

Thankfully, the smallest of families, and utterly impossible to forget. When the roulette wheel points on a gargoyle, it's almost fatal. It happened to me about three or four times, each one an eternity of despair in which I wallowed and bewailed my fate. You may as well be trapped in the claws of a monster since their size and weight would intimidate an Army Search & Destroy Unit. A true gargoyle bares several octaves of jagged edged keys, who like vampires eagerly await the taste of blood . . . yours. The music rack erratically snaps shut into your face, or collapses at the weight of a whole sheet of music. Due to the general progress of civilization, the species is almost extinct now. Who would create such weighty material in these days of casual house moves and lighter construction? Socially speaking, a member of this group of instruments has all the immediate charm of a tawdry, belligerent character with tainted breath. To know a gargoyle is not to love one, though I have worked myself to the point of pitying their plight. After forced hours of togetherness, both of you sign a pledge of mutual hostility.

The Kaput Family

If only these folks showed their true colors and flew a "Distressed Merchandise" flag, avoidance would be simpler. It is, after all, your own fault for not giving this piano a more thorough run that included the pressing down of each key. Doesn't matter if your oversight was neglect of innocence. Appearances can deceive, as is the case when each and every key seemed to be sitting up nicely at first scan. Concealed within their ranks are a few (and maybe more if it's damp weather) who have no intention at all of jumping to attention when struck. After too many times of falling into this booby trap, even your fingers get unhappy with your dumb oversights and seem to turn against you. The Kaput's prime special is its sleeping giant trait of the non-stop ringing key. It thrives on the element of surprise by throwing you this jolt in the very middle of a melodic passage, and then over-riding all else for the following ten measures. Like Chinese torture, it can break your spirit. Since you can't walk off the job, you stay.

And now away from the Kaput's keyboards to another hidden bomb, the pedals, so vital to smoothness and expression. Thank heavens malfunctions here are rare, but when it strikes, the party is over. You can live with a pedal promising to groan and squawk with each toe touch, but it is hell upon earth when one actually gives up the ghost. Sagging onto the floor prone and lifeless, it spells Doomsday to all expertise and class. Each note, instead of floating out into the atmosphere on wings, is aborted before takeoff in an instant choking and dying thud. The effect is that of putting a monstrous period after each and every note.

Irish Piano Clans

Meeting foreign pianos in Ireland was like a lesson in singing "Amazing Grace" with bowed head. I had not expected much and for once had not made my preconceived notions public. This was Irish luck for me, as I'd have found myself eating humble pie each time I sat down to play. Traveling along as music making guests of our son, Kenny Jr. (long since having become a Jesuit priest), Kenny and I played every type of music at every sort of stop during a two week Irish Pilgrimage. To my unending delight not one Insipid, Gargoyle or Kaput piano offered itself as the available instrument on the varied premises. Considering such contrasts as Killarney's "Great Southern Hotel" with a mirror-bright marvelous Grand, to others in like keeping, to the well kept and excellent uprights of wayside Inns and Pubs, there was nothing to do but smile and be impressed . . . and play. In my book, Irish eyes may be famous for more than their radiating smiles, but also for the loving and caring way they look upon their pianos.

The Loverlies Family

Well tuned and gracious pianos do exist within commercial territory. Not only in the plushier spots but often just standing by in an ordinary locale. Like driving a Rolls-Royce, exposure to them converts the player into a devotee, and sharpens his criticism of lesser and undistinguished models. To be truthful, most of the Loverlies are Grands with blue-blooded lineage, born into family names such as Steinway, Baldwin, Kimball, Wurlitzer and the Chickering, to name a few. Other fine specimens can be found in smaller or Baby Grands, some Spinets and, strange to say, good old solid uprights.

I will admit to a noticeable transformation when working on a fine Grand. My dress, which was often long and within the bounds of "evenish," became a high fashion gown that rippled and flowed, my arms took on more gracefulness and fingers ran away as if waxed. Voila . . . it was Magic! At times like this (and other sessions when we played within that mythical aura of musical ambience), my whole self sings "This Is A Lovely Way To Spend An Evening" and then continues the lyrics, "can't think of anything I'd rather do."

Adjuncts to the foregoing should not be dismissed lightly. Trivial as it may sound, what's beneath a pianist of the sit down and play type (stand up style rarely the norm in my era) deserves a place in this section. In the realm of commercially used pianos, the divorce rate between originally wedded piano and a seat thereto is alarmingly high. When wind-up stools with ornate glass clawfeet became a gleam in collector's eyes, many a wedded pair became separated. Even the less coveted piano benches were involved in the breakups. Where they went is a moot question, unless their identities were changed to that of a new fashion coffee table. What now stands in the stead of departed mates is a motley family of assorted dining table chairs and the ultimate insult to injury, the metal folding chair. They can all be summed up in one fell swoop— none offer proper heighth for good or even comfortable leverage at any given keyboard.

Not to forget is to what follows naturally—the posteriors forced into hours of intimate contact with these maverick and misplaced pieces of furniture. Their varied coverings and surfaces ranged from sticky leather to old prickly plush, and again the downright unfriendliness of cold metal. One time when an old and handsome cane-bottomed chair was kindly proffered as a well intentioned substitute for the missing piano chair only a fat pillow prevented an acquisition of matching imprints. A like incident involved the serious-faced man who, in a quick look around for a good chair to bring up on the stage for the pianist, struggled forward with an armchair. When all else fails and nothing can be dredged up in the form of a seat, there is a last resort. I'm sure I'm not the only one who has played a job seated upon a stiff instrument case or two, teetering across an impossibly low seat.

When out at large in strange piano territory and happily coming upon the classic scene of a piano in loving company with its original spouse, I am sufficiently moved to pause in a silent moment of gratefulness. My faith in old fashioned security and principle becomes restored.

38

Important Seasonings

Outside of actual travel, which could not be indulged in until later years, nowhere could we have had a better insight into other country's characteristics than we had right in Tacoma. Music and fortunate timing were the promoters. Though ethnic social dancing still exists, I don't believe it matches the flourishing scale of the Forties. The cleaving was a bit stronger then and weekly or monthly scheduled dancing took first place in their entertainment picture.

Luckily, our little open calendar in the '30's stood ready to receive some generous dashes of unaccustomed flavors. For me German traits were not strange, but German style fun nights and dancing events were, and rightly enough this was our first seasoning. Others, reading like a League of Nations, followed, with Scandinavians, Slavonians, Swiss (rare for they maintained their own group complete with yodelers), Croations, Lithuanians, Scotch and one Japanese formal dinner dance. Whoops . . . I forgot Italian weddings!

Thumbnail impressions not destined for a Social Studies book and viewed from a piano are as follows:

Swiss Dances . . . . Filled with indomitable energy, ruddy cheeks, high voices and an unknown fatigue factor.

Japanese Dance . . . . Exquisite politeness, shining faces and utmost regard for the parental guests and chaperones.

Polish, Slavonian . . . . . . Most begin in low gear before shifting to
& Lithuanian powerful overdrive with aroma of hearty food pervading.

Scotch (Bobbie Burns Concert & Dance)   Real patriotic fervor that's catching . . . Bagpipes to love with tears and stout drafts of whiskey.

Italian Weddings. . . . . . . Never a letdown. Spontaneous outbursts of romantic music, loads of flowers whose perfume must blend with aromatic food and the unforgettable "Tarantella."

German & Scandinavian Covered in depth later due to more exposure.

Always at hand and frequently resorted to was Green Book's precious pages, allowing us that personal touch. Not to have played for any of the "old country" people would have left us with a limited diet and a gaping hole in our musical bag.

39
Musical Kaffee Klatch

"Undt ve vant you should play r-r-r-right after the kaffee time. Schust for about an hour or so, undt den dey all go home." The time was in the early Thirties when beggars were not choosers. My brother Hans and I had joined the Saengerbund chorus in Tacoma, due largely to our German heritage and our mutual need of ethnic roots and ties. Many of the older members had either known or been patients of our doctor father some years back. Once a month the chorus, under the direction of Friederich Kloepper, performed at a Family Evening held in an historic Tacoma Avenue building, known as Fraternity Hall. Inside its three spacious floors were thousands of board feet of lumber, turned into ornate woodwork, flooring and doors that led into numerous separate halls whose airs were laden with the heaviness of closed doors and successive coatings of varnish.

Following the singing program, a local German baker (a Mr. Kuhnert) provided and presided over long pans of Streusel-encrusted coffee cakes. Moderately sized pieces were served with the club's Kaffee (included in a nominal admittance fee), after which the remaining hour or more was filled with dancing. Ours was the assignment of "making the muzzik."

The Committee (ever present in club or lodge affairs) was made up of German florists, jewelers and other merchants, each one endowed with a sparing hand. Their offer: They would be willing to pay me, and three others of my choice, for an exact one and a half hour of music. "Let us see . . . at vun dollar and a haff an hour (their rate) that makes chust exectly $2.25 apiece." The kaffee and kuchen were thrown into the bargain. As I said, beggars were not choosers. Another option was added. That of sitting through their program, which we frequently did as my brother still sang with them and the whole performance was of high quality as a whole, with many excellent voices, talented direction and choice of material.

Our inevitable welcome, this after having all scaled two inside flights of wooden stairs, laden to the hilt, was being brought to an abrupt halt at the hall's entrance door. Sitting squarely at the side of the door was an officious appearing ticket man. The serious responsibility of his admitting four people, none of them paying the small charge required, sent him to a pompous authority act worthy of a German Depot Meister. The obvious evidence standing before him of four huffing and puffing bodies, each with an arm-clutch of musical gear, did little to dismiss his suspicions. Searching glances, after all they could be imposters, and then a dubious wave of his hand to the inner hall, a gesture of one who had let go of all judgment and prudence. Musician's Union where were you then?

Once past Checkpoint Charlie, it became all German family atmosphere. All in all the evening was one of enjoyment, ambience and friendliness. The actual music playing was easy sailing. Once each night we broke into "Trink, Trink, Brüderlein Trink," a traditional brotherly drinking song. One chorus was never enough. Voice after stentorian voice joined in a thunderous imitation of a Heidelberg Bier Garten and lasted till lungs and legs gave way. All we had to do was provide a token background and sit back and absorb the Teutonic roar. In a small way it atoned for the salary.

Interruptions and complete cessation of music in mid-air was as frequent as if we were playing during the Blitz air-raids of London. And like the Londoners, we never knew when. Maybe in the middle of "Around the Corner" (very popular then) or a dreamy waltz. They were not particular. All of a sudden a Saengerbunder would mount the high stage with frantic arm-waving, his cheeks fanned into apoplectic red. "Schtop the muzzik . . . Schtop the muzzik," he would shout. He was obviously chosen for this function as his volume even surpassed normal German decibels (no microphones yet). He and the ticket-master seemed to be two of a kind.

After achieving a reasonable silence and the whole crowd had ground down to a halt (a feat of *any* kind of dance), he would drop his bomb: "VUN EAR-R-R-R-INK HASS BEEN FOUNDT . . . I HAFF IT HERE IN MY HANDT." And he would dangle one arm above the crowd, displaying the tiny earring. "IFF SCHEE CAN IDENTIFY IT, SCHEE CAN HAFF IT." Again, he took no chances for any skullduggery. Other interruptions of equal or less importance erupted quite regularly. Each and every one demanded the same treatment and after the first evening, in which we all had suspected at least a fire alarm, we took them as they came. Incidentally, the Saengerbund gave me my one claim to fame as the program folder listed the music thusly: "Ilse Reitz & Her Orchestra." When I saw it in formal print on dimpled paper for their impressive Spring concert held in a downtown hall (and usually a sell-out among Tacomans), I felt quite important. In fact I still have a copy.

We were with them for nearly two years of warm hearted people, good Streusel kuchen and countless choruses of walloping "Trink-Trink," and most of all for me, a feeling of belonging. It was only the first of the many ethnic experiences still lying in wait.

40

The Scandinavian Score

Countless times in early childhood, when Tacoma's Kay Street was a familiar area, I had walked by an old doorway whose overhead lettering read, "Valhalla Hall." An odd name such as this naturally led me to wonder what kind of things took place upstairs. It was not till years later in the Fifties when I was to see for myself. After two seasons, the name Valhalla had a most distinct meaning.

During a lull in the Fifties, Kenny and I joined an already set-up regime. In short, we filled in for two musicians of a group who had chosen to go elsewhere. Buildingwise the Valhalla Hall had much in common with Fraternity Hall, where we had played for the German Seangerbund group. Both were steeped in an odor a bit on the musty side, and enough varnished woodwork for a whole block of houses. The leader who hired us was an enigmatic and tireless accordionist rightly named, Ragnar Saldin (last name accented on last syllable). The dancers seemed to emulate his same characteristics by exhibiting an endurance beyond anything I had seen up to this point. Ragnar backed himself up by a dry-witted and casual drummer known as Bill Barrett. After our first hour of the debut night we knew for certain Ragnar was the apple of every dancing Scandinavian's eye. Ours was but to fit in, roll up our sleeves and think Nordic!

With the opening flourishing run on Saldin's accordion (he was showy), the descendants of Leif Ericson leaped to the dance floor as if shot from a cannon. The high point of each dance occurred when the magic of a particular Swedish waltz threw them all into abandoned joy with whirl upon whirl. The effect of this tune was impossible to forget.

157

Even in later years, whenever I played it at a nursing home, I could see the lights come on in Nordic faces. More than once older women would dance together briefly in a reliving of happier days. Ragnar did not lack for stage presence either, which added fuel to their fire. Posting himself on the very edge of the high stage he would begin the opening bars of "Vienni Su," a sentimental and slower waltz of definite Swedish origin. As the dancers waltzed by he literally became a part of them, swinging and playing his chromatic Accordion over their heads, the repeated arpeggio notes flying beneath his fingers. Encores were inevitable. Somewhere near mid-evening the second fuse was lighted. The Hambo dance was on tap. Here is where the experts were separated from the crowd, who all stood aside graciously to watch and applaud. How we loved the dips and half-circle swoops in which the feminine partner is momentarily airborne. We learned to neatly accent the second beat so necessary in this gymnastic feat and somehow got ourselves into the swing of this event. But we were not the pure thing. Musically rooted blood is also thicker than water and we knew full well we could never duplicate the bone-felt tempo, without Ragnar to prop us up.

We remained on a monthly basis for about two years. Long enough to see the phasing out of Valhalla dancing, due to many circumstances such as Ragnar's commute from Seattle and the reluctance of younger Nordics to keep the old boat afloat. During our stay short the incursion of pop dances varied the format and was no doubt the reason we were hired. Saldin's accordion did a creditable job on the Continental tunes of the Forties such as "The Third Man Theme," but he did rely on us for more jazzy numbers. For me it served as an exercise in sight reading again. Nowhere are more notes crammed into one measure than a Schottische or Polka, and I was not content to just fill in with chords. I liked to race notes with Saldin. Actually the piano was excess baggage; even Kenny's strident Banjo became second fiddle. We were only a trimming.

Prior to New Year's Eve (our first with Ragnar), Bill Barrett would intimidate me with: "Wait till you play a New Year's Eve here. The women throw their little kids down from the balcony!" While this never happened, the Valhalla nights were colorful enough just as they were.

41

Music with Strangers

Absence often makes a music leader's heart grow fonder. Fonder of the musician who for some reason cannot play an accepted engagement. As soon as the "can't make it" news surfaces, the action begins. What ensues is a telephone marathon (in busy seasons). Each succeeding "Gee, I'm sorry but I'm already busy that night" lessens the demands on his proficiency and preferences begin to drop a notch at a time. Obviously, within larger bands a gap is not so acute, but in a tightly knit combo, an absence can bode any number of dramas. Some are fairly smooth going with happy endings while others can drum upon a nerve-tingling evening.

Luckily for us, sickness rarely intervened within the group. But we had loopholes. With Al Meddaugh on top of the Seattle Local's list as trumpet man to call for special stage bands for backing up traveling big-name performers, he was at times unavailable to us. Morry's no-shows (fewer thank goodness) ran from being needed in a scheduled big band concert or *any* infringement on his annual July fly-fishing sabbatical in Montana. Fortunately, our Local's "At Large" list was fairly dependable, but on peak occasions even this well could run dry. Nail biting time came next. One note: Tact and diplomacy must come to the fore when casting about for help. It is not smart musical etiquette to phone musicians on Saturday nights (working ones that is), either for socializing or possible hiring. The rank implication of your assuming him to be at home, instead of out tootling somewhere, is the first faux pas. The second is that it's you who are exposing his nakedness. Therefore running down a replacement musician can be as complicated as the Act of God, or whatever created the vacancy in the first place.

Looking at both sides, when caller and callee are unacquainted the conversation goes like this: Caller hopes he's not hired someone capable of putting four square corners on his well rounded group. The callee wonders if he's committed himself to a combo whose measurements are precisely squared already! "Square" in our days suggested a corn-pone or stilted style.

Without fear of lawsuits and with relatively few evenings spent working with dubious replacements, I think them sufficient to foster a few observations. They are to be read with tongue in cheek and as being licensed into print by a feminine slanted and imaginative mind.

Bless the musician who comes to your rescue carrying along his own list of best bets to play during the evening. They usually are numbers he does well and serve as wonderful get-acquainted starters.

Beware the horn player who arrives carrying shiny and reputable instrument cases. He then makes polite inquiries, and without further ado steps smartly to a backstage corner and blows enough scales to warm up Sousa's band. He often plays with the verve of vanilla pudding. You've less concern if he just tootles away aimlessly on a few brief passages from one of his favorite tunes.

Be forewarned about the player who packs in his own music copies, offering to share them with all. Though you may be a whiz at sight reading, most of these little gems turn out to be mavericks, written in keys direly needing quick transposing. The paper they're written on is without body, flying away at a deep breath, and the size of print used is for microscopic purposes only.

Do not let faint heart overtake you if your fill-in musician's entry is similar to this: It has been a notably balmy and dry day with not a cloud in the sky, but he wanders onto the scene wearing a bona fide raincoat, perhaps of advanced age. Don't twitch if he rolls it up into a limp wad and proceeds to toss it out of sight among the props. And then he opens a scarred and much brunted case. The first escaping fumes warn you to keep a respectable distance. He usually fits in like a glove.

Really sit back and relax should your to-the-rescue horn player be able to execute the following: Give another player a spoken cue in mid-music, which somehow emanates from the only unoccupied corner of his lips. If he can do this without distortion or breaking of meter, he's a pro.

As a rule Bass players could be counted on as leaning close to a zany margin. A condition possibly brought on by the comparative dullness of their necessary contribution. After amplification, wirings and fuses, and musical technology caused them to wheel in skyscraper stacks of gear, their characters underwent noticeable change.

Waiting for a last minute and unrecognized pianist. At this piece of drama I am at an obvious loss to give a report. From what I've heard, this is when doubting heads suddenly bow and solemnly mumble, "Our Father, which art in Heaven." All modesty has not left me in quoting the above; it's just that bona fide pianists (before electronic keyboards and such) were not in large supply. I should add the fact that modesty is not necessarily a musician's chief virtue.

One more tip, brought into focus by our longtime musical accomplice, Morry Kenton. It was his first night at the Yacht Club and he had just skirted between many tables of seated club members, all ready to dance. He stepped up onto our kitty-corner bandstand and I imagine we all gave each other that momentary first glance. As yet we had not met Morry beyond telephone calls wherein arrangements had been agreed upon for him to take over the sax spot in our group, and a general checking of music levels had been made at either end. As he stepped on the stand, Kenny in his characteristic, affable manner paused with his drum assembling and offered an outstretched hand. Morry, never changing his expression said in an undertone, "Let's not shake hands up here now and do introductions—it could make the crowd uneasy!" We realized his point immediately. The more it looked like we were an acquainted and cohesive group the better . . . and we never forgot it.

42

What Is Musical Piety?

Like the sweet little country girl in the musical "Oklahoma" who laments, "I'm Just a Girl Who Can't Say No," the musician with the same problem is open to even greater frustrations than she. Finding that elusive middle path that lies between conscience and credence in the music work world is just as difficult as elsewhere. With the advent of the Musician's Performance Trust Fund, an endowment which after a bit of extra paper work repays the musician for services at approved locales, the incidences of having to issue callous sounding "NOs" fell to a much lower level. Understandably the funded locales are in the realm of service hospitals, nursing homes, mental institutions, etc. However for those years preceding this boon, it wasn't hard to find yourself frequently out on a limb.

How could a deaf ear be turned to, "Could you p—l—e—a—s—e come and play for our patients . . . it means so much to them." Or, "We're an entirely charitable organization and all we're asking for is your donation of some music to make our drive go over the top." Another more bargain-like plea went, "All you have to do is make a little music . . . we'll see you get a good dinner and have a fun time." And the one with a veiled reminder thrown in, "Business has been slow so we're putting on a dance to be sponsored by our Merchant's Association. We'd appreciate if you'd help out. We can't pay much but it's all for a good cause . . . we all live in the same town, you know." Decisions were even tougher when harried school principals (before resident rockbands) used to phone: "The kids are dying to put on a nice formal dance and of course you're aware our district just does not have the funds to afford any big outlay." Even if *you* were prompted enough to give in, the job of pursuading fellow musicians was yet another hurdle.

Should St. Peter be impressed with a high count of volunteered music hours, our double entry through the pearly gates stands a good chance. If still found wanting, I will blow my own horn and add hours of Ladies' Luncheons, Garden Clubs and other such fancy but non-paying fripperies. And I'd toss in the five years of providing a weekly music hour at the Orting Old Soldier's Home, which largesse was of my own making. On second thought, these five years may not apply, since they gave back by furnishing me insight into retired veterans' lives, loves, their heartaches and, believe it or not, a whole new world of humor and a new set of friendships. After five years I felt sure I had enough to write a book.

In the event St. Peter looks me straight in the eye with, "And when you gave freely of your musical talents, did you offer it with a heart filled with love and no thought of recompense?" "Well," would be my stuttering reply, "I can remember a street dance where my heart was not joyous and I was filled with ill will for the merchants who set us upon a makeshift stage no insurance policy would ever cover, and the wind blew the music back at the buildings instead of out into the street, forcing us to play in coats and scarves." "And one time," I would blubber on, "Out at Madigan Service Hospital during the Korean War I felt no love . . . just stark fear.

"In company with two Grey Ladies I was to cheer patients in an off-limits Ward, where burly orderlies locked the heavy doors behind us and everything looked either padded or metallic, and I was cautioned to choose my music carefully (this last with unspoken explanation of why a low profile was preferred)." Two weeks later the same patient who had cut the cake at refreshment time on the night of my debut ran amok with a butcher knife, drawing some blood before being restrained.

Then if St. Peter said, "That's not enough," I could reach deeper into the bag, for never would I leave it thus and omit the many, many good times when my heart all but overflowed with my love of playing music for people in instances where no paycheck was awaiting me after the last chord. Actually, as I consider and think of the many musicians we've talked with, joined notes with, or read and heard about, I get a confident feeling we'll all make it through the upper gates.

43

Cold Cuts

If ever a musician requires First Aid, it's after his musical soul has been cut to the quick. Without a doubt, a back-up supply of good humor is the best antidote. Be the cut delivered tactfully or radically, your good nature will serve as an astringent against prolonged bleeding. The unromantic truth of my piano offerings not being *everyone's* cup of tea drew blood almost immediately. I don't ever remember brimming over with laughter about it. Lots of them are thankfully forgiven or else forgotten. So what if people completely disregarded your self-approved original innovation? Or the ones that walked out in groups without a backward glance, while the whole band was playing at their very best. Others among the superficial wounds are the certain folk who had danced half an evening to your music, danced repeatedly right before your eyes, and then failed to even recognize you at intermission time? Morry's pithy answer to their shortsightedness was: "If I ever have to go incognito, I'd just sit and play in a band. No one would ever identify me later." Surface scratchers are the exhilarated dancers who can breathlessly rush up to the stand immediately after your last well executed touch on the likes of something tasty as "Stella By Starlight," or the melodious "Skylark." Your mind is already forming gracious phrases and modest "thankyous," which you'll accompany with a benign smile as your admirer showers kudos upon you. And then your little dream ends abruptly as the emissary blurts out with great urgency, "Can you play 'Alley-cat' next?"

Two rather personal cuts that still bring a smile are worth noting here. The first one I consider a classic of conciseness. In much the same fashion as the old after-dinner routine of adolescent years when I had been asked to "sit down and play while we clear the dishes," I had been asked the same after a community Potluck. This one was fairly rife with retirees and of course I had plenty of ammunition for their favorites. "You play and we'll clear the tables . . . it'll make our job more enjoyable." Still quick to pick up on such bargains, I lost no time in getting to their piano. I confidently sailed through many familiar and loved Green Book numbers, threw in a dash of Viennese waltzes and the ladies' apron strings fairly flapped to the beat. When I deemed it time to put a period on the little cleanup concert, I ended with the usual decisive and heavy chords of most Strauss waltzes. How this old gal timed it I'll never know. In split-second timing she got her words out into the open air, exactly within that tick of time that precedes an oncoming applause. It came from the direction of a cornered clutch of diehard card players. They had already picked up and studied the fan of cards in their hands, while others were still laying aside knives and forks. Loud and clear with a clearly marked trace of picque came the words: "I BID SIX HEARTS." She didn't need a mike and followed her irritation with a slanted look in my direction that said, "and it's about time." For some reason it hit my funny bone right on, erasing the lack of her appreciation for my thoughtfully chosen measures to please this casserole crowd.

The other incident proves the old axiom of never being a star in your home town, or your own family. This one took place in daughter Arlene's Sun Valley home and came from our then ten your old grandson, Andrew. Seeing him in the rare position of sitting on the davenport, in a listening attitude while I was playing their piano, had me positively beaming. Now was the time to seize an opportunity and expose him to something beyond junk music. Despite the ever present comic book lying upon his lap, he was definitely paying attention. Hoping to capture some value points in his young eyes, I had been running through "The Minute Waltz" as fast as I could and still not take the turns too quickly. I went into a warm glow when after the last tinkling note Andrew requested: "Play it again Grandma." Why I do believe, I said to myself, he's really recognizing some of the better things. Or perhaps my telling him the title had sparkled his interest. I turned about face on the piano stool looking for Andrew's look of approval, only to see him looking down intently at his wrist watch. "Gee Grandma," he gloated, "You didn't make it—that last time it took you a minute and *twelve* seconds!"

44

Some Odd Balls

In a world filled with such an infinite variety of people, it is entirely possible that some representatives from the group referred to as "fringies" are going to surface as chairman or members of a dance committee. Therefore it follows that somewhere during a dance musician's calling he will find himself seated up front supplying the music while peering down onto a dance-floor with great wonderment at the comedy of errors unfolding before him.

Once, and once only, we were hired to play a club dance where only two couples danced—briefly! Not adverse to adding new dancers to our list, we had taken the job though the name "Holidy Club" did not ring a bell for any of us. The place was also unfamiliar to Kenny and me as these people had obtained the old Tacoma Tennis Club for the evening, which was then housed in a large and charming old historic residence. It was an early October evening and a late Fall rain slanted against our headlights as we stared intently through a streaming windshield trying to spy something resembling an entrance road to the grounds. After a fruitless circling of heavily landscaped and treed blocks we took a wild chance by plunging the car through an unobtrusive gap in a tall bushy hedge, hoping not to land in a private yard. Luckily we emerged on a narrow paved roadway leading to the clubhouse. Once inside we were politely ushered into what looked like an early American parlor, complete with white brick fireplace, white wainscoting and flowery papered walls. With no further ado our greeter left for a room just across the hall, but out of our immediate view. Gay flowers and ribbons bespoke a merrymaking mood and a pleasant evening loomed before us. Good fellows that we were, four of us literally wedged ourselves into the fireplace and each other's laps, so as to give a fair amount of parlor space to the dancers. But where were they, we asked each other after three or four sets had only produced one or two lackadaisical couples from across the way. We rallied ourselves with, "Probably just slow to get going . . . doing a lot of talking" and "wait 'till they decide to dance, then they won't want to quit, we'll *have* to make up for lost time then. Oh well, we'll just keep vamping 'till ready." Amazement grew as time went on and not another human being crossed the threshold into our lonely parlor. Oh yes, the people were still in residence, we could catch bits and pieces of their laughter and banter. Did the two couples who had risked dancing soon after we began playing report it to be something less than desirable? Pangs of desertion beset us as it became increasingly apparent the entire club was choosing to remain in their own bailiwick with not even a twinge of curiosity as to who or what made the music possible. Only the thin theory of our music floating into the general atmosphere and possibly providing an added touch kept us from becoming stripped from our ego and lapsing into a combined morose state.

I can't remember just how many hours we hung on, but I do know it was not a laughing matter—yet. I can still see the striking lady who sauntered into our room soon after we'd decided to just fold our tents and quit. Like a fashion model in her beautiful white satined slither-eryness, she glided up to the fireplace, placed a crisp white envelope upon the mantel, bestowed a thankful but careful smile, uttered a sweet thankyou and flowed back from whence she came. For once no one thought of a remark of any kind, at least not at the moment. There just wasn't anything appropriate to say and we must have looked like four disgruntled Cinderellas huddling up against the fireplace. The check within the envelope neatly written with a pacifying amount on the dotted line, was in our combined opinion, the only thing that made any sense in the whole dance. Or was it a dance?

On another occasion, over a quick early supper, with one eye to the clock, we found a minute to think outloud. "Wonder what we're getting into tonight?" was our shared question. An undue note of uncertainty was justified as a few hours hence we'd be out in the middle of Puget Sound playing for a dance! Kenny had been contacted far in advance by a government official who seemed most happy to hire us for what he clearly termed would be a staff dance. When the locale entered their discussions Kenny almost backed away. "Getting there," he was ex- plaining to me as he hung up the phone, will be involved and take a lot of our time." I agreed when I heard the dance would take place at the Federal Penitentiary on McNeil Island. "But I think we should do it," he went on, "we'll even get a boat ride in the deal."

A pleasant nervousness hurried my heartbeat when a month later, Morry Kenton, Kenny and I stood alongside an official grey launch idling away at the 6th Avenue dock. Now that we were actually about to embark I felt like a cross between a hesitant sightseer and a dubious musician. McNeil Island and "The Pen," as it was called years ago by area residents, had been a familiar term since childhood, always evok- ing a fear in one's breast like no other. Only its watery seclusion kept this forbidding island at a comfortable distance, and bird's eye views from a Longbranch ferry to Aunt Lottie's years ago were close enough to boast you'd seen it.

With the first lap of the trip (the drive from Puyallup to Steilacoom) behind us, all was going as planned. Our host (the telephone voice) virtually gathered us under his federal wings as soon as introductions were made. "The men will load all your gear into the boat . . . just step on board and make yourselves comfortable. Isn't this a nice spring evening?" From then on we did not touch nor handle a single piece of our luggage till we were ready to play. Whether or if it was examined, I do not know.

Off we chugged at a fair clip on a Federal Prison Launch, carrying about a dozen of "the men," our polite leader and three unsuspecting musicians. Relentless rotating beams from high watchtower turrets were just beginning to light up a fading twilight. We were now in waters distinctly marked "No Trespassing," sidling across the fronts of several long docks. Everything loomed up into life-sized power and strength. We watched again as our things were quickly stowed into the rear of a waiting prison bus. To me the pre-arranging almost suggested we march ourselves to our seats, precisely and correctly. Gears were ground and shifted as the uncrowded large bus, only occupied now by the chaperone and the three of us, delivered us from shore level to the upper regions. Unconciously there is a quickening of pulse at the sight of massive buildings and an immensity of grey filling all visible space, and nowhere a sign of human life, just grey monotony. Next the driver halted briefly at another set of gates, where a few words were exchanged, and for one moment the entire bus interior was caught in one of the scanning tower beams and we seemed almost ablaze. Visible outlines of mounted guns marked each wall, a constant vigil against anyone's plans to slip away. However, Kenny and I could still recall Roy Gardner's miraculous escape in the '20's, and his daring swim through the cold and rough currents to freedom.

"The staff dance," our man was explaining, "will be held in the building to your right. It's our recreation hall." He went on despite my audible sigh of relief, "The folks are all ready for you." You couldn't mistake the accenting of "staff" each time. Was it to reassure apprehensive minds? Following on his heels we trooped up a set of broad steps to a long open veranda. With shining white siding and bright sets of patio chairs on the porch, the scene stood out like a millionaire's country lodge amid all the somberness. Once inside the mood was summer cottagey with lots of windows and wicker pieces pleasantly pillowed in flowered chintzes. Staff wives babbled and fussed over flowers, punch bowls and such, but we'd not be setting up here. Up another short stairway and then we were home. I did a quick appraisal of the piano.

We were to find out this was of minor importance tonight. All the instrument cases and drum regalia, as I looked about, had been carefully set upon the stage, just waiting for us. How strange it was.

And what could they do for us? Another man was seeing to our needs now. "If you could," was my request, "I'd much appreciate a pillow to bring this chair up to a better level." He vanished as if issued a top command. His return was not so swift. Surely there must be an available pillow in this large place, but it was time to fire off, low chair or not. Just then he reappeared with not one, but an armload of cushions under his chin. Didn't those pillow coverings look very similar to the ones on the downstairs rockers? When I noticed one or two heavy threads still dangling from the corners of them, putting two and two together produced a comical picture of his bodily uprooting them anyway after discovering too late they were much attached to their chairs. Someone was going to be unhappy! "Thought I'd bring a few so you could try them on for size," he smilingly offered. Shades of the old fairytale of "The Princess and the Pea." I chose one at random and quickly pounced upon it before Morry would have the perfect opening to chant one of his favorites, "I never saw a piano player who took so much time to settle. Reminds me of a dog making his bed." We were off, piano pointed correctly and pillow in place. Complimentary remarks came our way right after the first set and the many happy faces and feet effected a relaxed evening of Staff dancing ahead.

"Could we please clear the floor for just a minute," said a voice of a pleasant fellow on the sidelines. The music dutifully stopped, whereupon he began to march himself forth and back across the floor, briskly scattering the contents of an open carton. He was a living symbol of the old Kansas farmer out seeding his field. "Okay," he announced happily, "let the dance proceed." Which it did, for about two minutes, or as long as it took each pair of shuffling feet to stir up an alarming pall of powdery film into every square inch of space. It was like an Oklahoma dust storm. Morry was wailing, "Did you see what that clown was pouring on the floor? That was a box of 'DUZ'—you know, that awful new and strong detergent!" While he was predicting his own imminent sinus attack, a great chorus of staccato sneezes began to hit the air. Those who weren't sneezing were wheezing as handkerchieves, Kleenex and even shirtsleeves saw hasty action. The overall mopping of tear-filled eyes gave off a general appearance of a sudden and sad distress having taken place.

"Please," came the same voice, "we'll have to clear the floor again." But no one was left to accept his advisory, the dancers having taken to the steps as fast as they could. "Please leave the room," he went on

anyway, "we'll have to open some windows and do some sweeping."
We were right on the heels of mass retreat of snifflers and were amazed
at what was taking place below. Like volunteer firemen trained for
emergencies, the kitchen crew answered the alert and sprang into
feeding the dispossessed dancers. Trays of attractive food and all the
trimmings hit the tables before you could say Jack Robinson. Meanwhile we did some briefing. Should we count this as a regular intermission break, normally reserved for a later hour?

Once more we bravely went back to music on what, with a 5:00
o'clock departure from home, was becoming a long evening. The traces
of soap fumes still in the air were as nothing to what had preceded, and
the evening had resumed on a swept but still grainy floor. We had been
offering several peppy numbers and deemed this a good time to slow up
and do a waltz set, only to see the voice of doom approaching—what
now? He took the mike, "Better choose your partners, it's that time
again." What time again? The huge black hands of the institutional
clock on the wall pointed to 10:45. We couldn't believe the next sen-
tence: "This will be the Goodnight Waltz"! Why, we'd hardly gotten
into the swing of things yet, but no one registered complaint for they
knew what we did not. An eleven o'clock curfew, strictly enforced, was
the law of the island. Apparently staff people do not argue the point.

Departure was a reverse of our earlier trip, save for now being
attended to by only the crew. I reassured myself they were to be trusted.
The stop and go tempo of the shortest, sneeziest dance ever, had for the
time being put a halt on my imagination. Forgotten temporarily were
outbreaks, dramatic violence or anything else that might take place
right while we were on the island. Again we chose to ride out on the
deck as the grey launch shuttled us back to our own world. Arcs of light
were still cutting into the night breezes of Puget Sound, as I held a scarf
to my head and pondered the odd happenings of a prison staff dance.
When these men motored back across the waters to their isolated
island, would they be sleeping in better beds than those less privileged?
And what about the dangerous criminals in solitary confinement? And
why did lawbreakers and the islands for them like this have to be? Were
the inmates victims of bad luck or what might have brought them to
such a sad level of living?

As before, we carried nothing down to the boat. By the time we
stepped off on the wooden planked dock at Steilacoom again, the
prow's searchlights shone upon our baggage, all standing in wait. Good-
nights were exchanged, whereupon the busy launch pointed back to its
home berth. As for us still facing some road travel yet, we were well

armed with conversation to help speed us along. With the dance ending so abruptly, getting home time would be near regular dancenight's hours.

I don't believe we lost any sleep over accepting a moderately generous check for the brief amount of music performed. After all, they had sought us out and as almost everyone rationalizes, it was government money instead of having to come from civilians' pockets. By today's evaluations of job conditions, we had played in a "Hazardous Environmental Atmosphere." KERCHEW!

After playing away seventeen consecutive New Year dances at the Yacht Club we found ourselves, so to say, out on a limb one October with nothing as yet in view. Along came a juicy plum which we lost no time in picking off. I guess one forgets easily, for our old nemesis was destined to come into full bloom again—the one wherein the employer was a large lodge. But how could we miss, the job had all the earmarks of a winner. Over the phone came, "You'll have everything you need, a big stage, a fine Grand piano, and all kinds of sound equipment. We're all wired and we really got it all. By the way," the enthused voice continued, "the Lodge will be holding its first New Year's party in our new facility, and we're making big plans." All of his proud items were as stated, but he neglected to give us a thumbnail character analysis of the committees involved in this gala affair. (Committees are rarely singular in lodge structure.) It was therefore left for us to discover later that each member concerned was bent on creating a debacle and, I might add, without trying.

Our entrance, come the great Eve, was almost pure joy. A wide and functional stage door directly opposite a private parking area of the imposing building had us inside and set up without laborious ferrying of gear. Bless the builders with foresight. And bless all the attention showered upon us almost immediately, like visiting royalty. It included a guided tour of the spacious and well appointed quarters with a host of office suites befitting a giant corporation. Thank heavens, the job not only paid handsomely, but was landing us in a most attractive situation such as a large ballroom floor now sparkling in silvery streamers and ringed with silvery clothed floorside tables. All this and a shiny, easy playing piano on an adequate stage. Not bad. The euphoria was short-lived when our first discovery came to light. Not a microphone nor any speakers were in sight, and no amount of searchings or fetchings by concerned officials brought forth any sign of them. In fact, we joined in by ransacking the entire backstage. All to no avail. From here on our good fortune slid steadily downward. The passing of time did its best to add drama. Early revelers had been strolling in since our arrival, all of them carefully dressed with bottle-outlined brown bags clutched to each man's fancy vest and cummerbund. Without a doubt, they'd been ready since 3:30 in the afternoon. With the hour of nine fast approaching and still no equipment, there was only one thing to do—start playing and hope we weren't in for a hellish evening.

Frequent bulletins were issued to us: The equipment was *in* the building. The room in which it was stored was under lock and key. No one had the foggiest notion as to the whereabouts of the key-keeper. The key-keeper was not at the Ball. Meanwhile we carried on feeling we could muddle through at least until the midnight hour came due.

"By gosh fellows" (and this was no time for me to object to the term), we found out that Fred Turner is in charge of all the sound equipment." Well now, we were getting someplace. Not so. Fred Turner had taken leave with nary a qualm and with him had gone the keyring! The abashed figure before us ended the story with, "Someone said they thought they heard someone say he thought Fred left on a flight to Baltimore this afternoon." Thus ended the key search and we struggled on with what was now beginning to shape up like a night in the '30's.

At precisely 10:30, while casually glancing about the floor I saw a trio of happy committee members dispensing somethings from a large box. Oh no, it couldn't be. But it was. Noisemakers, funny hats, whirligigs and such were being bestowed upon each table already. A mild, dispirited honking and squawking ensued, but of course the desired effect died in midair, instead of creating the traditional midnite bedlam. We were at this hour still unaware of their twelve o'clock plans.

At long last, time was not flitting by, the big hour was nearing. We knew we'd be behind the eight ball trying to carry it off without a microphone, and I doubt our faces suggested unbridled merriment or great anticipation of the midnight hour. About then three or four men filed behind our stage and out the stagedoor. Committees are not prone to leave the premises, so where were they going? Never mind, all our watches showed less than a minute to go now, so let midnight happen. And it did. A tremendous blast, close enough to send each of us about a foot skyward from our chairs, rocked the entire building. All sense of humor was drained from our outraged senses. What were they thinking of? Out on the floor people shrieked and screamed, while shattering echoes reverberated from every corner. The awesome nearness of the concussion seemed to suck in the very walls, forcing all activities to a quick halt, leaving some couples frozen into whatever position of dance they'd been in. Instead of hiding out somewhere, back through the door marched the terrorists, wearing looks of devilish glee. Their triumph of success would have vanished had they paused to observe the band. Any

Happy New Year wishing went by the board in the ensuing babble, as did traditional hugging and kissing. We thanked our lucky stars when Kenny came back inside after checking our cars, reporting each to still be in one piece.

The rest of the dance dwindled down to a trickle and gave out at one-o'clock. "No, really, we appreciate the invitation to stay for the New Year's breakfast, but we'd just better get headed for home," had been our agreed reply to the kind offer, which is not standard behavior for most musicians. We had begun the dismantling process and barely looked up in surprise at the next bulletin. "Well fellows" (didn't they ever see me?), "the doggonedest thing has happened," which by now was not headline news. An apologetic-faced committee member stood before us, a dangling check clasped in his fingers. "Your check was left on the front office desk. I saw your name on the envelope and it's just a good thing I took a look inside, or you wouldn't have been able to cash it." No one dropped a music case as he went on to explain that all lodge checks must be co-signed and this one had no co-signature, nor was a co-signee in view. Would the next mailing of the corrected check be O.K.?" That would be fine, and we left. Two weeks later it appeared the Lodge gears had become disengaged again, for no word was coming, let alone a check. Just as Kenny was preparing to turn the matter over to our Local 117, the official envelope arrived with just the check inside, and no explanation of the delay. Oh well, who could explain such an Odd Ball as this had been?

45

Musical Confessions

Though one rarely receives the best of both worlds, we all give it a try. My two worlds were not so terribly unique—music and home keeping, at least I thought so. After the day a fourth grade pupil, during a discussion of their parents' avocations leveled our daughter with, "But your mother plays for *dances*," the word almost curling her little lip, I began to wonder if I was undesireably unique!

Fortunately, the two worlds blended easier than did music and boyfriends during the '30's. With the exception of dire circumstances, I fully supported the idea of wives and mothers inhabiting and anchoring the homefront. Therefore the world of commercial dance music, as I knew it, fit my conscience fairly well. In the case of a musician or artist being so richly endowed with a genius talent as to give the world first claim on their lives, all my ethics would have been waived. This not being my problem, I applied myself within both spheres as best I could.

While notes and melodies were indelibly written on my brain, dollar signs never kept them company. Had any controversy ever existed as to whose function it was to handle the music business and the finances thereof, our Mr. and Mrs. team would have gone asunder. All of which made Kenny the good contractor, negotiator and check handler that he was.

I have another confession which falls into the class of a perfect paradox. For no special reason there has always been a lack of fondness on my part for all-girl bands, or even female jazz musicians as a whole. Where this placed me and what I was doing is a moot question. Maybe I had a huge blind spot! To be entirely honest, I never saw myself as a true jazz pianist, which could be the answer. There were very few opportunites for making friends with other girl pianists as they could be counted on one hand, which is no excuse, since I would only have seen them as adversaries anyway. Later years found me slightly improved in this department. Like all the others who create music, the dream of getting recognition and "making it" to the upper circuits did come and dance around in my brain. Who knows, if one would have wished to pay the going price or had the stamina or capacity to handle such a thing? Putting it all together, temporary frustrations were not unknown. "Would you have been good enough?" is a question that affects many, and though its intensity wanes with time, it never goes away.

The next question is much simpler to answer. Why did I attempt writing up our small arrangements? Especially when doing so caused my most prominent musical shortcoming to blatantly come to light? To buy sheet music was like bringing home a naked store dummy, providing at best only a skeletal lead, and if you were lucky, a few unusual chords. Bona fide "charts," as they are termed, seem to be aimed at larger bands, and custom arrangers are as scarce as hen's teeth. Though my abiding desire was to play at my best, the eagerness for keeping our music supply fresh and interesting was equally strong. And so big egg-shaped notes leaned and clung haphazardly on or between the ruled lines of my purchased music paper. Not to mention incomprehensible timing. Now my former skimming by the boring technicalities, so doted on by Rose Schlarb years ago, left me without a professional leg to stand on. Were it not for the trained eyes of an Al Meddaugh or a Morris Kenton, who added and subtracted quarter, eighth and sixteenth rest symbols, inserting their own style and meter when needed, my goose would have been cooked. In defense I will say I learned to account for instrument key adjustments, making transposing unnecessary for them. In general we ended up with an equal amount of measures. Better yet, we ended up with a creditable library of show tunes and whatever else struck my fancy.

The funny part of all this is my reverting to the old screen door method once more. Elusive measures, chords and even lyrics (which were jotted in shorthand) were filched, so to say, from unlikely sources. The radio always had my ears at acute bend, but many a scrappy note staggered across margins of grocery lists. Even the droning background of supermarket music gave clues as I wheeled my cart among the shelves. "Whoops, I need that little measure," and out would come my pencil, or my memory bank was alerted.

Zooming elevators were not immune, though the music within them sounds about as full of heart as the apparatus propelling the cars up and down. One time I actually rode beyond my floor to pin down some tricky chords in the mid-section of "Sophisticated Lady." Who wanted to buy the whole piece for just a few chords? It may not be fair to blame everything on having been a part of the Depression, since a penurious nature could play a role too. Lyrics were hastily done in shorthand, which I have never let go to seed, and in their own way often set the phrasing and timing. It helps to be a compulsive listener, but in some instances it can be downright irritating. There is no fighting it, whether in a dentist's waiting room, a department store, or anywhere a series of notes floats into the air. The tune or any portion of it must be identified, classed and oftentimes even keyed for unusual harmony or interesting chords. So while others smile or munch their food or read abstractedly or peer at pricetags on merchandize and just allow the music to flow on by, the compulsive listener has to listen and work it all out.

174

The first debuts of my written efforts represented an enormous risk, since formal practices were almost unknown. When the reputation of good showtunes was on the line, the pangs of doubt were acute. Perhaps professional arrangers suffer likewise to a degree, and if so they have my sympathy. However, when notes were correctly dotted, measures jibed and the sound was pleasing, the pain would disappear. When they were otherwise, I always swore to do better on the next copy. My reams of hand-written music can best be summed up by a tune we used for a Cha-Cha: "Fools Rush In Where Angels Fear To Tread!" Somehow it evolved into a homely but sizable variety of desirable numbers, some of them echoes of lesser known Broadway shows and a bit off the trodden path—a library if you will.

It still makes me smile when I think of it. By way of my catch-as-catch-can system, we were among the first in Tacoma to tootle off what has since become a classic, "I Left My Heart In San Francisco." Not even Al or Morry had caught it yet and after our first rendition Al asked, "Did *you* write this?" I wish I had.

46
The "Dance Committees"
(Heaven Bless Them)

Great respect is due to High Schoolers' resourcefulness for an extraordinary job at romantic license. Someone in command had set up their Junior Prom as an evening of classic ballroom dancing with white gloves and receiving line yet! When contacted, Kenny had been issued suggestions to feature slow melodic ballads, waltzes and anything to promote a genteel effect.

Weeks later we were carefully picking a path towards the curtain through a backstage clutter such as I had never seen before. The affair was being held in a large cafeteria with a large stage at one end, and we had opted for a stage door entry and easier parking on a large campus-type facility. The cause for wonder was an assortment of old washtubs at either stage end, fronted by an unconnected portable fan. Inside the tubs were large chunks of dry ice. Not for the punch I hoped. In front of the curtain where we were to play, all was bathed in an icy blue glow, provided by footlights. Before a testing could be made on the piano, whose upright and informal appearance was benefited greatly by the soft glow, someone was guiding me through the dignified receiving line. "Just so the kids can get the feel of it," I was told as it was still early. I felt like a visiting dignitary in spite of being a test run, since orchestra members do not often fall into such favor.

While we sat up music and stands, the backdrop curtain revealed a look-into scene of silver birches and various murky objects too close to identify. About the second dance, vapors swirled from each stage side, ruffling into the cafeteria and across the stage like a billowing fog. The band was in a similar fog. Whatever were they doing? The source had been solved, tubs of dry ice and a now-connected fan, but what was it all about? The ice-encrusted panels along the walls (courtesy of the Art class) also gave no clue. Not until one of the chaperones tapped me on the shoulder with, "The students hope you have 'Lara's Theme' and would you play it often? You see, this is their 'Dr. Zhivago' night!" Ah yes. Later I stepped out front and there it was—the swirly fog, the symmetrical birches and the icy panels. We were in an Ice Palace. Truly, I reminded myself, today's flock is smarter.

And now to the pink tumbleweeds, a perfect case in point to illustrate the remote limits of one woman's vision for an utterly pink Christmas dance. Most December club dances made do with snowy flocked trees (Fire Department approved) and twinkly lights along with traditional reds and greens of hollies and other paraphernalia. Extra play nights for company dances were wedged between the regular holiday parties where bosses and management, like Scrooge, bestowed evenings of special dinners and dancing, many even with gifts for each employee. We savored these, as the long process involved the calling off and marching forward of each recipient. A needed breather amid the whole mad, musical Christmas rush. It must be said that after hundreds of "Jingle Bells" choruses and other favorites had been jangled away, Yule festivities began to pale. As if to make up for the jading, we were about to be taken aback one year by the last club on our holiday playing calendar. They were the established and venerable Wauna Club, with whom we had just signed a year's contract earlier in the fall.

Their bailiwick then was the upper deck at the Top of the Ocean, an actual replica of a ship built right over Commencement Bay. After pushing and clambering all instruments up the tilted gangway towards the top and maneuvering them through the ship-like doors, we just had enough breath left for gasping at what we saw. The impression was of stepping into an intimate fluffy pink boudoir. I almost expected little white dressing tables and negligees to appear. Everywhere one looked was PINK. Soft pink twinkly lights, pink tablecoverings, pink candles, all of which was only the bottom layer to what appeared overhead.

Acoustics to the wind! This committee head had exploited the low ceiling, built true to a ship's style and the bane of all bands, to fit her scheme. Now the clearance was lowered even further by what looked like endless clouds of feathery pink texture, each atwinkle in more pink miniature lights. What in the world, or how in the world had it been done?

By intermission time, glancing overhead had divulged the clouds of pink to be a most sophisticated version of tumbleweeds. Truckloads of them, from eastern Washington no doubt. The story was filled in while chatting with one of the members. Our informer was Jean Rock, one of my favorites. We had become acquainted while she and her husband Harold had reigned as Commodore and Shipmates President of the Yacht Club. Her tone was almost apologetic, and began with, "This really was not my idea of what to do for our Christmas dance, but our decoration chairman for December happens to absolutely *love* pink." Just about then the addicted pink lady floated by. Her gown of frothy pink made her difficult to locate among the scenery.

How was it achieved? Not easily, or not by any last minute makedo. Back in October the chairwoman had organized a caravan of cars which in a body trekked across the Cascades into eastern Washington for the purpose of hustling tumbleweeds. For anyone not intimately acquainted with the same, a brief explanation is due. After turning dry and bristly in the fall this weed, composed of one hundred percent brambles and sticky arms, rolls across open land in a drunken abandon. Bouncing along with the wind, kith and kin latch on with their equally spiny twigs until they snowball into colossal sizes. Their ultimate destination is a collision with fences, making the only safe and sane way to attempt gathering them to be at the time while they're still single. At that it's a test of anyone's nervous system.

Step Two began with the vexing job of disentangling the whole crop after their cramped ride in car trunks, where they now resembled mountains of ratted hair. The committee, now home again, converted the mass into single stalks again. Next came the dipping into vats and tubs of pink dye, followed by a final spray of glitter before the dye set. Presto—no more a drab desert nomad. More work loomed ahead, such as the transporting to the scene, and the frazzling job of cramming each prickly and frothy bouquet into a grid of a false net ceiling. When and how the little lights were attached has left me. What price a Pink Christmas! Not to forget is the later removal. How it ever managed to pass or escape the Fire Code was never known.

And now from the heavens of pink down to utter basics. I can still see the three glass canning jars in my mind, each one trying its best to revive and support what was inside. At 9:00 o'clock somewhere out on the Olympic Peninsula we were getting set up to play a large community dance for the local Improvement Club. The huge barn-proportioned building was raw-bone bare. Bare wooden walls stretched upward to a bare ceiling; matching splintery benches lined the floor edges. In combination with the bare-boarded and lumbering high stage where we were to be seated, the whole vista was a matched set of drear and dust. Just as we gazed disconsolately across the hall, feeling that obviously the Improvement Club's energies had been directed elsewhere, someone came through the door. He was a burdened figure, who with his tin watering pail almost looked like Mistress Mary on her way to the garden. he listed toward the stage, pail hanging from one arm and a clutch of glass objects under the same arm. I could hardly wait to see what was going to take place, hoping all the while he had *something* to contribute. I had to look quickly since it was all over in a few seconds.

With his free arm he first divested himself of three glass canning jars, which were rolling together precariously in their underarm niche. One jar was quickly plunked down at each end of the long stage apron, leaving the third to be placed in dead center, with miles of open space between. Next, from the pail hooked in the crook of his elbow, he withdrew what once had been three proud and aristocratically tall, pure white Calla Lilies. One . . . two . . . three . . . there. From out of the little bucket he now poured what was left of whatever amount of water he had started out with, which proved to be a short swallow per jar. The Lilies, already in the throes of a bad hangover, continued to discolor and fall into drooping postures right before our eyes as we played. We pondered doing a chorus of the Funeral March.

The unique direction of one particular committee is still not forgotten. Kenny had contracted this casual extra engagement with a young people's group who were planning an annual dancing party to be held within the confines of their church. As a rule most musicians are not overly struck by the prospect of playing a church basement job and, I might add, they are not common fare. However, extra dates upon calendars are seldom frowned upon by most of the musical gentry. And so there we were several weeks later, reluctantly descending a much worn set of stairs to the nether regions of a fairly large church. All four of us had almost sanctimoniously treaded across the back portion of its darkened and empty sanctuary. Our jazzily (or so I thought) dressed greeter left us at the top of the stairway with, "Just go on down and you'll walk right into the room. The committee is down there setting up things." Ah yes, the committee. What hath this one wrought? We'd seen a fair share of these lower levels, where all the twisted crepe paper streamers and bobbing balloons in the world still were an uneven match against resident linoleum floors, blackboards and Biblical posters.

The room we were to come upon immediately did nothing to announce itself. Or were we in it? Our feet had led us into a shadowy space that seemed to be staggering in the throes of a partial eclipse. With eye adjustment, visible objects began to loom from the dusky interior. With the help of flickering candles here and there we found our so-called music stand. Slowly a scene began to emerge against the backdrop walls sketched with pillars, vines and winding river. Scantily clad young women pranced about and between scattered café tables thankfully lighting yet more candles. Others were plunging long slender bottles into the silvery buckets atop each tiny table. Ice cubes clinked and rattled with each anchoring, and one couldn't help pondering the acute dissimilarity between the upstairs and the downstairs. What was the motif, I wondered, while musing over the former thought? Was it Spain? Perhaps it was Italian, since I could now identify red-checked tablecloths. The answer came shortly. Could we please include "C'est Si Bon," "Magnifique" or anything else Frenchy throughout the evening?

This committee, either in pure fun or in subconcious retaliation, had successfully brought to life their chosen theme of "A Night in Gay Paree." It was Basement into Bistro with amazing and faithful authenticity. I felt sure Maurice Chevalier would have felt right at home here. And if I may say it, and I must, they produced a spirited evening!

47

Grace Notes

I for one will never sell the general public short when it comes to imagination and innovation, especially when in pursuit of fun. Costume dances were at their height in early Crescent years, where announcing the annual Halloween Prize Costume Dance was like setting fire to dry prairie grass. Everyone was swept along in the path of burning creativeness. The orchestra too welcomed such a departure from the norm, especially the pianist who had by now been able to memorize everyone's regular attire. New dresses or suits in those lean years did not appear with great frequency upon the bodies of our clientele.

To see even the more prosaic of your patrons' inhibitions take wing made our role in the party almost as much fun as theirs. A masked ball has and always will allow people to strip off their acquired personalities and to the limits of their sense of the dramatic play at being someone else. What it took sometimes to achieve this plateau made for evenings to remember. And while these affairs date far back into history, I believe the depression era forced more individual talents into production. No one could afford going out and renting professional outfits, and the need to flip out and flaunt the everyday prevailing mood of the times, stored up now for too long was, to say the least, urgent.

The animated characters, like a particular man done up in a striped romper suit actually riding his kiddy-car 'round and 'round the big floor, were real attention getters. That was especially true when the person was one of the more gracefully endowed dancers whom every woman coveted as a romantic partner. And then there was one of our very portly gentlemen who had somehow squeezed himself into a bursting pair of knee-pants. He insisted on dancing with one hand trailing a red coaster wagon behind him. In between sets he offered free rides to the lounge or refreshment areas and had a lot of takers. No plush cruises or big money awards were offered as prizes, but whatever was to be won was sought after with just as much gusto, for competitiveness was always stirred to a full boil. It has been said countless times that the harder the times, the harder people scratched.

Little by little the big costume dance extravaganzas trickled away and slowly disappeared. However, old-time mixed dancing seemed to show no signs of fading as the national economy slowly began to creep upward. Gone, at least from our scene, were the one-night feathered Indians, the bosom-stuffed Mae Wests, dashing Pirates, eerie Ghosts, fearful Frankensteins, yipping Cowboys, straw-hatted Huckleberry

Finns, powder-haired George & Martha Washingtons, and swarthy Arabians who danced away their fantasies at the Crescent Ballroom. I'm so glad I didn't miss the performance.

Twice at later dates and at other locales, we played for what were called "Come as a Song" dances, with results definitely proving that some of the original spirit still remained. We hadn't seen everything yet! Four of them left lasting impressions on my brain and one will stay with me if I live to be two hundred. The first ever "Come as a Song" party and dance popped up at the old Tacoma Country Club, causing us to wonder how people would go about such an invitation. Before and after the stately and pillared Southern-style mansion burned, we were frequently on call with the Club's managers. I loved playing there (the original) not just for the prestigious address but for the indulgence of the Steinway Grand for an evening, which in this case was whipped cream icing. It didn't take long at the unique party to see not much had been spared for their presentations. However, the name of the song each person was attempting to portray was not to be announced until judging time and up till then it became a wild guessing game. Couples were dancing by the piano in eyecatching get-ups, only one of which I even came close to identifying. After about three whirls by my post of a lovely white haired woman romantically abloom with roses fastened upon a white gown and her escort shining a flashlight upon it, did I also see the light: "Moonlight and Roses"! Then suddenly I almost dropped a whole measure of whatever we were playing. All I could do was stare at what was nearing our stand—an honest to goodness Nun. Never had anyone done this before at any costume dance but here she came, attractive from white bordered cap and cape to the hem of her long inky black skirt. For added effect she nestled unsanctimoniously upon her escort's shoulder. She slid on by and as we all gazed at her retreating figure, all our chins dropped in unison. Her southern exposure, and a good portion of it, was visible, was breathtaking and eye-gluing. The sudden revelation of this seemingly pure nun from the rear view caught everyone unprepared. Mouths stayed agape at what was now a scantily clad chorus girl in briefest of lacy tights, with rhinestones ablaze and a whole highway of whistle curves. How could this be one and the same person? The odd thing about it was how the shock of the transformation remained constant for each member of the band! She would come dancing towards us, go on by and with the same startling effect each time. My mind ran more into the mechanics of how in the world the costume had been sewn together. She was an animated dancer and nothing seemed to slip out of place.

At long last the colorful contestants marched around the dancefloor for judging, each one holding a placard with their printed song title in view. Of course she received the unanimous vote, being the split personality of all time. The beautiful nun with the show-stopper backexposure had chosen a song that now was easy to guess, after reading the title. It read simply: "Body and Soul"!

For pure down-to-earth humor the second prize went to a poor woman who had wearily pushed a wicker baby carriage throughout the revelers. Sitting within the pram back to back were two life-sized toddlers (dolls of course) and strapped to her back was another one dangling out of a packsack. Her dowdy dress disclosed another pregnancy was imminent, but just what her song was had escaped everyone. The laughter as she wheeled the buggy around for judging was uproarious when her song title was unveiled in a one word explanation: "Careless"! For the many times we later played this ballad which enjoyed a long span of popularity, I would see the whole little charade in my mind. Anyone who may have watched me might have wondered why the rather sad lyrics of someone cast aside by a careless lover made me smile all over.

Some years later the "We Fifty" Club gave a similar type of dance, with more emphasis on graphics to serve as clues. At that time they were still dancing at the old Fircrest Golf Clubhouse, another old and charming place with a long verandah along one side overlooking the greens. Strangely enough it also became a fire victim, and along with the fine Country Club Grand went an excellent Baby Grand from the Fircrest fire. Counting the extraordinary Chickering back at the Cambridge Apartments, this now made three of my treasured friends reduced to ashes. We soon became used to the odd arrangement of space at Fircrest. Their dancefloor occupied the center of the main building, along with a large fireplace. On either side French doors (open on dance nights) led into dining and sitting rooms. The dancers used both siderooms for table space and socializing between dance sets, quite out of our range of view. So after each set we would sit quite alone in a suddenly empty scene, barring one or more of the members stopping to chat with us, as happened quite frequently.

When we would resume for the next numbered dance, carefully checking our scorecard with the printed danceprograms, the couples poured out from each side of the arched doors, almost like a school fire drill. The unique arrangement was the only one we have seen before or since. But back to the "Come as a Song" evening. Rightful top honors were captured by the clever graphics used in denoting "Nola" as his song. The man had simply (?) drawn five black lines of the music staff upon his white shirt. Sketched across his chest the black notes were placed in the correct order of an upward scale, do-rae-mi and so on. His song title lay in the fact that they read: Do, rae, mi, fa, so. . . .ti, do. Everyone bit with their great discovery, "But there's no "la." "That's right," he'd chortle, "you got it . . . it's "No—la." I can't remember whether or not he had great competition, beyond a dancer whose blouse-front was painted with three pink lambs. We even got this one as the song "You, You, You" was currently popular. These were some of the times when the musicians had almost as much fun as the crowd.

48

Mortified

Imagine my chagrin at being called by a casual friend to "fill in for me at the Mortuary, temporarily of course." The Pacific Northwest was in a state of shock over a prolonged snow and ice condition. "I'm marooned on top of our hill 'till our driveway thaws out. If you would play for me today, I'll suggest you go ahead and take the whole week to make it worth your while." I gave way when she added, "There's not much to it. Sometimes I read in *The Reader's Digest* during a service to keep from boredom. *You* wouldn't have any trouble at all." Nothing but ice and snow and her final phrase would have swayed me. It would begin with tomorrow's 1:30 p.m. service.

At one o'clock the next day I was crunching over several snowy blocks, after parking the car. I preferred to forego the offer of private parking at the rear of the premises. The farther away from the business end of this place the better. Entering through filmy curtained front doors, the veiled and muffled atmosphere took hold immediately. Instead of sitting down to play, I wanted to turn around and leave. In this mortuary the organ was placed within the last two rows of seats, making you one with the folks who had come to the service, close enough to shake hands if so moved. A man ushered me behind the solid door to the offices and more mundane objects such as files and type-writers. With not much time to spare he addressed me quickly with, "The family requested hymns are standard. Here is the list. You'll know Al Isenberg the soloist (I did already). He doesn't rehearse, just pops in from his office down the block when it's time for his solo, and goes back to work after that. As for your check, we pay (and he stated an unstaggering amount) for each service." It was peanuts. At my reference to that effect and claiming a union affiliation, he raised his eyebrows and the per diem. A wish to keep this just between us was added. No time now to ponder over the contrast between the compassion inside the office and out in the sanctified air of the chapel.

The first funeral solemnly slid through the allotted thirty minutes, without incident except for one unnerving moment when suddendly in the dim and muted lighting I sensed a figure standing behind me. Ah yes, Al Isenberg whose marvelous voice I so admired at church. His phantom-like entrance had startled me. We consulted in brief whispers and after his beautiful songs, which I knew were heart consoling to everyone, including me, he melted away again to the outside world.

The week wore on. Each service was touching and I could not find it in my heart to assume any semblance of a blasé manner, much less open *The Reader's Digest*. However, I was new at this and resolved each day to remain that way. The strain did lessen to being able to slip out between two consecutive services one day and hastily drink a strawberry milk shake. But getting back to the main theme, there was a very large and impressive funeral on my last scheduled day—one completely under the auspices of a local and large lodge.

"This will be well attended," I was being coached. "Mr. Blank is well known . . . no minister to deal with; they'll go by lodge ritual. The fellow was to leave the explanatory booklet here for you to read beforehand. Where is that book . . . he must not have dropped it off. I'll have him phone you tonight and arrange to meet you here one hour early with the book. That should do it. O.K.?" Clouds of foreboding were gathering. The tedium of lodge mumbo-jumbo had always distressed me and now I was to fit in with cued music.

The car was parked at greater distance the next day. Extra cycle patrolmen were already wheeling into position. I was quaking even though the lodge man had phoned, confirming the early meeting in a voice brimming with confidence and assurance. Soon I was seated among the gathering patrons awaiting the sight of this steady assuring fellow, *and* the all important book. A semi-circle of empty chairs occupied the pulpit stand. This *was* different. Flowers, wreaths, sprays and emblems were crammed into every available niche. But where was my man? The mortuary director sidled up, intoning into my ear, "Just keep playing . . . it's very fine . . . he'll be here any minute." Now *I* was getting his sympathetic word. Near the end of my prelude section up came a man, striding, in relation to the situation, quite briskly. We didn't even murmur "How-do-you-do." Quickly he placed a small and tightly

184

bound booklet upon the organ's lighted music stand and spread it open to Page One. Page One immediately flapped shut. "Just follow along with the printed paragraphs," he lipped. "That's where I'll be reading and whenever you see a blank place, play *something*." He was gone. In frantic desperation I snatched the obstinate book from the rack with one hand while holding a sustained chord with the other and placed it on the bench beside me. My purse served as a doubtful anchor to the bouncing pages. There was no time for being indignant. It was sit down and *pray!*

Naturally the fine print from that distance, far removed from the beam of the organ light, was barely readable. The only way to get a positive sighting was by assuming a jack-knife position during the entire service. As each blurred blank appeared, I cautiously advanced a few notes in case the man began talking again. The maneuver was as daring as plunging into traffic at only a blinker-lighted intersection. Suddenly I went from jack-knife to upright position. One of the brothers was calling the roll and was slowly but insistently intoning the name of the deceased! A dreadful silence hung after the calling of his name. I half expected Mr. Blank to sit up in his coffin and say, "Can't you tell I'm not present . . . I'm dead." Finally from within the semi-circle another brother chanted, "Mr. So and So Blank is not present. Mr. Blank is dead." At least someone said it. The period after the last word was as heavy as a cannonball. No meeting with the reader ensued after all had cleared away. Just as well . . . I could assume that I had made it.

After the whole week was over the family thankyou cards began to appear in the mail, one of which I kept. It expressed handwritten thanks for my choice of "Trees" as most appropriate for their father's funeral. He had spent his lifetime in the woods at logging, a fact casually dropped by the Director as "This old logger sure had a rough life." On that last day I walked out the mortuary doors alone, my modest check for the lodge service in hand. It would have taken a hefty amount written on the designated line to atone for my acute anguish. Could they possibly have realized a little extra was only fair? But the figure was exactly the same . . . possibly sufficient, I thought, to cover the cost of one hinge for today's elaborate coffin.

Any further contact with this branch of the music world would have to come *much* later and only under pressing circumstances. Wasn't music designed for dancing and fun?

49

My Very Own Music Boxes

Much like reaching into Fräulein Fritsch's box of wooden notes so long ago, my mind often reaches into its store of music material, perhaps all filed away in boxes too. If life's incidents and moods are file indexed in the brain, I would believe most of mine are classified under the letter "M." This is the one that gets the most use in my case. The constant use must keep it in good repair, for it doesn't seem to wear out. I can dip into the box and pull out needed notes, measures, tunes and to my delight, whole scenes when music filled my whole being with pure joy. But who's to understand this marvelous recall system built into the human body? Come to think of it, that little exercise in childhood of placing the notes drawn from a box might have been an omen. Seems like I've been dipping into my own box ever since. But on to what sometimes runs across the screen.

Sometimes the picture flashes with the band holding forth at Tacoma's Winthrop Hotel, once the Queen Mary of hostelries and now demoted to the mothball fleet. The occasion shows a Grand Ball, capping a Railroad convention during the Fifties, with all the banners and trappings. The scene is from the index captioned, "Pure Joy Music." Much as convention dances are considered by most musicians to be the aberration of all playing jobs, you rarely turned one down. Certainly not when the company was the one employing Kenny for so many years now. I had copied off the latest little Northern Pacific ditty currently being aired on T.V. and we were tootling if off whenever the mood struck us. Railroad brass was in great evidence and an air of pleasant hullabaloo and togetherness filled the long crystal chandeliered ballroom. Kenny was in a bit of limelight of his own, for it isn't often the host city's division of such a large company can provide an orchestra headed by one of their own. Co-workers and officials waved and smiled as they went by and it was fun to see and meet visiting VIP's, whose names heretofore had only been scrawled signatures. Add the fact of them now dancing to our tune. Though it rarely happens in a large throning crowd, the tempo, the setting, the melody ("Getting Sentimental Over You") created a like mood between dancers and music makers. We were happy, they were happy. We saw ourselves, within this brief little flash of time, as Tommy Dorsey & Co. And they probably did too. The whole magic still remains an undefinable phenonomen. Every musician, great or small, has experienced it and, like us, longed to bottle it up for keeping when needed. Each time the mystical combination took place, I would ask myself, addressing the question to the innermost part of my being, "Where in God's world would you rather be than right here?"

My next favorite pull from out of the music box are the humorous incidents, too many for one book to hold. Many still contain full potential for a good laugh, if sometimes at my own expense. The many weddings kind of fuse together in an overall aura of white satins, laces, swishing trains, surrounded with pastel blooms and flickering candles. The few that chose to stand up on their own, by eclipsing all the frills with the sheer drama of circumstances, are of course the ones stored in special boxes. Now, out in the open, they've fallen into the category of "Musical Comedy."

There is a pitfall with a recall mind, which is no news to anyone. There are times when you cannot turn them off, when melodies or parts thereof relentlessly turn in endless replays. The timing often conflicts with a good night's sleep, and though it is a common condition for the whole human race, the memorizer (by instinct) suffers a more acute case. During our most crowded playing years, often the entire drive to the job was a mental run of as many repetitions of a certain way I wanted to play one number, or a little phrase I was unsure of, or an intro, as could be completed with each turn of the car's wheels. Impromptu piano flings do not work well in a written arrangement, much to my sorrow. However, we played enough "off the cuff" to take care of everyone's personal ideas.

50

When the Chemistry Goes Awry

"I'll bet you have a good time playing for so many dances. It looks like a lot of fun. I wish I could sit up there and play like you." These remarks are often heard by musicmakers and often in a tone tinged with wistfulness. If your answer is an assertive, "Oh yes, I do . . . it *is* fun," you are only veering slightly from the truth. In my own estimation, music playing enjoyment level hovers around ninety percent, which is an excellent ratio for any creative, yet commercially slanted work. When the crowd is abuzz and the dancefloor aswirl with happy and pleased dancers whom you have sprung into action, and the music is coming out the way you put it in, I truthfully agree it to be fun—like no other.

But who would want a Nirvana level to prevail? So in keeping with the general balance of things, I must deal with a possible ten percent subtraction from total bliss. Muddling through dance nights with runny nose, or groaning stomach, or other minor discomforts not meriting your being replaced, do not count. They are apparent facts you can at least, with a little help from the drugstore, recognize and challenge. It's when the unseen pixies and gremlins common to all endeavors decide to zero in on your party. When they exercise their pranks to the beat of a live band, your goose is all but cooked. Negative ions abound as they move in and about gleefully putting a hex on the whole affair, and it's not long before you're at their mercy.

After several ill-fated attempts at being in charge of your quality level and adjudging your musical output to be mediocre at best, you know it's time to pull out all the stops. Should this fail, you face the prospect of hearing your musical foundations crumble right before your and everyone else's eyes and ears. Song titles heretofore at the tip of your tongue are beyond recall and empty holdover measures, always so ripe and ready for your own little inventions of jazzy fill-ins, remain just that— empty holdover measures. Announcing the predicament to a compatriot is unwise since the eerie condition is highly contagious. The only useful antidotes I ever found were the summoning up of moral discipline, a kind word from another, and the thought of losing your job.

When the entire dance concept is invaded, everyone is in for a night of stiff upper lip. The reasons can be as undefinable as the wrong mix of people, the inappropriate location or heaven knows what. Certainly within the ten percent non-enjoyment is the inevitable final act of the dance. Only the most stoic of musician can avoid being caught up in the poignant drama of the crestfallen committee whose innocently laid plans for an evening of delight and moneymaking all went up in smoke. The acceptance of their methodically written check amid the shambles can lower your self approval to a Shylock level. Luckily I was not the transactor, since compassion might have bent the union rules more than once.

Who's to blame for the following, I do not know. May as well blame it on the gremlins too, though poor planning and inexperience often are at fault. The persons in charge hired a three or four piece combo for legitimate financial reasons, unaware that even an eight piece band would hardly dent the expanse of the square footage involved. Or perhaps expectations of a crowd were dim, and so they chose a smaller place. The first blunder, in the days prior to just turning up a volume button, caused the small group in a very large hall to flail and slave away at creating enough of a commanding sound to stem a gathering roar. It's blood and sweat time.

The second deceptive trap into which most combos have fallen more than once is the anticipated slim turnout which, for some reason, turns into a throng of unexpected bodies all cramming themselves into inadequate quarters. The small band, upon suddenly looking around at the gathering monster, feels unarmed for something bigger than they—THE CROWD! Frustration and resentment at either faux pas were easy emotions to achieve. The possibilities for being stormed were rife at times like these. A few remembrances of them are still quite clear.

Last, but not least among the ten percent faction, is one that was very hard for me to work with. Unflattering remarks or wisecracking hecklers, few as they were for us, always carry enough power to nip at your cool. Perhaps not for the most hardened of souls, the likes of which I've met only a few. Even a lone agitator among a large crowd was enough to shake my balance and I feared them like the plague. Kenny could deal with them reasonably but firmly, and Al could continue on course in clear tones, while Morry, unless restrained, only wished to end the whole matter in a few seconds, verbally or physically. Two alternatives are open, both non-violent. Either play on like one possessed or assume a royal attitude of rising above the trivia. Unfortunately, I was not good at the game and bared my suffering to any or all. These annoyances occur mainly at the more open or public functions and our inflictions were few.

51

We Go Continental and Catholic

Borrowed from a page in my Irish diary, written in the early Eighties: We were aboard an Aer Lingus plane, prior to landing in Ireland as "carried by the tour" musicmakers on Jesuit son Kenny's "Irish Pilgrimage Tour."

"Everything looks fresh and new in the dawn's early light. Look below, those were glimpses of a dim faraway earth! A deep Irish voice up front gave out a cheery 'Good Morning,' followed by estimated arrival time, weather at Shannon Airport and other such good news. Then the lovely light disappeared and we passed through fog layers, down, down, before coming out into a kind of green luminescent half-light. Shannon's modest complex of airport buildings was next and suddenly we lowered ever so gently to a featherbed landing. You could have had a teacup on your knee. Green, green, green, just like they said. All the green checkerboard seen from above was now flattened into green fields. The long winding river turned out to be the much sung about "River Shannon," flowing by on its way to the Western sea. Houses were few for Shannon is not a city, just an airport facility used as an International re-fueling stop and terminal for Irish flights. We were in IRELAND!" (End of diary quote.)

In continuance the following day: "Mass was said before dinner by Kenny Jr. and the other priests in our group." Strangeness between our party of 27 Catholics and the three rebels (Kenny and I along with another stray Methodist had named ourselves thus) was in the first stages of dissolving. We had all, for the sake of creature comfort and solace, shared body heat by sitting as close together as possible inside this large and stone-cold Cathedral. By after dinnertime, served in a rather elegant white and green dining room of the Great Southern Hotel, everyone was ready for a change of pace. Tonight was an introductory night out at a typical Irish pub. Along with the Guinness Stout it was to be the entrée of Kenny and me, not as soloists but as "sit-ins" with the local Pub ensemble. The affair did not go exactly as hoped for by Kenny Jr., but was a great success just the same.

Due to the spasmodic power outages brought about by an ongoing electrical strike throughout Ireland, Kenny became the sole attraction. The place was only equipped with an electric organ (no piano) which of course made it inoperable. The outage had already happened as we strolled in a body across another of Killarney's stone bridges, turned the corner and made our way in gathering darkness to "The Laurels." Of streetlights, there was none. Life at The Laurels was carrying on too with myriads of fat white candles inserted (carefully I hoped) into bottles. In unison they all sputtered and reflamed at every door opening. There seemed to be hundreds, almost like the finale of a Christmas Eve Candlelight service.

About mid-evening Kenny was introduced. He may as well have been Eddie Peabody with all the fanfare and hooting. Song after folksong, with attached verses that hung onto each chorus like a long bridal gown's train, had been sung. And no one showed any signs of tiring, not with the rows of chocolate-colored foaming beers frothing at all tables. The timing was perfect. They were ready for an American import. Let's bring him on in real Irish style. I enjoyed all the hurrah so much, I didn't mind being on the sidelines this time.

At the likes of Kenny and his lively Banjo, Irish eyes not only smiled but lighted up like the Vegas strip.

One day of the tour together and the music resolved whatever line might have existed between the religious preferences of our troupe. Their Masses, and there were many, were staffed by the six priests among us and one Methodist organist and we all worshipped and sang together. I will admit to vast spaces of Abbeys and Cathedrals along with their unknown and cold organs taking precedence over the fact that this was live ecumenism. My immediate thought was always, "Lord help me select the right stops and may the first chord not take the roof off." Preliminary runs just never happened, since the scheduling of a Mass came at the convenience of whatever place we chanced to be. The services were for our own immediate walk-in group, rather than the regular parishioners, with the music at my disposal, or I would have headed for the nearest exit in a hurry!

Though the better part of an Irish day was spent at "Knock," the site of many miracles, I had my own miracle the following day at the next sanctuary along our way, the Columban Abbey. A spoken wish to hear "something by Bach" had come from the resident priest who, besides being elderly, very learned and world-traveled, was a-bubble with Irish wit and refreshing charm. My mind raced ahead with, "You could give 'Prelude and Fugue in C' a try, but you've never really played it without the music. This is hardly the time to rely on memory . . . and don't forget, Bach is not "cover up" material. How nice it would be to be found not wanting."

Seconds ticked by as the front pews began to take occupants. What to do? How much volume would be needed in this high vaulted chapel? Two closed music books leaned on the organ rack and my eyes skimmed over them briefly. One read, "Songs for the Sacred Mary," no help there. Cold hands became colder as I turned about to spy several priests stepping towards an altar, at least a city block from my perch. It was time to get going. My right hand, now turning blue in an expanse of atmosphere totally unacquainted with any heating system, flicked open the second music book, a manuscript-like folder. At the top of the sheet it said, Page One and my startled eyes jumped in disbelief at the title of the first number printed directly below: "Prelude and Fugue in C," by Bach. I could almost hear it say, "Here I am, play me!" A miracle? No doubt about it.

52

Hazards

Is it safe to say, physically speaking, the playing of dance music per se is a safe occupation? From what I've seen I would say it is, excluding of course the transportation to and fro. Even an accident prone person is out of harm's way. Should you see musicians playing away with visible bandages, casts or crutches, you can be reasonably sure the reasons for such had little to do with playing music. Broken down lips, muscular complaints or smoke-teared eyes will not qualify for an insurance adjustment. Nor would heavy blooper notes, dropping on your toes with a thud, maim or disfugure. However, a knowing policy writer still has a chance. He could look into performance periods of horn soloists with a penchant for playing on the brinks of high stages. Or pack-laden drummers who must conserve space by using telescopic drum stools. Since I've witnessed both hazards, with each being excrutiatingly funny, I know for certain they are possibilities. Happily, the two comic accidents were incidents, rather than injurious accidents. Both also prove that people, given the right circumstances, are sometimes the best comics of all.

The first mishap came about at the Crescent Ballroom back in the Thirties. Ole Lund's face-lifting job did not include any lowering of a too-high stage built in the mode of the day. Only the long limbed and agile could even attempt jump-offs or jump-ups. A set of steps had wisely been placed at each end of the stage, ignored by us at times. It was yet another night of mixed dancing when up walked Hallie Eaton, leaving his chair for stage front, trombone to lips. He was ready to play a close range solo (no microphones in evidence yet). Lights were lowered and up above the giant crystal ball checkered the filled dance-floor beneath with light and shadows. Hallie had called out "Dreamy Melody," as the chromatic descending bars could slide from his trombone very effectively. The rest of us had settled back in a thirty-two bar respite, as he stood poised on the dimly lit stage. All of a sudden he vanished from sight, but we could hear "Dreamy Melody" still filling the air. One extra, miscalculated step had sailed him downward, still holding on and sliding the correct notes, where he made himself one with the swirling crowd below. Here he calmly finished the chorus. Like a cat he had landed deftly on his feet. The dancers, most of whom were preoccupied with being moonstruck, hardly noticed his descent or presence. However, the rest of the band loved to relive the whole act at any given opportunity. I for one can still see it all, complete with Hallie's look of "Well, I did it, so what?" As one brother expressed it afterwards, "You know . . . he could have wrecked his trombone!"

Now on to telescopic drum stools. For correct leverage their seats are those of a racing bike, except for the fact they rise upward in umbrella fashion, by being released from a metal tripod at floor level. Hence the possibilities for a sudden surprise, if not in perfect order or too hastily assembled. Kenny was to prove the point soon after his conversion to drumming. Of course it didn't happen at home, but right in the middle of a "We Fifty" evening. The dance was proceeding at the usual spirited pace of this fun club, with Kenny making full use of cymbals and other accents contained in his newly acquired equipment. Without warning a loose clamp gave way and it was goodbye drummer. At least the upper portion of him. At hearing an alien sound behind us, four heads of the band turned just in time to watch him go down, not quickly but slowly like a setting sun. No one ceased playing, not even Kenny. Like a captain going down with his ship he remined in control. We could see a pair of hands with brushes attached still making a contact with the snare drum above. Again, no injuries sustained. The humor of it failed to reach him immediately. To be sure, on the next trip out, a brand new and reliable stool was packed into his gear. It never happened again, but the memory of it goes on. Other minor hazards came along for him such as "creep-aways," when a drummer vainly tries to clutch at his whole set before it inches out of his working sphere. A sure trip rug compensated and was added to his luggage (and sometimes forgotten). Portable stages with drop-offs also merit extra attention, especially when a well stocked drummer finds himself fighting for every inch of space.

We like to think of this musical comedy act as poetic justice. I can't remember how much time elapsed between the collapsing drum stool and this episode, but it did happen at the same club. On this night of Western motif dancing, fancy little dance programs were done in cut-outs of horses, with all the trimmings in like design. Ten gallon hats and cowboy paraphernalia were dancing by the bandstand with much fun and appropriate remarks. We had been advised in advance to please take note and come as Western as possible, and of course to use the music accordingly.

"I think I'll make it a real Western," said Kenny as we prepared to leave home, and he tucked an empty "38 Special" revolver he had once inherited into his drum case. For added authenticity several blank cartridges were added. He would choose the proper moment and then shoot off the blanks . . . harmlessly into the air of course. Unfortunately, "up in the air" at the Fircrest Golf building was somewhat curtailed by a low ceiling.

The cowboy fun and western regalia evening was at its crest. This is a point every dance musician can pinpoint quite accurately. We had just played ourselves into a western sweat with a racing set of "The Eyes of Texas," "Don't Fence Me In," and others. At the breathless finish we tacked on the old true western, "Shave & a Haircut . . . Six-Bits" tag. During the number Kenny had his revolver poised (unseen by any of the crowd) and ready to fire right on target and meter with the finale. This made the old tag come out as "Shave & a Haircut . . . BLAM BLAM! His quick draw hit it right on the nose with an ear-splitting report. The entire crowd did an instantaneous rise of feet from the floor—shakily followed by a great roar of laughter. In all the uproar we saw a quite serious faced Dr. Tweit striding towards the bandstand. Had we gone too far? Without a pause he looked Kenny square in the eye and said in an even tone, "Please don't do that again, Kenny. I only brought along one pair of trousers!"

53

Wrong Cue or Tempted

With playing what came naturally rarely backfiring on me, I trusted too heavily one night and wound up demonstrating how to play a Freudian slip. Friendly pressures had twisted my arm into something I considered to be out of my comfort range—a piano solo for a seated audience. Though not a concert affair, the listeners would at least be expecting something above the basics at this informal Sunday evening family program. Compounding my reluctance was the locale—a fairly large church. "Just play anything that comes to your mind," friends had cajoled. "We are all so fond of music here." What neither he nor I suspected was that my mind would be prompted to prove one of Freud's well known theories. It would direct an inner repressed but not expressed thought to come out into the open, without my willing it so.

Truthfully, even while walking up the carpeted aisle from the pew where daughter Arlene and I were sitting, no particular song had entered my head as yet. Not a good habit, but something always popped about the time I sat down, so why worry? But it didn't. I stared at the shiny front panel of a quite new golden oak upright, plugged in the trusty wires to my mind, and waited. Nothing. Before even a gaping silence could open, my fingers involuntarily sprung me into what was, without doubt, the least appropriate number to fill a Sunday evening sanctuary: "TEMPTATION"! Once the opening bars were loosed there was no turning back and though not a word was sung, the sultry suggestive lyrics seemed to shout out among the vestments. "You came, I was alone. I should have known, you were temptation. It would be thrilling, if you were willing. . . ." Try as I would to put out the flames, on they went, "take me . . . I am yours . . .," but by now I had it cooled to a sputtering ember, or so I hoped. More than anything else, my wish was for some way to make an invisible return to the pews when I finished.

All I had to do then was to face a daughter who was having obvious difficulty in concealing her utter amazement. The applause was polite.

Poor Politics

"We got the piano all warmed up for you, even put a pillow on the chair, so sit down and play us something to liven up this job." If I never lay claim to fame, the taking up of this offer may qualify me a spot in the Hall of Musical Variety. The invitation was hardly a new idea, as many a dinner, pot-luck and buffet aftermath had been cleared to my music since way back in Firgrove days. I looked about me with a brief moment of doubt. The lady pleading for action was one of three seated at a long table fronting a single classroom of a historically registered country schoolhouse. No dishes or food were in sight and I had just finished voting in a statewide November election in what I considered the most delightful polling precinct possible! At one side of the table a pot-bellied stove glowed out the temperature of a July scorcher, and to the other side stood an old warhorse of an equally historic piano.

The next twenty minutes or so of such bipartisan selections as "Twelfth Street Rag" and a string of similar peppy requests bounced off the old slate blackboards as straggling voters came through the door and creaked across the old wooden floor. At each ending of a piece would come, "Jazz it some more honey, things have been pretty slow this morning." No one seemed to mind at all, least of all the voters, some of whom jigged up the center aisle. The presiding ladies always seemed to have the registration books opened to the proper page by the time the folks arrived up front. Some remained to visit with neighbors and listen to some more music before returning to their cars, parked knee-deep in the pasture grass outside.

We were not to find out till some months later that the whole musical incident, innocent fun as it seemed to be, was highly out of line, in fact illegal. Someone had talked! Furthermore, anyone desiring to remain on said election board would not be a party to any future occurrence of same. What a way to conduct the great American franchise of voting! And so with bowed head, this sit-down-and-play remains as a one and only one-time performance.

Wedding Music Strains

Sometimes I wonder about the relationship between "The Lord's Prayer" and me. Ever the romantic soul, I have an incurable case of loving to play weddings. To be honest, it took years before the bride's set of nerves and mine did not jangle a duet, and that was before I could emanate any tangible aura of a musical anchor so often needed at these times. Nevertheless, give me a church, a bride and groom and a friendly organ, and the world is a happy place where love still reigns supreme. Unfamiliar churches and cranky organs can dim the glow, as can the telephone brides. These are the ones you never see in the flesh till the day of the wedding. All details, such as the one omitting a need for a rehearsal with the organist present, had been taken care of via telephone. It would take more than the five fingers on one hand to count the times this has taken place, with often some rather startling results. Still, my convictions remain unshaken.

On my honor, a lot of the Hollywood scripts and storybook depictings of various disastered weddings are not overdone. I participated in one which, had it been on screen or in a book, would have been rated as just too silly for words. I shall try to condense one of them, though it was a long ordeal for all concerned.

When I entered the church in which this ill-omened affair was to be held, I already felt a foreboding, and for no reason. Right away it was announced the ceremony was on hold, pending the arrival of the best man's overdue flight. While we waited, the singer and I opted to use the time for a quick rehearsal. We did this to the tune of a great baring and gnashing of teeth between the bride and the soloist at my side. It didn't fit well with "The Lord's Prayer" at all. As I filled in the obligato measures the soprano threatened, "I came a long way to sing at this wedding, but I'm walking out, right now!" Mine was but to play and wonder. When the wedding finally got underway, it was mine again to figure whether she'd hit the road already, or whether someone had prevailed, or whether I would have to hastily pull something out of my head to play in the allotted time slot. While I was playing away in my dense cloud, wondering whatever had brought this all on, the irate singer marched up to my back and hissed loudly in my ear, "I'm going to do it, but it's the last time I'll ever do anything for *her* again." And so we did "The Lord's Prayer," and despite the histrionics, it came off surprisingly well, though I doubted I was in a corresponding mood by then. We were launched, but not for long. Just about in the middle of the spoken vows, everyone up front (including the organist) was severely jarred by an ominous and deep thud . . . a dead weight thud like someone falling out of bed in the middle of the night. It was none other than the best man. I had thought him to look a hectic pale after his frantic late arrival. He chose to end his misery by fainting at the feet of the groom. I looked over the organ to the wedding party, he was gone. The next act could have been in a Laurel & Hardy film. Two of the men in the same group, instead of getting down and ministering to the prostrate brother, simply raised him upright again, propping him up bodily on either side. There he stood, with glazed eyes and limp limbs, until the ceremony was completed. I never found out what had caused all the fireworks, choosing to exit myself as quickly as possible after the Recessional.

I had a close brush with the theatrical at one particular wedding played, one I know will never happen again. Or I should say, the likes of which are not likely to repeat. Kenny and I were attending a large wedding, this time as guests. As we casually chatted with folks prior to entering the church sanctuary, a highly distraught stranger pulled at my sleeve with a firm jerk. Not even an "excuse me." "We heard you could play," her voice was quaking. "Oh, I hope you can help us . . . our accompanist for the soloist has not shown up, and it's almost time to start!" Seconds later the stranded Contralto rushed forward, sheet music in hand. "Oh, thank heavens you've found someone," she wailed. And what was the sheetmusic? "The Lord's Prayer," but written in the proper key range for a Contralto—five flats, hardly within immediate sight reading comfort zone. Luckily, I had seen it before. The wedding proceeded without a hitch.

What I enjoy with any wedding is the exhilarating mood that fills you from head to toe, the importance and hopeful finite meaning of spoken words, the happiness, the joy, and being able to share in the whole thing. Next on the list, if anyone should ask me, I love playing the Postludes, especially the ones following an exceedingly well done ceremony, not necessarily ostentatious or plush, but just well thought out, and most of all sincere and filled with bright hopes. Recessionals at weddings, in my book, give forth marvelous free air for any innovative organist to throw stereotyped music to the winds. Even if the traditional processional has been requested, one can still abbreviate and then veer off to whatever suits the occasion. By this time no one is checking out the details anymore. My all-favorite fling was at a niece's large church wedding, one late Fall afternoon. It was nobody's fault the chosen hour for the ceremony fell perilously close to the last quarter of a momentous football game. Not just any old game, but one between the two arch rivals of Washington State, The Huskies from Seattle vs. the Cougars from Pullman. The winner was slated for the Rose Bowl.

As we had moved to the beach now, Kenny and I had driven up to Olympia, the site of this huge church, and taken a motel there for the weekend. In this way we could take in the rehearsal dinner, etc. An hour before the wedding the two of us were torn between the TV screen and putting on our good clothes. The split-haired Husky victory kept us on a relay between the front room and the bathroom. As it was, my lace jacket was left behind. Getting to the church across town was too speedy to vent any jubilation over the Husky win. By the thickness of the traffic, it seemed the whole town was going in our same direction. As we made our way toward the elevated choir loft and large pipe organ I was privileged to play, I spied the minister. I already knew what I wanted to do. Still enveloped in the gleeful victory, I asked his permission to play "Everything's Comin' Up Roses," which I assured him I would only insert after the regular recessional. It should be added, this number was almost as traditional for use as a Rosebowl promoter, as any Lohengrin exit music. "Sure . . . go ahead," he answered with a grin, while adjusting his snowhite surplice.

Not till later during the reception did I learn he was not the resident pastor of the large edifice, but rather from an out of city branch of the denomination.

Postscript: The congenial and also young pastor was also a University of Washington (Huskies) graduate! We had a good laugh as we heaped our plates from a most bountiful buffet. Not a negative comment was ever heard.

56

A Different Tune

Like a country cousin striving to take on city airs, Firgrove and South Hill began shedding their basic clothes and trying on designer models. All was being temptingly spread before them. Having intimately participated in our tenure with the old, we too gaped in amazement at all the new. Amazement surrendered to aghast when the first oh-so-convenient bank begat another, and another, and another, and when cowpath and field's friendly faces were paved into one vast and blank countenance of cement. We waived the remaining alternative of taking prescribed immunity shots for suburbia virus, feeling sure they would not help the condition. Each bulldozer's mighty scoop of formerly well used earth placed us a mile closer to a woodsy lot behind the dunes near Ocean Park, Washington. This was our shock absorber, bought several years back and used for weekends and holidays. Like the dispossessed, we were fleeing. The A-frame would soon be claimed as full-time home.

All signs leading to our next chapter in future living seemed to point in a southwest direction now. For us they read: "This way for two musicians whose long producing well of commercial music has been considerably tapped." "This way for a couple whose children already lived elsewhere." "This way to some semblance of continued country living." In other words, our minds were made up.

In consideration of all the foregoing, putting our quickly sold home and acreage behind us was not a traumatic wrench, but leaving my mother was. Now nearing 91, she viewed our move as a tolling bell to a long chapter of her own life. No amount of reasoning about the beach only a 3½ hour drive changed her mood. For her it wasn't farewell, it was goodbye. To not feel like the deserter, I had to remind myself constantly that she was still an independent housekeeper within shouting distance of my brother and family. There was also the fact that my elder sister lived within ten miles. And then when mother, during our frequent moving discussions, with her characteristic sense of fairness wished us both well in our new home, the wrench gave an extra twist.

The clouds dotting our departure scene carried a few unanswerable questions. Would mother go into too much of a depression over what she felt was a definite blow? Would we have an outlet for the music so much a part of our life, in this under-populated area? Knowing full well commercial dance music, as we knew it, was fading, we also knew its chances for reblooming there were even slimmer. And oh, pray tell us, what in the world would we do on Friday and Saturday nights?

In mid-August of '76, after pinning an old Thanksgiving poster of Tiny Tim uttering, "God Bless Us Everyone" to the kitchen wall, we closed the door on our hand-wrought Firgrove house. No weekend departure this time, we were off, trundling along behind a lurching truck whose bulging sides swished the overhanging maple boughs of our tunnel-like driveway. Taking our directions from the beckoning "This way" signs, corners were turned toward the South I-5 Freeway. We left the streaming flow at Olympia for the lesser roads leading to the nether end of our state. My mind tumbled with such large issues as: "Will the Havens remember, come next May, to clip off the spent blooms of the nearly one hundred clumps of daffodils bordering our long driveway." I must send them a card.

Before our vacated home had a chance to cool off, the Havens family had walked inside, read Tiny Tim's message with a smile and rolled up their sleeves. It was as if music went out the door, only to turn around and come right back in. With Mr. Havens' position as choral director of the Puyallup schools, his Grand Piano was immediately fitted into the front room! How fitting. Live music hadn't even been granted a decent intermission before coming back up on the stand. Conversely, serious room footage had been measured months ago to accommodate our Spinet into a window spot of the A-frame. First things first.

The real music-as-a-business foldup came several months hence. Commuting the distance was just not worthwhile, no matter how stubborn the cause. No one needed to drop a heavy object upon our heads. It was time to go.

57

Nadir

In early November, three months into our beach living, mother had her oft-spoken wish fulfilled: If she could evade her dread of becoming a nursing home resident or patient, and just go to sleep some night without awakening, she would count herself both lucky and satisfied. A bone-setting surgery, following a minor hip-breaking fall, proved too much for the heart condition she had successfully lived with for so many years. My personal diary of that November date reads: "Last night was the worst night of my life." This after receiving the unexpected phone call.

Subsequent long solo walks on our ocean beach did much to dull the pain, but the diary's message remains intact. Never did I dream that soon I would be claiming a timely musical Providence again. My music angel was still in circulation, for quite soon thereafter I was asked to fill in at our local Ocean Park Methodist church. The organist was in need of some Sundays off. "But," I told myself, "you're not a church organist per se, even if you've helped with many a Sunday School's music. This is different. You'll play with too much beat and will have to curb yourself constantly against lapsing into jazzy routines." On the other hand, who knows? Could one make a satisfactory transition from Saturday night's swinging beat and hoopla and go right into Sunday morning's sedateness? After seven years as resident organist now (the other well-loved one having passed away in the meantime), I'm still trying with now and then a feeling of gaining on it. And here is where Providence steps in. Like Rip Van Winkle, Bach, Mendelssohn, Schumann and others have all re-awakened and found themselves up front again on the music rack of our Spinet. Not to forget was mother's large library of Piano Classics, some of the editions in beautifully bound books whose pages still remain first quality material. While playing dance music and such will always be my love, choosing the music within my realm, to make a congregation happy reading from mother's music and playing it, created space for another love.

58

The Fox & the Grapes

"Oh, it's just as well. I didn't want those sweeter grapes up above my head anyway." So sighed the wily old fox of Aesop's Fables as he contented himself with a possible sour feast. I will hope I don't echo his philosophy when mentioning some of my own convictions. Even had I qualified in all areas and burned with higher ambition than I did, the whole concept of success or possibly popular acclaim may well have flopped. Given my same fortunate components of husband and children, a double load of career seeking and home keeping would have overtaxed my backbone. However, some manage to bring it off and enjoy their grapes too. So was the old fox really all that sly? Or is he dated?

And so it goes. I still love pianos and still always share a personal kind of sadness with the ones that stand by, so to say. They may be in dusty halls, restaurants or someone's home. À la Alice in Wonderland, each one displays a little sign that reads, "Play Me." If the unused instrument is a Grand, the sign stands out in neon lights! Evidently there is no cure. I still love it when people dance to our music, or listen from another church, a community program, or wherever. Pardon me for just one moment, the phone is ringing.

"You're planning your wedding for next month?" A glance at the kitchen calendar follows. "Yes, the date is fine. Oh, it's going to be in the old Oysterville Church, and you'd prefer all traditional music?" I do not add that this formula is a winner, but chat on. "Yes it does lend itself well with its quaint and historic charm." We discuss the amazing acoustics of this precious and restored glimpse of the past, the short wooden-floored aisle, and the old pump organ that brings it life. Of course her traditional music fits in well, but in a desire to please one bride, an all-Bach wedding was played without incident. Or the surprising challenge of setting up "For Once in My Life" as a mid-ceremony solo. A pleasant agreement between bride-to-be and organist, with all the mutual expectancy involved, generates enough good feeling to make a day. Love and romance still bloom.

As I was saying. Oh dear, the telephone call has just reminded me of a weekly detail that is close to deadline time. It's Thursday afternoon and the Offertory selection for this Sunday's service at our Methodist Church has not been phoned in yet. It is to everyone's benefit, I feel, when the music played during Offertory time is listed by title in the congregation's bulletin. One does want people to know what is going on!

Let's see . . . what to sit down and play this Sunday?